A Suetonius Reader

Selections from the
Lives of the Caesars and
the *Life of Horace*

Josiah Osgood

Bolchazy-Carducci Publishers, Inc.
Mundelein, Illinois USA

ℬ𝒸 LATIN Readers

These readers provide well annotated Latin selections written by experts in the field, to be used as authoritative introductions to Latin authors, genres, topics, or themes for intermediate or advanced college Latin study. Their relatively small size (covering 500–600 lines) makes them ideal to use in combination. Each volume includes a comprehensive introduction, bibliography for further reading, Latin text with notes at the back, and complete vocabulary. Nineteen volumes are currently scheduled for publication; others are under consideration. Check our website for updates: www.BOLCHAZY.com.

Series Editor: Ronnie Ancona
Volume Editor: Laurie Haight Keenan
Contributing Editor: Laurel DeVries
Cover Design & Typography: Adam Phillip Velez
Map: Mapping Specialists, Ltd.

A Suetonius Reader
Selections from the Lives of the Caesars and the Life of Horace

Josiah Osgood

© 2011 Bolchazy-Carducci Publishers, Inc.
All rights reserved.

Bolchazy-Carducci Publishers, Inc.
1570 Baskin Road
Mundelein, Illinois 60060
www.bolchazy.com

Printed in the United States of America
2011
by United Graphics

ISBN 978-0-86516-716-2

Library of Congress Cataloging-in-Publication Data

Suetonius, ca. 69-ca. 122.
  [Selections. English. 2011]
  A Suetonius reader : selections from The lives of the Caesars and The life of Horace / Josiah Osgood.
     p. cm. -- (BC latin readers)
  Includes bibliographical references and index.
  ISBN 978-0-86516-716-2 (pbk. : alk. paper)
  I. Osgood, Josiah, 1974- II. Title.
  PA6701.E14O84 2011
  937'.07092--dc22
  [B]

                                                                                    2010048906

Contents

List of Illustrations

Preface

For many years now I have enjoyed reading Suetonius, and after preparing this textbook I appreciate him only more. Not only does his outspoken *Lives of the Caesars* entertain readers even today, it played an important part in the development of the art of biography; and for historians Suetonius lights up a momentous period, the transition in Rome from the Republic with its colorful nobility to rule by the monarchical Caesars. And yet Suetonius is not often read in Latin classes—largely, I suspect, because of a distaste by Latinists for his seemingly "colorless" style and a preference for the more obviously wonderful Tacitus.

With this reader, I hope to make clear Suetonius' attractions to students of Latin while also showing that he is in fact an excellent author to teach. His syntax is not too involved but reinforces all major constructions; his subject matter facilitates acquisition of new vocabulary; and his works are easily broken down into manageable sections. When you read Suetonius, frustrations are mild and passing.

I must thank Ronnie Ancona for her invitation to write this book, and all of her good ideas about how to shape it—including incorporation of the *Life of Horace* found in manuscripts of that poet and based on Suetonian material: it gives an excellent sense of another largely lost masterpiece of Suetonius, his *Lives of Famous Men*. I also am indebted to Laurie Haight Keenan at Bolchazy-Carducci for all her enthusiasm and assistance, and to the press's two superb referees for substantial guidance that improved a number of the notes in particular. David Byers heroically produced first drafts of the Latin text and vocabulary for me, for which all thanks; and I thank too students at Georgetown University in my class on imperial biography in the fall of 2009, who put a draft of this book to the test. Their instant affinity to Suetonius was most encouraging, while they also helped to root out some errors and identify passages inadequately explained.

The Latin text of *De vita Caesarum* printed here is that of M. Ihm's Teubner edition of 1908, *De vita Caesarum libri*; the *Vita Horati* is taken from C. L. Roth's Teubner edition of 1904, *C. Suetoni Tranquilli quae supersunt omnia*. Several proposed changes are noted at the start of the Latin text. Reference is made throughout the notes to C. E. Bennett's classic *New Latin Grammar*, first published in 1908 and available in reprinted form from Bolchazy-Carducci Publishers.

JOSIAH OSGOOD
Washington DC

Introduction

∽ LIVES OF THE CAESARS

Imperial biography has often been dismissed by Roman historians. Ronald Syme, for instance, the Camden Professor of Ancient History at Oxford University from 1949 until 1970, claimed that biographies of emperors "are a menace and an impediment to the understanding of history in its structure and processes"; they lead to "a distortion of historical perspective" (Syme 1986: 14). And a later Camden Professor, Fergus Millar, once posed the question "whether Imperial biographies, or histories of individual reigns, should be written at all" (Millar 1966: 243). A single emperor's actions, Millar suggested, could not be studied, "until the whole social context of the Imperial power has been examined over a substantial period" (244–45). Millar went on to produce in his *The Emperor in the Roman World* (1977) a pointedly impersonal study of emperors from Augustus to Constantine, organized around such themes as "The Imperial Wealth" or "The Emperor at Work." What the emperors did in their free time, how they were educated, whom they married: questions of this sort were deliberately excluded.

Professional historians of modern eras, too, have expressed concerns about biographical approaches to their subject. As one scholar has explained: biography "only involves one life, derives from a belles-lettres tradition rather than a scientific or sociological one, and is often written by non-academic historians who attract a lot of readers" (Banner 2009: 580). So again, not enough structure and process—and the added stigma that biographies are often written for lay audiences. "Biography," another scholar asserts, "remains the profession's unloved stepchild, occasionally but grudgingly let in the door, more often shut outside with the riffraff" (Nasaw 2009:

573). Leading historical journals tend to exclude biographical articles; biographies are not encouraged as doctoral dissertations. Most universities do not have a department of Biography (as Hamilton 2007: 4 ruefully observes).

And yet it is no coincidence that precisely as historians continue to denounce biography, biography has risen up to become a dominant area in nonfiction publishing, and a major focus of broadcasting, from television to the Internet. Society's curiosity about the lives of others, alive and also dead, can hardly seem to be sated, and that curiosity is now well catered for. One inspiration for this development was the publication of Lytton Strachey's iconoclastic group biography, *Eminent Victorians*, in 1918, in which Strachey proclaimed, "Human beings are too important to be treated as mere symptoms of the past." His hope was to detach biography from history and set it on a new course, to pierce through the idealizing, and usually massive, lives written of distinguished Victorians, to find real human beings with all their quirks and flaws. In doing so, Strachey looked back over the nineteenth century to arguably an even more important figure in the development of English biography, Samuel Johnson, who famously remarked (to his own biographer, James Boswell), "If a man is to write *A Panegyric*, he may keep vices out of sight, but if he professes to write *A Life*, he must represent it really as it was."

A younger coeval of Strachey—and, quite likely familiar with Strachey's work—Ronald Syme raised another, less philosophical objection to Roman imperial biographies: even if one's aim was not to write some kind of history, still to write a biography, in the modern sense, was very hard with the materials at hand. "Now you can write a biography of Cicero," Syme said. "But probably not of Caesar" (Syme 1985). There just is not the evidence you need—the letters, diaries, interviews, and so forth, on which modern biographers rely. You end up, instead, with "political biography" or "slices of historical narrative," as Syme put it (Syme 1988: 329). Such depersonalized studies did (and always will) get written, Syme acknowledged, and with some frequency. But in fact what fascinated Syme, throughout his career, was precisely the *personality* of certain of the Roman emperors, Tiberius, Domitian, and Hadrian in particular—and also

Julius Caesar himself. A paper Syme wrote, "History or Biography: the Case of Tiberius Caesar," tries to come to terms with the man, looking for clues in the ancient sources, as well as invoking modern parallels—King Philip II of Spain, even a character in Marcel Proust.

Fascination, at least, with the lives of Rome's emperors and their characters went back to ancient times. Indeed, the surviving masterpiece of Latin biographical writing, to which this textbook will introduce you, is Suetonius' *Lives of the Caesars* (*De vita Caesarum*), an account of Roman emperors, although beginning not with Augustus (commonly reckoned first by modern historians) but Julius Caesar (100–44 BCE), whose name was assumed by Augustus, and all of Augustus' successors, including Domitian, Suetonius' last subject. Written under Hadrian (who ruled 117–38 CE), this work was a pioneering effort, the first, in Latin, to treat collectively the lives of Rome's rulers; it would have continuators in ancient times, and also would contribute to the development of biography in the modern era.

Suetonius set out on a quest for the smaller, but telling, details surrounding his subjects. He was interested not just in great events, like Julius Caesar's brutal murder on the Ides of March, but in Caesar's baldness: "of all the honors voted him by the Senate and People," Suetonius remarks, "there was none he accepted or made use of more gladly than the privilege of wearing a laurel wreath on all occasions" (*Iul.* 45.2). Suetonius' zeal in collecting such evidence has led to the charge that he was little better than a gossip. Yet, it can be replied, he was living up to the biographer's challenge of finding real human beings, with all their idiosyncrasies. Divine Augustus had rotten teeth, was weaker on his left side, and wore special platform shoes to make him look taller. Tiberius was a hard drinker, liked peep shows, and was a child molester. Caligula loved his racehorse, and gave him a marble stable, an ivory stall, purple blankets, a jeweled collar, as well as a house, furniture, and slaves—and was said even to have planned to award him a consulship.

The reader becomes incredulous, and that is part of the point. Suetonius may seek to know his subjects, but they are not ordinary men. They are able to construct their own weird worlds. A modern reader, though, still can ask: is *everything* Suetonius says true? And how did he come to write such a book? Did he use reliable methods? Why have modern writers such as Syme, even when posing biographical questions, found Suetonius less than satisfactory?

❧ *Biography at Rome*

For all the continuities between ancient biography and modern, key differences must be recognized. At Rome, biography's origins, which were never entirely forgotten, lay in commemoration of the dead. At the funerals of nobles, family members delivered *laudationes* celebrating the deceased's accomplishments, and the accomplishments of his (and later her) forebears. These eulogies were arranged not chronologically, but thematically. They dwelt a great deal on virtues. They were to be inspiring to the younger generations. Families came to preserve copies of the *laudationes*, and kept them along with *imagines*, sculpted likenesses of the ancestors, which were displayed in the *atrium* of the house, together with brief inscriptions recounting the deeds of the deceased (*tituli*). Whenever a family member died, the *imagines* were taken out and worn by actors in special processions through the center of Rome.

All such practices stemmed from the very competitive behavior of Roman aristocrats, a further offshoot of which was an outburst of memoir-writing in the later Republican period. Already Cato the Elder (234–149 BCE) had worked into his *Origines*, the first history written in Latin, copies of his own speeches and a defense of his career—and such personal justifications continued to feature in historiography (the prefaces of the historian Sallust are a famous example). But then, in freestanding works, others aimed to set the record straight on their own lives—feisty Aemilius Scaurus, *princeps senatus*; Lutatius Catulus, whose military glory was eclipsed by the new man Marius; the unfairly condemned Rutilius Rufus, who at his trial took Socrates as his model. Even the Dictator Sulla wrote extensive memoirs—while others had their own exploits written up for them, Pompey the Great, for instance, by the Greek writer Theophanes. Caesar and Cicero, the great geniuses of their age, characteristically wrote up their exploits themselves, Caesar in his spellbinding commentaries on the Gallic War; Cicero in a series of works, in Latin and also Greek, in prose and also in verse.

The fierce struggles between such men led to pamphlet wars after their deaths, a further development of great importance for biographical writing in Rome. Caesar, and Caesar's foes Cato and Brutus, as well as Cicero, all were treated to admiring posthumous accounts by their friends (and Cato also to a few attacks). Not only was the Roman *laudatio* an important model here, but also one of the earliest forms of Greek biographical writing, the *encomium*, the first notable examples of which were written in the fourth century BCE; especially popular among Roman readers was Xenophon's *Agesilaus*, which discussed first the Spartan king's achievements in chronological order, and then gave a long non-chronological review of his virtues. Oppius may have structured his (no longer extant) life of Caesar along these lines, for at least part of the work seems to have avoided chronological arrangement to concentrate on evidence for Caesar's virtues.

The ongoing civil strife of the late Republic also inspired a great deal of reflection on the Greeks' own turbulent history, and the lives of its leading figures in particular. And this harmonized with another trend, intense interest in Greek scholarship, and its cooption by Latin writers: a perfect illustration is Cornelius Nepos' *Chronica*, the work mentioned in the opening poem of the Catullan corpus. Drawing inspiration from Apollodorus of Athens' chronicle, which listed events from the fall of Troy to its time of writing, Nepos, in three volumes, conjoined Roman events with Greek. Nepos is significant too as being among the earliest Latin biographers proper, who also included (according to the late antique scholar Jerome) Varro and Santra, and then the Augustan writer Hyginus.

Nepos and Varro's biographical works are known in some detail, and are partially extant. Both were looking to make Roman the techniques, even to some extent the contents, of Greek biography proper, which was primarily a phenomenon of the Hellenistic period—brief lives of literary figures and also others who might inspire curiosity, lawgivers, for instance, and tyrants. The prolific Varro, who during his long life produced hundreds of books on an encyclopedic range of topics, wrote on the lives of the Roman poets—trying to extract, as

Hellenistic scholars did, clues from their own works. Varro also produced a work *Imagines*, which reproduced portraits of 700 famous men
(kings and statesmen, dancers and priests among them), accompanied
by brief epigrams and a discussion of the evidence for the portraits: it
was a remarkable fusion of Greek scholarship with the Roman tradition of *imagines* and *tituli*. Nepos fused Greek and Roman in a major
biographical undertaking, *Lives of Famous Men* (*De viris illustribus*), a
series of perhaps as many as 18 books and 400 lives, organized by category (e.g., historians, generals), with foreigners treated first (Greeks,
Carthagininians, Persians), then Romans. The extant life of Nepos'
friend Atticus, from the book on Roman historians, shows in its arrangement the influence of *encomium*, and also the *laudatio*.

Atticus himself was interested in biographical writing. He wrote
books on the distinguished families of Rome, and also a work that
paired portraits of praiseworthy Romans with epigrams on their
achievements. This surely was an inspiration for the later Forum of
Augustus, whose long porticoes were filled with statues of great Romans and inscriptions recounting their deeds—biography put to patriotic purpose. Little survives of the *De viris illustribus* of Hyginus,
a freedman and librarian of Augustus, but what does suggests a work
similarly patriotic. Suetonius likely drew on it, as he surely did on
Varro's work, when he came to write his own *De viris illustribus*, becoming, as it were, the new Varro of emperor Trajan's Rome, an era
in which much biography was being written (e.g., Tacitus' account of
his father-in-law Agricola).

∾ *Suetonius the scholar*

The evidence for Suetonius' own life is relatively extensive, and comes
through a variety of sources. His *Caesars* reveals some details of his
background and early life. He speaks, for instance, of a recollection
of court life under Caligula passed on to him by his grandfather (*Gai.*
19.3, included in the selections in this book). And in the life of Otho
(10.1) he says that his father, Suetonius Laetus, fought as commander
of the Thirteenth Legion under that emperor in the civil war that
followed the death of Nero; this means that the elder Suetonius was

of equestrian status, with property worth at least 400,000 sesterces, a substantial sum. After witnessing Otho's suicide, the Thirteenth Legion transferred its loyalty to the side of Vespasian, who shortly was to prevail, become new emperor, and found the important Flavian dynasty; Laetus probably went over too. It has been suggested that the biographer, Suetonius Tranquillus, was born just after the war in 70 CE, thereby explaining his final name Tranquillus. Somewhere around 70 CE is certainly likely, as Tranquillus described himself as a young man (*adulescens*) in the year 88 CE, when report of the false Nero reached Rome (*Ner.* 57.2). Rome was, evidently, where Suetonius was at this time—and we seem to see him there in another story he tells, set in the reign of the last Flavian emperor, Domitian (*Dom.* 12.2, included in the selections in this book). There Suetonius would have studied the main subjects of Roman education, *grammatice*— that is, the classics of literature and their interpretation—and rhetoric (cf. Suet. *Gramm.* 4).

Suetonius makes only one significant reference in *Caesars* to his life after this point, his gift to the emperor Hadrian of a small but rare bronze statue of the young Augustus, which Hadrian placed in his own bedroom (*Aug.* 7). But evidence does survive in the published letters of an important contemporary, Pliny, who was consul under Trajan in the year 100. Through the letters we see Pliny doing favors for Suetonius; in letter 1.18, addressed to "Tranquillus," Pliny promises to try to get an adjournment for a case Suetonius was to argue. Suetonius was therefore it seems at least for a time (c. 98 CE) acting as a legal advocate—though not, apparently, too confidently, since the reason he sought an adjournment was that a bad dream made him fearful of the case's outcome. Another letter (1.24) shows Pliny trying to help his friend get a good price on a small country estate he wished to purchase—a place where he could "clear his head, restore his eyes."

Pliny also secured for the equestrian Suetonius a military tribunate, but Suetonius wished the office passed on to a relative (according to *Ep.* 3.8). The tribunate, the post Suetonius' father held, was the launching point for the military career that an equestrian could enjoy, but which Suetonius evidently declined. He was instead becoming absorbed by a new pursuit, scholarship. By about 107 CE at the latest, Pliny writes (5.10), Suetonius was on the verge of publishing a major work—though as with his court case, was having doubts. Pliny urged him on.

A final letter comes from book 10, a book different from all the rest in Pliny's corpus as it contains letters written to Trajan (mostly during Pliny's governorship of the province of Bithynia-Pontus on the coast of the Black Sea in 109–11 CE), and also Trajan's responses. Trying to do Suetonius one more favor, Pliny wrote Trajan (10.94), praising Suetonius and asking that Trajan give Suetonius, *eruditissimum virum*, the so-called "right of three children" (i.e., legal privileges for those who had produced three children), even though Suetonius' marriage was childless. It may seem odd that Trajan should be asked to grant a favor to a man who seems to have avoided military service for scholarship, but this is to misunderstand the place of scholarship in imperial Rome. In quite a few other letters, including letters of recommendation for official posts, Pliny praises men's intellectual achievements. Military men and administrators were expected to be erudite too, or at least to commend erudition in others. And so Trajan assented to Pliny's last request (see letter 10.95). There is, however, a strong likelihood that Suetonius was on Pliny's staff in Bithynia-Pontus, and may have helped Pliny with his correspondence, for instance (so that it was not his erudition alone that commended him). It seems clear that Pliny died while on service in the east, and it may even be that it was Suetonius himself who arranged for publication of the final book of letters.

A list of Suetonius' scholarly works is preserved in a Byzantine encyclopedia, and can be supplemented with other titles. Most are lost, though some are quoted briefly in later sources, and there are also Byzantine epitomes of two essays written in Greek, *Words of Insult* and *Greek Games*. Other works included *Roman Spectacles and Games*, *The Roman Year*, *Critical Signs in Books*, *Cicero's Republic*, *Names and Types of Clothes*, *Rome and Its Customs and Manners*, *Famous Prostitutes*, *Kings*, *Institutions of Offices*, *Physical Defects*, *Weather Signs*, *Names of Seas and Rivers*, and *Names of Winds*. The list is instructive. Unlike many ancient scholars, Suetonius appears to have produced no editions of texts, or commentaries on them. But he did use the methods of the grammarians, which were the methods of scholarship more widely—above all, the discussion of words, their meanings, their usages, and their appearance in old or obscure texts. Related to this was antiquarian research, into legal, religious, or social matters. Much in Suetonius' lost works seems to have been lexicographical and antiquarian. As one scholar has put it, he was predominantly interested in "Life and Manners" (Wallace-Hadrill 1983: 46). From that it was a short step to biography, and some of the works, e.g., *Famous Prostitutes*, seem pretty clearly to have been biographical. Aside from the *Caesars*, the most important of these, and the only to survive in any form, was *On Famous Men*.

In *On Famous Men*, the preface of which named such predecessors as Varro and Nepos, Suetonius confined himself to the lives of literary figures, who were arranged into categories—grammarians and rhetoricians, poets, orators, historians, philosophers, and so forth. The segment *On Grammarians and Rhetoricians* survives, and the biographies of poets such as Terence, Horace, Lucan, and Vergil, found in manuscripts containing their works, to varying degrees reflect what Suetonius wrote in his book *On Poets*. (The *Vita Horati*, included, in its entirety, in this textbook, is thought to be fairly close to the Suetonian original.) Also useful for reconstructing this major work is the chronicle of Jerome, who used Suetonius extensively—just as Suetonius himself used the work of earlier scholars. Study of these scholars and of the authors' works themselves was Suetonius' main method, though he also was able to add into his *Vita Horati* quotations from letters of Augustus, apparently not widely circulated.

From what survives of *On Famous Men*, it has been concluded that Suetonius had a special interest in the age of Augustus, and the late Republic; and also that a particular interest throughout the work was the relations of authors with figures of authority. The *Vita Horati*, for instance, concentrates on the poet's patronage by Augustus, and Augustus' powerful friend Maecenas. Almost certainly written before his imperial biographies, the work may have prompted interest in doing more research on the lives of the Caesars. But there was likely another reason Suetonius warmed to the topic of the Caesars. By the time he published his masterpiece, he had come to work for them.

∾ *Suetonius' career*

An unexpected source for Suetonius' life turned up in Algeria, in 1950, from the coastal city of Hippo Regius (where Augustine would later serve as bishop and die in the Vandal sack). A now fragmentary inscription, originally intended to accompany a statue erected by the town council, reveals that Suetonius was a priest (*flamen*), likely in Hippo, and that he held a series of distinctions in Rome, including almost certainly a place on the equestrian jury panels, appointed by Trajan (see Townend 1961). Why would such a text have been found in Hippo Regius? The likeliest guess is that the town was honoring a famous local son. Roman authors came from all over the empire, but had to go to Rome to make their name. The latter part of the inscription reveals that Suetonius also held three crucial equestrian posts in the imperial court, at Rome, the first two probably appointed by Trajan—*a studiis* and *a bybliothecis*.

What do these titles mean? A phrase with *a* or *ab* and a noun functions in Latin idiomatically to indicate a department in which one worked, or which one headed. The *a studiis*, then, handled *studia* for the emperor—that is, his literary and cultural pursuits, which, given the prestige attached to literature by men like Pliny, it was important for him to promote. Emperors did so by holding readings, for instance, bestowing privileges on teachers of rhetoric or grammar, and, from the time of Vespasian, appointing chairs of Greek and Latin rhetoric in Rome. The *a studiis* presumably helped with such matters. The *a bybliothecis*, a post first held by freed slaves of the emperor such as Hyginus, but then in Suetonius' day by equestrians, headed the public libraries, already founded by Augustus. Trajan himself constructed a great library in his Forum, comprising two buildings (one each for Greek and Roman authors) that flanked the famous column that still stands in Rome, paid for with Dacian spoils. Perhaps Suetonius had a role in organizing them; very likely he used them for his own work.

Both jobs required scholarly skills, and typically were filled by scholars. The last job held by Suetonius (under Hadrian), the highest post an equestrian without military experience typically could hold in his day, need not have been. It was the real plum, the *ab epistulis*, the Secretary of Correspondence. What was needed here was a sense of how to compose. The secretary would compose all sorts of letters for the emperor, if not make the decisions that lay behind them. Emperors had to issue thousands and thousands of letters, to provincial governors (such as Pliny), to officers, to their subjects. In *Lives of the Caesars*, Suetonius evinces interest in the correspondence of emperors, including such seemingly mundane matters as their orthography. As *ab epistulis*, Suetonius and his staff likely had to look through letters written by Hadrian's predecessors. It has sometimes been thought that the position therefore gave him access to otherwise unavailable archives, including the letters of Augustus, which Suetonius says to have seen firsthand (*Aug.* 87–88), and made ample use of.

A further piece of evidence—and the last remaining clue for the reconstruction of Suetonius' life—has been brought in here. In a biography of Hadrian, part of the *Historia Augusta* written in the late antique period but based on earlier sources, it is revealed that the *ab epistulis* Suetonius and the praetorian prefect Septicius Clarus (head of the imperial guard) were more familiar with Hadrian's wife Sabina than was appropriate and were dismissed from service by the emperor, most likely in 122 CE (*Hadrian* 11.3). It is difficult to evaluate this information. Certainly, it does connect with another point, namely that Suetonius dedicated his *Lives of the Caesars* to Septicius (the dedication, along with the first few pages of the life of Julius Caesar, is lost from our manuscripts, but is referred to elsewhere). Pliny's first book of letters was also dedicated to Septicius, and so perhaps Septicius and Suetonius rose together, under Pliny. It was, evidently, while Suetonius served as Hadrian's *ab epistulis* that Suetonius made the dedication, since it referred to Septicius' prefectship. It has been suggested that after the dismissal, Suetonius was cut off from access to sources such as the letters of Augustus, and that this would explain a curious fact—namely that while the lives of Julius Caesar and Augustus are very full, and those of Augustus' successors through Nero reasonably full, the later lives, especially of the last three Flavian emperors, are surprisingly thin. These later lives, the hypothesis goes, were written only after Suetonius' dismissal.

But there may be another explanation: if *On Famous Men* came before *Lives of the Caesars*, Suetonius was already interested in—and had access to—the letters of Augustus. (This in fact may have commended him to Hadrian, who modeled his rule on Augustus, and even used a portrait of Augustus as the seal on his own letters: Birley 1997: 96). And *On Famous Men* as a whole showed the same bias as the *Caesars* for the late Republican and Augustan periods. It may be, therefore, that the period of later emperors was simply of less interest to Suetonius—it was more familiar to him (and his contemporaries), and arguably less foundational. A further consideration relevant for the *Caesars* is that by the accession of Hadrian, Tacitus had finished a historical masterpiece, his *Histories*, which covered exactly the period of Suetonius' last six lives (Galba to Domitian). To be sure, Tacitus' *Annales*, covering Tiberius to Nero, may have been finished by now too. But Suetonius' work would be distinguished by starting earlier, with Julius Caesar, and by covering Augustus, the emperor Hadrian most wished to emulate. But was that really why Suetonius made the choice to start with Caesar? And what, for that matter, prompted a serial biography at all, lives of rulers in sequence?

༽ *Emperors and biography*

From the start there had been interest in lives of individual emperors—and Julius Caesar too. Augustus wrote, in the 20s BCE, a (lost) autobiography; so too did Tiberius and Claudius, as did also Claudius' last wife, Nero's mother, Agrippina. Augustus also wrote a brief account of his major achievements (the so-called *Res Gestae Divi Augusti*), to be inscribed in front of his mausoleum, and surviving now in several provincial copies. This was for the most part organized thematically, rather than chronologically, covering the offices Augustus held, the honors he, and his sons, received; the lands and money he gave his soldiers and the Roman people, the buildings he built, the games he held; the wars fought, territories annexed, distant lands explored.

Retrospectively, emperors tended to be treated in works of historiography, which, under the empire, came to show ever more interest in the personality of the emperor, and used the reigns of emperors as a structuring device (Tacitus' *Annals* is the prime example). Humorous pamphlets might also circulate, such as Seneca's still extant, and quite amusing, *Apocolocyntosis*, a burlesque on the deceased Claudius' arrival on Olympus. Biographies, interestingly, focused more on the victims of the Caesars, an outgrowth of the Cato and Brutus tradition. Gaius Fannius wrote three books on Nero's victims, Titinius Capito *Deaths of Famous Men* after Domitian. Tacitus' *Agricola*, also written soon after Domitian's death, is an artful variation on this form, recounting the life of a near-victim of the late emperor, and thereby attacking Domitian.

It was under Domitian that the first collective biography of emperors appeared, in Greek, by Plutarch. This was a series of eight lives, covering Augustus through Vitellius, two of which (*Galba* and *Otho*) are extant. Though he would go on to write his renowned *Parallel Lives*, joining Greeks with Romans, as Nepos had, but this time in pairs (e.g., Caesar's life is recounted alongside that of Alexander the Great), Plutarch embarked on this earlier work likely without any experience in writing biography, and certainly none in history. To judge by what does survive, his basic method appears to have been to slice up narrative history: *Otho* picks up seamlessly from *Galba*. Still, it was a novel idea, perhaps to be related to the firmer notion in the Flavian period that there was an office of emperor, allowing a collective portrait, such as the earlier Hellenistic lives of tyrants.

Suetonius, writing in Latin, adopted an approach very different from Plutarch. For one thing, he would start with Julius Caesar. Under Trajan, the notion developed—and came to be accepted even by Plutarch himself—that Caesar was the first Roman emperor, in part because of the military Trajan's veneration for this great general; commemorative coinage of Trajan included Caesar alongside later emperors. And even as Plutarch came to his own new way of writing biography, *Parallel Lives*, a format that allowed greater attention to questions of character (and moral judgment), so too would Suetonius find a way to include more of the small, but telling details that he thought were crucial to biography.

∾ *LIVES OF THE CAESARS: scope and subject*

Lives of the Caesars is divided into twelve biographies, extending over multiple books, as follows:

Book 1	*Divus Iulius*	Julius Caesar (100–44 BCE)
Book 2	*Divus Augustus*	Augustus (63–14 CE)
Book 3	*Tiberius*	Tiberius (42 BCE–37 CE; accession 14 CE)
Book 4	*C. Caligula*	Caligula (12–41 CE; accession 37 CE)
Book 5	*Divus Claudius*	Claudius (10 BCE–54 CE; accession 41 CE)
Book 6	*Nero*	Nero (37–68 CE; accession 54 CE)
Book 7	*Galba*	Galba (3 BCE – 69 CE; accession 68 CE)
	Otho	Otho (32–69 CE; accession 69 CE)
	Vitellius	Vitellius (15–69 CE; accession 69 CE)
Book 8	*Divus Vespasianus*	Vespasian (9–69 CE; accession 69 CE)
	Divus Titus	Titus (39–81 CE; accession 79 CE)
	Domitianus	Domitian (51–96 CE; accession 81 CE)

The individual lives themselves have a distinctive pattern. They are *not* accounts of a man's life from birth to death, in chronological order, as Plutarch's biographies (in *Parallel Lives*) were. Rather, Suetonius (with a few exceptions) arranges his lives thus: the emperor's family background; his birth; his life up to gaining power; his public life as emperor; his private life; his death and the omens foretelling it. Reaching the point in *Augustus* where his subject gained power, Suetonius makes his method explicit; he says that he will tell the rest of Augustus' life not chronologically (*neque per tempora*) but topically (*sed per species*), so that the details "may be more clearly set out and recognized."

This is a key statement for understanding Suetonius' whole enterprise. While there is some respect for the biological rhythm of life—birth, death, and what comes between—most of the material Suetonius discovered he arranged thematically, by rubrics, as it were, which he typically makes clear at the start of each section, or subsection. Thus, within the section on the emperor's public life, he ususally includes sections on the emperor's games and shows (*ludi*, *spectacula*), on his building projects (*opera*), and so forth. This easily allows material other than great events to be fitted into the lives (e.g., the emperor's literary pursuits, or his wives and children). From this an important consequence follows: Suetonius' arrangement facilitates comparison of one emperor against another, on such matters as games given, or building projects, or literary pursuits. The selections in this textbook from *Lives of the Caesars* have been chosen to give you a sense of all the typical parts of the Suetonian life.

∾ Suetonius' biographical method: sources and structuring

In writing his imperial lives, Suetonius appears to have made little use of oral sources. Fundamentally, his method was to read. A fair amount of what he needed could actually be found in the narrative histories written in the first century; other, choicer, bits could be dug out of pamphlets, or even the emperor's own literary corpus (Claudius' autobiography, for instance). How much did he consult the sort of documentary sources on which a modern historian, or biographer, would rely? Famously, there are the letters of Augustus, which Suetonius is willing to quote at some length *verbatim*—something an ancient historian, aiming for a uniformly "high" style, would avoid. And occasionally, Suetonius can back up assertions with documentary evidence—public records, for instance, provided verification for the birthplaces of Tiberius and Caligula; copies of the wills of Caesar and Augustus revealed their bequests to the people of Rome; Nero's notebooks, which Suetonius says he has seen, show that the poetry he wrote really was his, not a ghost-writer's. Yet the naming of specific sources such as these is most pronounced in the first two lives, and in the earlier phases of the lives of Tiberius, Caligula, and Claudius. This is one part of their greater richness, remarked on above. (If indeed Tacitus' *Annals* was well underway when Suetonius began his research for *Lives of the Caesars*, this could be an explanation for why he focused his reading on the Caesarian and Augustan age.)

From his materials, Suetonius then had to *compose* a life, and this is where a lot of the work lay—organizing and structuring. The great philologist Friedrich Leo had a theory that when it came to composition, Suetonius applied the method used for telling the lives of literary men (as in his own *On Famous Men*), imported to Rome by Varro: background, birth, and early life, followed by treatment of the author's work, and then his death. This, Leo suggested, accounted for Suetonius' abandonment of chronology in the main section of each of his imperial lives. But scholars have pointed out that the Roman tradition of *laudatio*—and the Greek *encomium*—must be kept in mind too. Augustus' *Res Gestae* is arranged thematically; so too is the still extant *Panegyric* that Pliny delivered in celebration of Trajan in 100 CE. In the published version of the speech, Pliny covers such topics as Trajan's campaigns, his grain distributions, his gladiatorial shows, and also his recreations, his wife, and his attitude to his freedmen—much as Suetonius would do in his lives. This speech, and others like it, may well have been an important model.

Still, the scholarly method employed by the *grammatici* had some relevance for the task at hand. Taking material and placing it in the right category, with only the most relevant points extracted to form a judgment—this was the basic method of scholarly exegesis, and Suetonius adopted it for his imperial lives, to meet his biographical needs. So, when it came time to treat (say) Augustus' execution of justice—an important part of the Roman emperor's "job"—the emphasis is on Augustus' personal style in judging, not the detailed content of the judgments themselves, which Suetonius excluded. In an age without computers, without even index cards or the like, and where the unwieldy scroll was still the main form books took, it was no mean feat for Suetonius to organize the evidence as he did. Most likely, he relied quite a bit on his own memory, which may explain occasional minor errors that he makes.

Suetonius was not, however, straitjacketed by his method. While some headings are repeated from one life to the next, others are more particular (e.g., a section on Claudius and his freedmen, or on Claudius' anger, or on Tiberius' avarice). There are also larger variations in structure. For Caligula, Nero, and Domitian—the three really "bad" emperors (as Suetonius, like other later authors, saw it)— the reigns are divided between good and bad actions, rather than public and private; Tiberius' reign is divided into public and private, but the public section in turn is divided into the positive and (a far longer section) the negative. Such structuring proves a very powerful device in Suetonius' hands: it contributes to the unmasking of the bad emperor's character, itself only fully exposed (rather than caused) by his acquisition of seemingly absolute power.

∾ The achievement of Suetonius

After Plutarch and then Suetonius' efforts, imperial biography has never ceased to be written. Suetonius' distinctive version proved especially influential, later in Rome and beyond. The Senator Marius Maximus carried Suetonius' series forward by producing a second installment of twelve, appropriately culminating with another notorious emperor, Elagabalus (who died in 222 CE). Traces of at least one other major biographer of second-century emperors have been detected in later sources, while Suetonius himself was used in the construction of several fourth-century historical epitomes organized by emperor.

The late fourth century, too, is the likely date of an extraordinary work, the so-called *Historia Augusta*, a collection of lives of emperors, princes, and usurpers, from Hadrian through Numerian (who died in 284 CE); the work purports to be that of six different authors, writing in the time of Diocletian and Constantine the Great (c. 300 CE). The content of the work never seemed very reliable, and in 1887 the historian Dessau argued that the work was in fact from the later fourth century, and came from the pen of only one author. Most now accept the view, but the question of this author's purpose is still debated. Syme, who wrote extensively on the topic, came to think that the author was a "rogue grammarian," who as he continued working, fabricated more and more—not just the names of the six authors attached to the work, but entire documents included in the lives themselves. According to the historian Ammianus Marcellinus, Marius Maximus was in vogue in the late fourth century; the author of the *Historia Augusta* may well then have been exploiting, with the use of fiction, a fascination with the eccentricities of emperors first catered to by Suetonius. (Biographical forms had long appealed to writers of fiction, and would certainly do so into the Christian era.)

Suetonius provided a model for the life of St. Ambrose (c. 340–97 CE), written by Paulinus, and then, quite remarkably, for a *Life of Charlemagne*, written by the monk Einhard in the early ninth century CE. A copy of *Lives of the Caesars* was available in the monastery at Fulda, where Einhard was educated and where he retired, and Suetonius, especially in his life of Augustus, supplied Einhard not just with the structure for his life, but also all of his vocabulary. The oldest extant manuscript of Suetonius was probably copied at nearby Tours in 820 CE, and perhaps derived from the Fulda manuscript, on which the whole textual tradition of Suetonius may therefore rest. Modern scholars, including M. Ihm, who produced the Latin text that appears in this book, reconstruct the original text as best they can using the Tours manuscript, along with a variety of later manuscripts. Later manuscripts are numerous, as were early printed editions, reflecting the great interest shown in Suetonius in the Renaissance.

Readers found Suetonius interesting for his own sake, and his work also influenced the development of early modern biography—helping to end the medieval era of idealization, and fiction. Samuel Johnson could think back to Suetonius when he set out to write his *Lives of the Poets*, his curiosity having been aroused about their lives, their "real character," as he put it. Perhaps paradoxically, then, in the twentieth century, biography's golden age, it was above all through a *fictional* response to Suetonius that *Lives of the Caesars* continued to arouse widespread interest in the English-speaking world. The two great historical novels of Robert Graves, *I, Claudius* and *Claudius the God* (published in 1934), were inspired by a reading of Suetonius, and

drew heavily on him; Graves went on to produce a popular translation of *Lives of the Caesars* for the Penguin Classics, and his novels
reached an even wider audience through the television dramatiza-
tion *I, Claudius* in the 1970s.

Supplying entertainment to millions, nearly two thousand years
after his death, Suetonius, meanwhile, was often being criticized by
professional historians—though often for unfair reasons. Upset that
Suetonius provided so little context for the episodes he includes, they
failed to remember that his work was intended as biography, not history, as its title asserts, *Lives of the Caesars*. And it is not Suetonius'
fault that modern historians have to rely on him for major undertak-
ings of the emperors, in the absence of the fuller historical narratives
that existed in his day. More recently, scholars tackling social and
cultural topics—instead of the more traditional historical topics of
politics and war—have found much of interest in the picture Suetonius evokes of imperial society. Suetonius' interest in dreams and
their significance, or in astrology, or in the place of Greek culture in
Rome, reflects important developments of the first and second cen-
turies CE, related in part to the displacement of the old Republican
nobility that ruled Rome by the monarchical Caesars.

Suetonius, recent interpreters have also suggested, was contributing, through his biographical work, to an ongoing debate on what
the ideal ruler should be in imperial Rome. The serial structure of
his work, and the breakdown of individual lives by rubrics, positively
encourage the reader to compare one Caesar against the next. The
ample discussion of the emperors' private lives was not, it should
be noted, extraneous to judging them as rulers—the private lives
of high-ranking Romans had long been a matter of public discussion, as Cicero's attacks on the sexual and sumptuary vices, or even
physical appearance, of his Senatorial colleagues show, or as Pliny's
Panegyric also shows. There are in Suetonius relatively few norma-
tive judgments—none of the detailed prescriptions that Pliny, for
instance, provides, and little of Cicero's thunder—but a sense does
emerge of what is praiseworthy, and what is not, with the earlier,
fuller lives—especially those of Caesar (Trajan's hero) and the ultimately more successful Augustus (Hadrian's model)—setting up

clear paradigms. Tensions detected in Suetonius' presentation, at the same time, may to some extent reflect tensions inherent to the position of emperor, which lay uneasily between that of a royal monarch, on the one hand, and a citizen magistrate, on the other.

How is Suetonius to be judged as a biographer? Again, it is important to avoid anachronistic judgments. His lack of interest in the childhood of his subjects is typical of ancient biography as a whole, which shows less interest in the exploration of why individuals *become* who they do. But some ancient biographers, notably Plutarch, do at least explore with some depth why a man such as Julius Caesar *did* what he did. Suetonius has less interest in giving coherent and explicit ethical characterizations of his subjects. Some readers even wonder how coherent his subjects are at all, whose lives in Suetonius' hands can seem more like a patchwork quilt than a coherent tapestry—hence criticisms such as Ronald Syme's.

This raises another question, that of reliability, one important to ask, even if, once more, anachronistic censure should be avoided. Given the distance of time separating him from his early subjects, Suetonius was often at the mercy of written sources, some of which, especially the narrative histories, might not have been entirely reliable. As Tacitus famously suggested (*Ann.* 1.1), contemporary histories of the emperors tended to flattery, and those written afterwards to falsification, out of hatred. Important transactions were often quite secret; even those hoping to set out the unvarnished truth might have relied on guesswork or imagination. Such reconstructions are now treated with caution by modern historians, and rightly so. When Suetonius cites his sources, as he does more often in the early lives, he at least gives readers some basis to evaluate his claims. He might then be fairly criticized for abandoning the practice in the later lives. But frequent and laborious discussion of sources risked bogging down the reader. And Suetonius very clearly aimed to write accessibly, as his clear and concise prose style shows.

Suetonius also has sometimes been criticized for a lack of literary artistry, but once again this is to miss the point. The biographer patently aimed for his prose to be unadorned—his is the business-like writing of a scholar, perhaps the imperial bureaucrat too. Where there is color is in the vivid details he so often includes—the costumes worn, the foods consumed, the shows staged, the animals sacrificed, and so on. Inclusion of such details helps quietly to persuade the reader. And his seemingly deadpan style can often be appreciated, after all, as an ironic counterpart to the enormity of his subject. Compactly worded sentences end shockingly, humorously, or both (e.g., *ignotissimum . . . amphoram, Tib.* 42.2; *Incitato . . . destinasse, Gai.* 55.3, *ut . . . semesa, Vit.* 13).

From its first flowering in the Hellenistic period, it was the purpose of biography to entertain. Here, surely Suetonius' achievement was great, for he continues to entertain to this day.

ᕽ *Addendum 1: Suetonius' Latin (and Greek)*

Given his goals of clarity and concision, Suetonius' Latin is relatively easy to read, especially after a little practice. His syntactical usage usually can be explained by the standard rules set out in a work such as Charles Bennett's *New Latin Grammar,* to which the notes in this commentary refer. It is, though, helpful to keep a few general points in mind. One way Suetonius packs a large amount into a small space is to leave unexpressed the subject of his sentences—virtually always the subject of the life in question. Another is very generous use of participles (one scholar has counted over 3,000 in *Lives of the Caesars*). Ablative absolutes abound, as do perfect participles combined with nouns in substitution of longer phrases (Bennett sec. 336.6), and participles, or adjectives, used substantively. There is frequent omission of the verb *esse,* whether as auxiliary or main verb. Objective genitives are also freely used to attain brevity. Suetonius' compact style is well suited to driving home anecdotal points about his subjects, sentence after sentence after sentence.

Suetonius' vocabulary is not exactly what one finds in the highest styles of oratory and historiography (the first Latin prose most students read). Unlike more literary authors, Suetonius is not afraid to use technical terminology, whether in the realms of law, bureaucracy, or the arts. Sometimes he is the first, or only, author to use a particular word, e.g., the verb *confisco* (which gives the English "confiscate"). Related to this is his willingness to cite verbatim documents, including the letters of Augustus but also imperial edicts, speeches, wills, graffiti, verses sung out in the theater, and so forth; a historian, if he were to include such material at all, typically would rewrite it to conform with the rest of his style. For modern scholars Suetonius' willingness to cite such material directly is a precious feature of his scholarly methods.

Suetonius also uses many Greek words (for some examples, see the passage **Nero the artist** below), which again would be excluded by orators or historians, who felt them alien to their style. Users of Latin, though, did freely incorporate Greek words into their discourse; and un-translated Greek phrases, including famous lines of poetry and proverbs, regularly featured in the conversation of educated Romans; it also featured in less formal or grandiose types of writing, especially letters, light essays, and scholarship. Greek was also sometimes used to discuss sensitive matters, with the idea that "plain Latin" would be too blunt. Suetonius regularly includes un-translated Greek in his writing, especially when quoting others, as will be seen in a number of the selections in this book.

∾ Addendum 2: A brief note on Roman names, dates, and sums of money

The following information will be of help in reading and comprehending the selections in this book.

Names

1. Free Roman men of the late Republican and early imperial periods typically had a threefold name, e.g., Gaius Julius Caesar. The middle name (here, Julius) was his *nomen* and marked his clan (*gens*); the first name (such as Gaius), the *praenomen*, marked him as an individual; the last name, the *cognomen*, marked divisions within the clan.

   Some clans did not mark divisions, so that a man might only have two names, e.g., Marcus Antonius. Also, while used in formal documents, the threefold name was not typical in daily conversation, where one might be simply "Gaius" or "Gaius Caesar" (with the *nomen* omitted).

2. The number of *praenomina* was quite small, never more than thirty, in the late Republic eighteen. Because of this, names were, when written out with the *nomen* and/or *cognomen*, abbreviated. These abbreviations were:

Ap.	Appius
A.	Aulus
D.	Decimus
C.	Gaius
Cn.	Gnaeus
K.	Kaeso
L.	Lucius
Mam.	Mamercus
M.	Marcus
M.'	Manius
Num.	Numerius
P.	Publius
Q.	Quintus
Ser.	Servius
Sex.	Sextus
S.	Spurius
Ti.	Tiberius
T.	Titus

3. The all-important *nomen* is often called, for greater clarity, the *nomen gentile* or *nomen gentilicium*. It was inherited by a child, as a surname is now; there was no choice about it. If one's father was a Claudius, one was a Claudius. One belonged to the Claudii (or the *gens Claudia*).

4. In addition to the *cognomen*, sometimes a fourth and even fifth name were added to the *nomen*. These were also at first called *cognomina*, later *agnomina*. They fall into four categories:

    a. a fourth name might mark a further sub-division of the branch of a family, e.g., P. Cornelius Scipio <u>Nasica</u>;

    b. when a man passed from out of his family into another by adoption, he took the threefold name of his adoptive father and added as a fourth name his own *nomen* modified by the suffix -anus; thus when L. Aemilius Paullus was adopted by P. Cornelius Scipio, he became P. Cornelius Scipio <u>Aemilianus</u>;

    c. an additional name, sometimes called *cognomen ex virtute*, was often given by acclamation to a great statesman or general, e.g., P. Cornelius Scipio <u>Africanus</u> (to mark his defeat of Hannibal);

    d. a fourth or fifth name, given as a nickname, might pass to a man's sons, e.g., Q. Caecilius Metellus <u>Celer</u>.

5. In the early imperial period, *praenomina* were used less and less to distinguish individuals of the same father; instead, sons would take on different *cognomina*. Also, for some individuals, an illustrious *cognomen* of some relevance to the family's past might be substituted in place of a *praenomen* (e.g., <u>Paullus</u> Aemilius Lepidus). Very famously, early in his career, the future emperor Augustus took as his *praenomen* the title *Imperator* (abbreviated *Imp.*).

6. After 27 BCE, Augustus' official name was Imperator Caesar Augustus: note that instead of using a regular *nomen* (Iulius), Augustus used the *cognomen* of Caesar; "Augustus" itself was an unprecedented name and meant something like "revered." Subsequent emperors, though all given a threefold name at birth, all marked their entry into imperial office by taking on new names, as follows:

Tiberius:	Tiberius Caesar Augustus
Caligula:	Gaius Caesar Augustus Germanicus
Claudius:	Tiberius Claudius Caesar Augustus Germanicus
Nero:	Nero Claudius Caesar Augustus Germanicus

Galba:	Servius Galba Imperator Caesar Augustus
Otho:	Imperator Marcus Otho Caesar Augustus
Vitellius:	Imperator Aulus Vitellius Caesar
Vespasian:	Imperator Caesar Vespasianus Augustus
Titus:	Imperator Titus Caesar Vespasianus
Domitian:	Imperator Domitianus Caesar Augustus

Shortened names were used to refer to the emperors. For instance, "Tiberius," though an old *praenomen*, served simply to distinguish the second emperor from the first, and so "Gaius" the third emperor from the previous two (note that "Caligula" was a nickname, never officially used). "Titus" distinguished this emperor from his father Vespasian.

7. For free women, the threefold name was largely unknown. Women, in principle, had only the *nomen gentilicium*, inherited from their father. So the daughter of a P. Cornelius Scipio was Cornelia, and all of her sisters would be named Cornelia too. Sometimes the addition of such qualifiers as *maxima* ("eldest") or *minor* ("younger") or an ordinal (e.g., *tertia*) helped clarify, and might be used informally as the woman's name (e.g., Tertia). Sometimes a distinguished woman might use a feminine *cognomen* too, e.g., Caecilia Metella.

8. Male slaves by law did not have the threefold name reserved for male citizens. They took a single name, given to them (frequently) by their master, e.g., Epaphroditus; female slaves also took a single name, e.g., Lais. When a slave was freed, he kept as a sort of *cognomen* his slave name, and added to it the *praenomen* and *nomen* of the man who freed him. So Cicero's secretary Tiro, upon manumission, became M. Tullius Tiro. A female slave, after being freed, would take the *nomen* of her patron while also retaining her old slave name; so, if Lais was freed by Aulus Atilius, she became Atilia Lais.

Dates

1. Romans had a twelve-month calendar. The name of each month (e.g., *Martius, Aprilis*) was an adjective, with *mensis* understood.

2. Individual days were reckoned from three points in the month:

    a. the *Kalendae* (Kalends, abbreviated *Kal.* or *Kl.*), the first day of the month

    b. the *Idus* (Ides, abbreviated *Id.*), the fifteenth day of the month in March, May, July, and October, otherwise the thirteenth;

    c. the *Nonae* (Nones, abbreviated *Non.*), the seventh day of March, May, July, and October, otherwise the fifth.

3. From these points, the days of the months were calculated backwards, as so many days *before* the Nones, Ides, or Kalends. Note also that Romans counted inclusively, so that (for instance) "the third day before the Ides of March" would be 13 March. (Bennett sec. 372 gives a convenient conversion chart.)

    Note also: (1) the name of the month appears as an adjective in agreement with *Kalendae, Nonae, Idus*; (2) the number of days before one of these dates is expressed by a Roman numeral followed by a period; if the day is just one before, in place of a Roman numeral one would use *pridie* (abbreviated *pr.*)

4. Three examples from passages in this book:

    Idus Martiae = "Ides of March" = 15 March

    IIII. Kal. Mai. = "fourth day before the Kalends of May" = 28 April

    VI. Idus Decembris = "sixth day before the Ides of December" = 8 December

5. The year is expressed by the names of the consuls in the ablative absolute, often without a conjunction, e.g., *Camillo Arruntio Domitio Ahenobarbo cons.* = "when Camillus Arruntius and Domitius Ahenobarbus were consuls" (i.e., 32 CE; note that *cons.* is a standard abbreviation for *consulibus*)

Sums of money

1. The *sestertius* was the basic unit of value in the late Republican and early imperial period, and the word for coin, *nummus*, often is equivalent simply to *sestertius*. It is impossible to give a modern equivalency, but one can note that a legionary in the army of Augustus was paid 900 sesterces a year; in Cicero's day, three sesterces a day was considered a normal wage for an unskilled worker.

    Four sesterces made a silver *denarius*, and twenty-five *denarii* made one gold *aureus*.

2. *Sestertia*, the neuter plural, commonly refers to the sum of 1,000 sesterces (i.e., *milia sestertia* is shortened simply to *sestertia*); hence *sestertia ducenta* = 200,000 sesterces or *sestertia quadringenta* = 400,000 sesterces.

3. When *sestertium* is combined with a numeral adverb (e.g., *uicies*, "twenty times"), then typically *centena milia* (100,000) is to be understood; hence, *uicies sestertium* = "twenty times 100,000 sesterces" = 2 million sesterces or *decies sestertium* = "ten times 100,000 sesterces" = 1 million sesterces.

❧ *A note on further reading*

The bibliography included here lists works cited in the introduction, as well as other important scholarship that informs the introduction and the textual notes. For those interested in learning more about Suetonius and his *Caesars* the single best book to read is Wallace-Hadrill (1983). Also worthwhile would be to read the whole of the *Caesars* in English. Robert Graves' translation of the *Caesars* for the Penguin Classics has been revised by James Rives and reissued (Graves 2007); and there is an Oxford World Classics translation by Edwards (2000). Most faithful is the Loeb edition of Rolfe, as revised by Keith Bradley and Donna Hurley, which also includes the remains of *Lives of Famous Men* (Rolfe 1998). Those seeking to read more of Suetonius in Latin might try the life of Claudius, brilliantly edited by

Hurley (2001), or the very entertaining life of Nero, edited by Warmington (1999). On Suetonius' Latin itself, see Mooney (1930: 611–39). All of these works contain ample bibliographies.

As for other topics touched on in this introduction: Hamilton (2007) is a general, but stimulating, introduction to biography written by a practitioner, as well as a *cri de coeur*, with Hamilton (2008) serving as a "how to" companion. On the development of ancient biography Momigliano (1971) is a classic; and see also Lefkowitz (1981) on Greek lives of the poets. Baldwin (1983: 66–100) gathers much material on Roman biography, as do various papers in Smith and Powell (2009). Bowersock (1998) is a brilliant treatment of the genre of imperial biography. On the so-called *Historia Augusta* Syme (1971) is a spirited introduction, while Griffin (2005) sensitively contextualizes Syme's work on this topic and his thoughts on imperial biography. On Suetonius' afterlife Townend (1967) is a good introduction; Bowersock (2009: 52–64) uncovers Suetonius' influence on Dr. Johnson in particular. Papers from an interesting roundtable "Historians and Biography" are printed in *The American Historical Review* 114 (2009): 573–661.

On the Roman emperor see, in addition to the landmark study of Millar (1977), the important papers of Wallace-Hadrill (1981 and 1982) on the ideology of imperial rule. Saller (1980) treats stories told about the emperor and how they might be used historically; Edwards (1993), looking at the rhetoric of immorality, has much of relevance too. Representations of Nero in literary texts are discussed in Elsner and Master (1994) while Vout (2007) explores stories told about the emperors' sex lives. Studies of particular emperors are numerous and are listed in the general works referred to above; and see also for guidance volumes 9–11 of *The Cambridge Ancient History* (second edition). The Latin text of Augustus' extant *Achievements* can be found in Wallace (2000) and see also now Cooley (2009).

↜ *Suggested reading*

Baldwin, B. *Suetonius*. Amsterdam: A. M. Hakkert, 1983.

Balsdon, J. P. V. D. *Life and Leisure in Ancient Rome*. New York: Mc-Graw-Hill, 1969.

Banner, L. W. "Biography as History." *The American Historical Review* 114 (2009): 579–86.

Birley, A. *Hadrian: the Restless Emperor*. London and New York: Routledge, 1997.

Bowersock, G. "*Vita Caesarum*." In *La biographie antique*, edited by W. Ehlers, 193–210. (Foundation Hardt Entretiens 44.) Geneva: Foundation Hardt, 1998.

———. *From Gibbon to Auden: Essays on the Classical Tradition*. Oxford and New York: Oxford University Press, 2009.

Bradley, K. R. "The Imperial Ideal in Suetonius' 'Caesares.'" *Aufstieg und Niedergang der römischen Welt* 2.33.5 (1991): 3701–32.

Carcopino, J. *Daily Life in Ancient Rome*. Revised edition. New Haven and London: Yale University Press, 2003.

Cooley, A. E. *Res Gestae Divi Augusti: Text, Translation, and Commentary*. Cambridge and New York: Cambridge University Press, 2009.

Edwards, C. *The Politics of Immorality in Ancient Rome*. Cambridge and New York: Cambridge University Press, 1993.

———, transl. *Suetonius: Lives of the Caesars*. Oxford and New York: Oxford University Press, 2000.

Elsner, J., and J. Masters. *Reflections of Nero: Culture, History, and Representation*. Chapel Hill: University of North Carolina Press, 1994.

Fraenkel, E. *Horace*. Oxford: Clarendon Press, 1957.

Graves, R., transl. *Suetonius: the Twelve Caesars*. Revised edition. London and New York: Penguin Books, 2007.

Griffin, M. "'Lifting the Mask': Syme on Fictional History." In *History and Fiction: Six Essays Celebrating the Centenary of Ronald Syme (1903–89)*, edited by R. S. O. Tomlin, 16–39. Grime and Selwood: London, 2005.

Hamilton, N. *Biography*. Cambridge, Mass., and London: Harvard University Press, 2007.

———. *How To Do Biography*. Cambridge, Mass., and London: Harvard University Press, 2008.

Hurley, D. W. *Suetonius: Divus Claudius*. Cambridge: Cambridge University Press, 2001.

Lefkowitz, M. *The Lives of the Greek Poets*. Baltimore: Johns Hopkins University Press, 1981.

Lewis, R. G. "Suetonius' 'Caesares' and Their Literary Antecedents." *Aufstieg und Niedergang der römischen Welt* 2.33.5 (1991): 3623–74.

Lounsbury, R. C. *The Arts of Suetonius—an Introduction*. (American University Studies: Classical Languages and Literature 3.) New York: P. Lang, 1987.

Millar, F. Review (in English) of F. Grosso, *La lotta politica al tempo di Commodo. Journal of Roman Studies* 56 (1966): 243–45.

———. *The Emperor in the Roman World*. London: Duckworth, 1977.

Momigliano, A. *The Development of Greek Biography*. Expanded edition. Cambridge, Mass.: Harvard University Press, 1993.

Mooney, G. W. *C. Suetoni Tranquilli de vita Caesarum libri VII–VIII*. London: Longmans, Green and Co., 1930.

Nasaw, D. "*AHR* Roundtable: Historians and Biography: Introduction." *The American Historical Review* 114 (2009): 573–78.

Rolfe, J. C., transl. *Suetonius*. Revised edition. 2 volumes. Cambridge, Mass., and London: Harvard University Press, 1998.

Saller, R. "Anecdotes as Historical Evidence for the Principate." *Greece and Rome* 27 (1980): 69–83.

Smith, C., and A. Powell. *The Lost Memoirs of Augustus and the Development of Roman Autobiography*. Swansea: Classical Press of Wales, 2009.

Syme, R. *The Historia Augusta: A Call of Clarity*. Bonn: Rudolf Habelt, 1971.

———. "History or Biography: the Case of Tiberius Caesar." *Historia* 23 (1974): 481–96. Reprinted in R. Syme, *Roman Papers* vol. 3, 937–52. Oxford: Clarendon Press, 1984.

———. "Caesar: Drama, Legend, History." *The New York Review of Books* 32.3 (February 28, 1985). Reprinted in R. Syme, *Roman Papers* vol. 5, 702–7. Oxford: Clarendon Press, 1988.

———. *The Augustan Aristocracy*. Oxford: Clarendon Press, 1986.

———. "Oligarchy at Rome: a Paradigm for Political Science." *Diogenes* 36 (1988) 56–75. Reprinted in R. Syme, *Roman Papers* vol. 6, 323–37. Oxford: Oxford University Press, 1991.

Townend, G. "The Hippo Inscription and the Career of Suetonius." *Historia* 10 (1961): 99–109.

———. "Suetonius and His Influence." In *Latin Biography*, edited by T. A. Dorey, 79–111. London: Routledge and Kegan Paul, 1967.

Vout, C. *Power and Eroticism in Imperial Rome*. Cambridge and New York: Cambridge University Press, 2007.

Wallace, R. E. *Res Gestae Divi Augusti*. Wauconda, IL: Bolchazy-Carducci Publishers, 2000.

Wallace-Hadrill, A. "The Emperor and His Virtues." *Historia* 30 (1981): 298–323.

———. "*Civilis princeps:* between Citizen and King." *Journal of Roman Studies* 72 (1982): 32–48.

———. *Suetonius: the Scholar and His Caesars*. London: Duckworth, 1983.

Warmington, B. H. *Suetonius: Nero*. Second edition. London: Bristol Classical Press, 2000.

Latin Text

Please note the following divergences from the texts of Ihm and Roth: *Tib.* 44.2, lines 66–67 has been repunctuated; at *Galb.* 3.2, line 21, I print *Viriathini*; *Vesp.* 22, line 16 has been repunctuated; at *Vita Horati*, line 2, I print *vero*; at *Vita Horati*, line 13, I print *Ninnio* for *Innulo*; *Vita Horati*, line 16 I have added <*ut*> and repunctuated; at *Vita Horati*, line 34 I print *Saeculare*; at *Vita Horati*, lines 50–51 I mark a *crux*; *Vita Horati*, lines 56–58 are not obelized; at *Vita Horati*, line 69 I have obelized *Humatus et*; throughout *Vita Horati* consonantal *v* is printed as *u*

∾ *The assassination of Julius Caesar, IUL. 81.1–82.3*

Sed Caesari futura caedes euidentibus prodigiis de- **81**
nuntiata est. paucos ante menses, cum in colonia Capua deducti lege Iulia coloni ad extruendas uillas ue-
tustissima sepulcra dis[s]icerent idque eo studiosius
5 facerent, quod aliquantum uasculorum operis antiqui
scrutantes reperiebant, tabula aenea in monimento, in
quo dicebatur Capys conditor Capuae sepultus, inuenta
est conscripta litteris uerbisque Graecis hac sententia:
quandoque ossa Capyis detecta essent, fore ut
10 illo prognatus manu consanguineorum necare-
tur magnisque mox Italiae cladibus uindicaretur. cuius rei, ne quis fabulosam aut commenticiam **2**

putet, auctor est Cornelius Balbus, familiarissimus Caesaris. proximis diebus equorum greges, quos in trai-
15 ciendo Rubiconi flumini consecrarat ac uagos et sine
custode dimiserat, comperit pertinacissime pabulo abstinere ubertimque flere. et immolantem haruspex Spurinna monuit, caueret periculum, quod non ultra
Martias Idus proferretur. pridie autem easdem Idus   3
20 auem regaliolum cum laureo ramulo Pompeianae curiae
se inferentem uolucres uarii generis ex proximo ne-
more persecutae ibidem discerpserunt. ea uero nocte,
cui inluxit dies caedis, et ipse sibi uisus est per quietem interdum supra nubes uolitare, alias cum Ioue
25 dextram iungere; et Calpurnia uxor imaginata est con-
labi fastigium domus maritumque in gremio suo con-
fodi; ac subito cubiculi fores sponte patuerunt.

   Ob haec simul et ob infirmam ualitudinem diu   4
cunctatus an se contineret et quae apud senatum pro-
30 posuerat agere differret, tandem Decimo Bruto adhortante, ne frequentis ac iam dudum opperientis desti-
tueret, quinta fere hora progressus est libellumque
insidiarum indicem ab obuio quodam porrectum li-
bellis ceteris, quos sinistra manu tenebat, quasi mox
35 lecturus commiscuit. dein pluribus hostiis caesis, cum
litare non posset, introiit curiam spreta religione Spurinnamque irridens et ut falsum arguens, quod sine
ulla sua noxa Idus Martiae adessent: quanquam is
uenisse quidem eas diceret, sed non praeterisse. assi-   **82**
40 dentem conspirati specie officii circumsteterunt, ilico-

que Cimber Tillius, qui primas partes susceperat, quasi
aliquid rogaturus propius accessit renuentique et gestu[m] in aliud tempus differenti ab utroque umero
togam adprehendit: deinde clamantem: 'ista quidem
45   uis est!' alter e Cascis auersum uulnerat paulum in-
fra iugulum. Caesar Cascae brachium arreptum gra-   2
phio traiecit conatusque prosilire alio uulnere tardatus
est; utque animaduertit undique se strictis pugionibus
peti, toga caput obuoluit, simul sinistra manu sinum
50   ad ima crura deduxit, quo honestius caderet etiam
inferiore corporis parte uelata. atque ita tribus et
uiginti plagis confossus est uno modo ad primum ictum
gemitu sine uoce edito, etsi tradiderunt quidam Marco
Bruto irruenti dixisse: καὶ σὺ τέκνον; exanimis diffu-   3
55   gientibus cunctis aliquamdiu iacuit, donec lecticae impositum, dependente brachio, tres seruoli domum rettulerunt. nec in tot uulneribus, ut Antistius medicus
existimabat, letale ullum repertum est, nisi quod se-
cundo loco in pectore acceperat.

❧ The work habits of Augustus, AUG. 78

Post cibum meridianum, ita ut uestitus calciatusque   78
erat, retectis pedibus paulisper conquiescebat opposita
ad oculos manu. a cena in lecticulam se lucubratoriam
recipiebat; ibi, donec residua diurni actus aut omnia
5   aut ex maxima parte conficeret, ad multam noctem
permanebat. in lectum inde transgressus non amplius
cum plurimum quam septem horas dormiebat, ac ne

eas quidem continuas, sed ut in illo temporis spatio
ter aut quater expergisceretur. si interruptum somnum   2
10 reciperare, ut euenit, non posset, lectoribus aut fabu-
latoribus arcessitis resumebat producebatque ultra pri-
mam saepe lucem. nec in tenebris uigilauit umquam
nisi assidente aliquo. matutina uigilia offendebatur; ac
si uel officii uel sacri causa maturius uigilandum esset,
15 ne id contra commodum faceret, in proximo cuiuscum-
que domesticorum cenaculo manebat. sic quoque saepe
indigens somni, et dum per uicos deportaretur et depo-
sita lectica inter aliquas moras condormiebat.

∾ The work habits of Augustus (continued), Aug. 33

ipse ius dixit   **33**
assidue et in noctem nonnumquam, si parum corpore
ualeret, lectica pro tribunali collocata uel etiam domi
cubans. dixit autem ius non diligentia modo summa
5 sed et lenitate, siquidem manifesti parricidii reum, ne
culleo insueretur, quod non nisi confessi adficiuntur
hac poena, ita fertur interrogasse: 'certe patrem
tuum non occidisti?' et cum de falso testamento   2
ageretur omnesque signatores lege Cornelia tenerentur,
10 non tantum duas tabellas, damnatoriam et absoluto-
riam, simul cognoscentibus dedit, sed tertiam quoque,
qua ignosceretur iis, quos fraude ad signandum uel
errore inductos constitisset. appellationes quotannis   3
urbanorum quidem litigatorum praetori delegabat ur-

15 bano, at prouincialium consularibus uiris, quos singulos
cuiusque prouinciae negotiis praeposuisset.

∾ *Tiberius on Capri, Tib. 40–44*

Peragrata Campania, cum Capuae Capitolium, Nolae   **40**
templum Augusti, quam causam profectionis praeten-
derat, dedicasset, Capreas se contulit, praecipue delectatus insula, quod uno paruoque litore adiretur, saepta
5   undique praeruptis immensae altitudinis rupibus et profundo mari[s]. statimque reuocante assidua obtestatione
populo propter cladem, qua apud Fidenas supra uiginti
hominum milia gladiatorio munere amphitheatri ruina
perierant, transiit in continentem potestatemque omni-
10 bus adeundi sui fecit: tanto magis, quod urbe egrediens
ne quis se interpellaret edixerat ac toto itinere adeuntis
submouerat.

Regressus in insulam rei p. quidem curam usque   **41**
adeo abiecit, ut postea non decurias equitum umquam
15 supplerit, non tribunos militum praefectosque, non
prouinciarum praesides ullos mutauerit, Hispaniam et
Syriam per aliquot annos sine consularibus legatis
habuerit, Armeniam a Parthis occupari, Moesiam a
Dacis Sarmatisque, Gallias a Germanis uastari neglexe-
20 rit: magno dedecore imperii nec minore discrimine.
ceterum secreti licentiam nanctus et quasi ciuitatis   **42**
oculis remotis, cuncta simul uitia male diu dissimulata
tandem profudit: de quibus singillatim ab exordio referam. in castris tiro etiam tum propter nimiam uini

25 auiditatem pro Tiberio Biberius, pro Claudio Cal-
    dius, pro Nerone Mero uocabatur. postea princeps in
    ipsa publicorum morum correctione cum Pomponio
    Flacco et L. Pisone noctem continuumque biduum
    epulando potandoque consumpsit, quorum alteri Syriam
30 prouinciam, alteri praefecturam urbis confestim de-
    tulit, codicillis quoque iucundissimos et omnium hora-
    rum amicos professus. Cestio Gall[i]o, libidinoso ac   2
    prodigo seni, olim ab Augusto ignominia notato et a
    se ante paucos dies apud senatum increpito cenam ea
35 lege condixit, ne quid ex consuetudine immutaret aut
    demeret, utque nudis puellis ministrantibus cenaretur.
    ignotissimum quaesturae candidatum nobilissimis ante-
    posuit ob epotam in conuiuio propinante se uini am-
    phoram. Asellio Sabino sestertia ducenta donauit pro
40 dialogo, in quo boleti et ficedulae et ostreae et turdi
    certamen induxerat. nouum denique officium instituit
    a uoluptatibus, praeposito equite R. T. Caesonio Prisco.
    secessu uero Caprensi etiam sellaria excogitauit, sedem   **43**
    arcanarum libidinum, in quam undique conquisiti
45 puellarum et exoletorum greges monstrosique concu-
    bitus repertores, quos spintrias appellabat, triplici
    serie conexi, in uicem incestarent coram ipso, ut aspectu
    deficientis libidines excitaret. cubicula plurifariam   2
    disposita tabellis ac sigillis lasciuissimarum pictura-
50 rum et figurarum adornauit librisque Elephantidis in-
    struxit, ne cui in opera edenda exemplar impe[t]ratae
    schemae deesset. in siluis quoque ac nemoribus passim

Venerios locos commentus est prost[r]antisque per antra
et cauas rupes ex utriusque sexus pube Paniscorum et
55 Nympharum habitu, quae palam iam et uulgo nomine
insulae abutentes 'Caprineum' dictitabant.

Maiore adhuc ac turpiore infamia flagrauit, uix ut **44**
referri audiriue, nedum credi fas sit quasi pueros
primae teneritudinis, quos pisciculos uocabat, insti-
60 tueret, ut natanti sibi inter femina uersarentur ac
luderent lingua morsuque sensim adpetentes; atque
etiam quasi infantes firmiores, necdum tamen lacte
depulsos, inguini ceu papillae admoueret, pronior sane
ad id genus libidinis et natura et aetate. quare Par-
65 rasi quoque tabulam, in qua Meleagro Atalanta ore 2
morigeratur, legatam sibi sub condicione ut, si argu-
mento offenderetur, decies pro ea sestertium acciperet,
non modo praetulit, sed et in cubiculo dedicauit. fertur
etiam in sacrificando quondam captus facie ministri
70 acerram praeferentis nequisse abstinere, quin paene
uixdum re diuina peracta ibidem statim seductum constupraret simulque fratrem eius tibicinem; atque utrique mox, quod mutuo flagitium exprobrarant, crura
fregisse.

❧ Tiberius on Capri (continued), *TIB. 60*

In paucis diebus quam Capreas attigit piscatori, qui **60**
sibi secretum agenti grandem mullum inopinanter obtulerat, perfricari eodem pisce faciem iussit, territus
quod is a tergo insulae per aspera et deuia erepsisset

5 ad se; gratulanti autem inter poenam, quod non et
lucustam, quam praegrandem ceperat, obtulisset, lucusta quoque lacerari os imperauit. militem praetorianum ob subreptum e uiridiario pauonem capite puniit.
in quodam itinere lectica, qua uehebatur, uepribus
10 impedita exploratorem uiae, primarum cohortium centurionem, stratum humi paene ad necem uerberauit.

∾ *Tiberius on Capri (continued)*, Tib. 62.2

carnificinae eius ostenditur locus   **62.**2
Capreis, unde damnatos post longa et exquisita tor-
menta praecipitari coram se in mare iubebat, excipiente
classiariorum manu et contis atque remis elidente ca-
5 dauera, ne cui residui spiritus quicquam inesset. ex-
cogitauerat autem inter genera cruciatus etiam, ut
larga meri potione per fallaciam oneratos, repente
ueretris deligatis, fidicularum simul urinaeque tormento
distenderet.

∾ *Caligula's capers*, Gai. 19

Nouum praeterea atque inauditum genus spectaculi   **19**
excogitauit. nam Baiarum medium interuallum †Pu-
teolanas moles, trium milium et sescentorum fere
passuum spatium, ponte coniunxit contractis undique
5 onerariis nauibus et ordine duplici ad anc[h]oras conlocatis superiectoque terreno ac derecto in Appiae uiae
formam. per hunc pontem ultro citro commeauit biduo   2
continenti, primo die phalerato equo insignisque quercea

corona et caetra et gladio aureaque chlamyde, postridie

10   quadrigario habitu curriculoque biiugi famosorum equorum, prae se ferens Dareum puerum ex Parthorum
obsidibus, comitante praetorianorum agmine et in esse-
dis cohorte amicorum. scio plerosque existimasse talem   3
a Gaio pontem excogitatum aemulatione Xerxis, qui

15   non sine admiratione aliquanto angustiorem Helles-
pontum contabulauerit; alios, ut Germaniam et Bri-
tanniam, quibus imminebat, alicuius inmensi operis
fama territaret. Sed auum meum narrantem puer audiebam, causam operis ab interioribus aulicis proditam,

20   quod Thrasyl<l>us mathematicus anxio de successore
Tiberio et in uerum nepotem proniori affirmasset non
magis Gaium imperaturum quam per Baianum
sinum equis discursurum.

ᔐ *Caligula's capers (continued), GAI. 55*

Quorum uero studio teneretur, omnibus ad insaniam   **55**
fauit. Mnesterem pantomimum etiam inter spectacula
osculabatur, ac si qui saltante eo uel leuiter obstreperet,
detrahi iussum manu sua flagellabat. equiti R. tu-

5   multuanti per centurionem denuntiauit, abiret sine
mora Ostiam perferretque ad Ptolemaeum regem in
Mauretaniam codicillos suos; quorum exemplum erat:
'ei quem istoc misi, neque boni quicquam ne-
que mali feceris.' Thr<a>eces quosdam Germanis   2

10   corporis custodibus praeposuit. murmillonum armatu-
ras recidit. Columbo uictori, leuiter tamen saucio,

uenenum in plagam addidit, quod ex eo Columbinum
appellauit; sic certe inter alia uenena scriptum ab eo
repertum est. prasinae factioni ita addictus et deditus,
15 ut cenaret in stabulo assidue et maneret, agitatori
Eutycho comisatione quadam in apophoretis uicies
sestertium contulit. Incitato equo, cuius causa pridie 3
circenses, ne inquietaretur, uiciniae silentium per mi-
lites indicere solebat, praeter equile marmoreum et
20 praesaepe eburneum praeterque purpurea tegumenta
ac monilia e gemmis domum etiam et familiam et
supellectilem dedit, quo lautius nomine eius inuitati
acciperentur; consulatum quoque traditur destinasse.

ᔕ *Caligula's capers (continued), GAI. 45–46*

Mox deficiente belli materia paucos de custodia **45**
Germanos traici occulique trans Rhenum iussit ac sibi
post prandium quam tumultuosissime adesse hostem
nuntiari. quo facto proripuit se cum amicis et parte
5 equitum praetorianorum in proximam siluam, trun-
catisque arboribus et in modum tropaeorum adornatis
ad lumina reuersus, eorum quidem qui secuti non
essent timiditatem et ignauiam corripuit, comites autem
et participes uictoriae nouo genere ac nomine corona-
10 rum donauit, quas distinctas solis ac lunae siderum-
que specie exploratorias appellauit. rursus obsides 2
quosdam abductos e litterario ludo clamque praemissos,
deserto repente conuiuio, cum equitatu insecutus ueluti
profugos ac reprehensos in catenis reduxit; in hoc

15 quoque mimo praeter modum intemperans. repetita
    cena renuntiantis coactum agmen sic ut erant loricatos
    ad discumbendum adhortatus est. monuit etiam no-
    tissimo Vergili *<Aen. I 207>* uersu durarent se-
    cundisque se rebus seruarent.

20   Atque inter haec absentem senatum populumque   3
    grauissimo obiurgauit edicto, quod Caesare proeliante
    et tantis discriminibus obiecto tempestiua con-
    uiuia, circum et theatra et amoenos secessus
    celebrarent. postremo quasi perpetraturus bellum,   **46**
25 derecta acie in litore Oceani ac ballistis machinisque
    dispositis, nemine gnaro aut opinante quidnam coepturus
    esset, repente ut conchas legerent galeasque et sinus
    replerent imperauit, spolia Oceani uocans Capitolio
    Palatioque debita, et in indicium uictoriae altissi-
30 mam turrem excitauit, ex qua ut Pharo noctibus ad
    regendos nauium cursus ignes emicarent; pronuntiato-
    que militi donatiuo centenis uiritim denariis, quasi
    omne exemplum liberalitatis supergressus: 'abite,' in-
    quit, 'laeti, abite locupletes.'

∾ *Claudius the scholar, CLAUD. 41–42*

    Historiam in adulescentia hortante T. Liuio, Sul-
    picio uero Flauo etiam adiuuante, scribere adgressus
    est. et cum primum frequenti auditorio commisisset,
    aegre perlegit refrigeratus saepe a semet ipso. nam
5   cum initio recitationis defractis compluribus subsellis
    obesitate cuiusdam risus exortus esset, ne sedato qui-

dem tumultu temperare potuit, quin ex interuallo subinde facti reminisceretur cachinnosque reuocaret. in
principatu quoque et scripsit plurimum et assidue
10 recitauit per lectorem. initium autem sumpsit historiae post caedem Caesaris dictatoris, sed et transiit
ad inferiora tempora coepitque a pace ciuili, cum
sentiret neque libere neque uere sibi de superioribus
tradendi potestatem relictam, correptus saepe et a matre
15 et ab auia. prioris materiae duo uolumina, posterioris
unum et quadraginta reliquit. composuit et de uita
sua octo uolumina, magis inepte quam ineleganter;
item Ciceronis defensionem aduersus Asini Galli
libros satis eruditam. nouas etiam commentus est
20 litteras tres ac numero ueterum quasi maxime ne-
cessarias addidit; de quarum ratione cum priuatus adhuc uolumen edidisset, mox princeps non difficulter
optinuit ut in usu quoque promiscuo essent. extat
talis scriptura in plerisque libris ac diurnis titulisque
25 operum.

Nec minore cura Graeca studia secutus est, amorem
praestantiamque linguae occasione omni professus. cui-
dam barbaro Graece ac Latine disserenti: 'cum utroque,' inquit, 'sermone nostro sis paratus'; et in
30 commendanda patribus conscriptis Achaia, gratam
sibi prouinciam ait communium studiorum com-
mercio; ac saepe in senatu legatis perpetua oratione
respondit. multum uero pro tribunali etiam Homericis
locutus est uersibus. quotiens quidem hostem uel in-

35 sidiatorem ultus esset, excubitori tribuno signum de
more poscenti non temere aliud dedit quam <*Il.24, 369
Od. 21, 133*>:

ἄνδρ' ἀπαμύνασθαι, ὅτε τις πρότερος χαλεπήνῃ.

Denique et Graecas scripsit historias, Tyrrhenicon
uiginti, Carchedoniacon octo. quarum causa ueteri
40 Alexandriae Musio additum ex ipsius nomine <nouum>;
institutumque ut quotannis in altero Tyrrhenicon libri,
in altero Carchedoniacon diebus statutis uelut in audi-
torio recitarentur toti a singulis per uices.

∾ Nero the artist, NER. 20–21

Inter ceteras disciplinas pueritiae tempore imbutus **20**
et musica, statim ut imperium adeptus est, Terpnum
citharoedum uigentem tunc praeter alios arcessiit die-
busque continuis post cenam canenti in multam noctem
5 assidens paulatim et ipse meditari exercerique coepit
neque eorum quicquam omittere, quae generis eius
artifices uel conseruandae uocis causa uel augendae
factitarent; sed et plumbeam chartam supinus pectore
sustinere et clystere uomituque purgari et abstinere
10 pomis cibisque officientibus; donec blandiente profectu,
quamquam exiguae uocis et fuscae, prodire in scaenam
concupiit, subinde inter familiares Graecum prouerbium
iactans occultae musicae nullum esse respec-
tum. et prodit Neapoli primum ac ne concusso qui- 2
15 dem repente motu terrae theatro ante cantare destitit,
quam incohatum absolueret nomon. ibidem saepius et

per complures cantauit dies; sumpto etiam ad reficien-
dam uocem breui tempore, impatiens secreti a balineis
in theatrum transiit mediaque in orchestra frequente
20 populo epulatus, si paulum subbibisset, aliquid se
sufferi tinniturum Graeco sermone promisit. captus   3
autem modulatis Alexandrinorum laudationibus, qui de
nouo commeatu Neapolim confluxerant, plures Alexandria euocauit. neque eo segnius adulescentulos eque-
25 stris ordinis et quinque amplius milia e plebe ro-
bustissimae iuuentutis undique elegit, qui diuisi in
factiones plausuum genera condiscerent—bombos
et imbrices et testas uocabant—operamque nauarent
cantanti sibi, insignes pinguissima coma et excellen-
30 tissimo cultu, pu[e]ris ac sine anulo laeuis, quorum duces
quadringena milia sestertia merebant.

Cum magni aestimaret cantare etiam Romae, Nero-   **21**
neum agona ante praestitutam diem reuocauit flagitanti-
busque cunctis caelestem uocem respondit quidem in
35 hortis se copiam uolentibus facturum, sed adiuuante uulgi preces etiam statione militum, quae tunc
excubabat, repraesentaturum se pollicitus est libens;
ac sine mora nomen suum in albo profitentium citharoedorum iussit ascribi sorticulaque in urnam cum
40 ceteris demissa intrauit ordine suo, simul praefecti
praetorii citharam sustinentes, post tribuni militum
iuxtaque amicorum intimi. utque constitit, peracto   2
principio, Niobam se cantaturum per Cluuium Rufum consularem pronuntiauit et in horam fere deci-

45 mam perseuerauit coronamque eam et reliquam certa-
   minis partem in annum sequentem distulit, ut saepius
   canendi occasio esset. quod cum tardum uideretur,
   non cessauit identidem se publicare. dubitauit etiam
   an priuatis spectaculis operam inter scaenicos daret
50 quodam praetorum sestertium decies offerente. tragoe-   3
   dias quoque cantauit personatus heroum deorumqué,
   item heroidum ac dearum, personis effectis ad simili-
   tudinem oris sui et feminae, prout quamque diligeret.
   inter cetera cantauit Canac[h]en parturientem, Oresten
55 matricidam, Oedipodem excaecatum, Herculem insa-
   num. in qua fabula fama est tirunculum militem positum ad custodiam aditus, cum eum ornari ac uinciri
   catenis, sicut argumentum postulabat, uideret, accurrisse
   ferendae opis gratia.

∾ *Galba's family, GALB. 2–3*

   Neroni Galba successit nullo gradu contingens Cae-   2
   sarum domum, sed haud dubie nobilissimus magnaque
   et uetere prosapia, ut qui statuarum titulis pronepotem
   se Quinti Catuli Capitolini semper ascripserit, impera-
5 tor uero etiam stemma in atrio proposuerit, quo pater-
   nam originem ad Iouem, maternam ad Pasiphaam Mi-
   nonis uxorem referret.

   Imagines et elogia uniuersi generis exequi longum   3
   est, familiae breuiter attingam. qui primus Sulpiciorum
10 cognomen Galbae tulit cur aut unde traxerit, ambigitur.
   quidam putant, quod oppidum Hispaniae frustra diu

oppugnatum inlitis demum galbano facibus succenderit; alii, quod in diuturna ualitudine galbeo, id est
remediis lana inuolutis, assidue uteretur; nonnulli, quod
15 praepinguis fuerit uisus, quem galbam Galli uocent;
uel contra, quod tam exilis, quam sunt animalia quae
in aesculis nascuntur appellanturque galbae. familiam   2
illustrauit Seruius Galba consularis, temporum suorum
†et eloquentissimus, quem tradunt Hispaniam ex prae-
20 tura optinentem, triginta Lusitanorum milibus perfidia
trucidatis, Viriathini belli causam extitisse. eius nepos
ob repulsam consulatus infensus Iulio Caesari, cuius
legatus in Gallia fuerat, conspirauit cum Cassio et
Bruto, propter quod Pedia lege damnatus est. ab hoc   3
25 sunt imperatoris Galbae auus ac pater: auus clarior
studiis quam dignitate—non enim egressus praeturae
gradum—multiplicem nec incuriosam historiam edidit;
pater consulatu functus, quanquam breui corpore atque
etiam gibber modicaeque in dicendo facultatis, causas
30 industrie actitauit. uxores habuit Mummiam Achaicam,   4
neptem Catuli proneptemque L. Mummi, qui Corinthum
excidit; item Liuiam Ocellinam ditem admodum et pul-
chram, a qua tamen nobilitatis causa appetitus ultro
existimatur et aliquanto enixius, postquam subinde
35 instanti uitium corporis secreto posita ueste detexit,
ne quasi ignaram fallere uideretur. ex Achaica liberos
Gaium et Seruium procreauit, quorum maior Gaius
attritis facultatibus urbe cessit prohibitusque a Tiberio
sortiri anno suo proconsulatum uoluntaria morte obiit.

✧ Otho's youth, Отн. 2–3

Otho imperator IIII. Kal. Mai. natus est Camillo   **2**
Arruntio Domitio Ahenobarbo cons. a prima adulescentia prodigus ac procax, adeo ut saepe flagris obiurgaretur a patre, ferebatur et uagari noctibus solitus
5 atque inualidum quemque obuiorum uel potulentum
corripere ac distento sago impositum in sublime iactare.
post patris deinde mortem libertinam aulicam gratiosam,   **2**
quo efficacius coleret, etiam diligere simulauit quamuis
anum ac paene decrepitam; per hanc insinuatus Neroni
10 facile summum inter amicos locum tenuit congruentia
morum, ut uero quidam tradunt, et consuetudine mutui
stupri. ac tantum potentia ualuit, ut damnatum repetundis consularem uirum, ingens praemium pactus, prius
quam plane restitutionem ei impetrasset, non dubitaret
15 in senatum ad agendas gratias introducere. omnium   **3**
autem consiliorum secretorumque particeps die, quem
necandae matri Nero destinarat, ad auertendas suspi-
ciones cenam utrique exquisitissimae comitatis dedit;
item Poppaeam Sabinam tunc adhuc amicam eius, ab-
20 ductam marito demandatamque interim sibi, nuptiarum
specie recepit nec corrupisse contentus adeo dilexit,
ut ne riualem quidem Neronem aequo tulerit animo
creditur certe non modo missos ad arcessendam non   **2**
recepisse, sed ipsum etiam exclusisse quondam pro
25 foribus astantem miscentemque frustra minas et preces
ac depositum reposcentem. quare diducto matrimonio
sepositus est per causam legationis in Lusitaniam. et

satis uisum, ne poena acrior mimum omnem diuulgaret,

qui tamen sic quoque hoc disticho

30 enotuit:

> cur Otho mentito sit, quaeritis, exul honore?
> uxoris moechus coeperat esse suae.

Prouinciam administrauit quaestorius per decem

annos, moderatione atque abstinentia singulari.

∾ *Vitellius the glutton, VIT. 13*

Sed uel praecipue luxuriae saeuitaeque deditus   **13**

epulas trifariam semper, interdum quadrifariam disper-

tiebat, in iantacula et prandia et cenas comisationes-

que, facile omnibus sufficiens uomitandi consuetudine.

5 indicebat autem aliud alii eadem die, nec cuiquam minus

singuli apparatus quadringenis milibus nummum con-

stiterunt. famosissima super ceteras fuit cena data ei   2

aduenticia a fratre, in qua duo milia lectissimorum

piscium, septem auium apposita traduntur. hanc quoque

10 exuperauit ipse dedicatione patinae, quam ob immensam

magnitudinem clipeum Mineruae πολιούχου dicti-

tabat. in hac scarorum iocinera, phasianarum et pauo-

num cerebella, linguas phoenicopterum, murenarum

lactes a Parthia usque fretoque Hispanico per nauar-

15 chos ac triremes petitarum commiscuit. ut autem   3

homo non profundae modo sed intempestiuae quoque

ac sordidae gulae, ne in sacrificio quidem umquam aut

itinere ullo temperauit, quin inter altaria ibidem statim

uiscus et farris †paene rapta e foco manderet circaque
20 uiarum popinas fumantia obsonia uel pridiana atque
semesa.

∾ The work habits of Vespasian, VESP. 21–22

Ordinem uitae hunc fere tenuit. in principatu ma-   **21**
turius semper ac de nocte uigilabat; dein perlectis
epistulis officiorumque omnium breuiariis, amicos ad-
mittebat, ac dum salutabatur, et calciabat ipse se et
5   amiciebat; postque decisa quaecumque obuenissent ne-
gotia gestationi et inde quieti uacabat, accubante ali-
qua pallacarum, quas in locum defunctae Caenidis
plurimas constituerat; a secreto in balineum tricliniu-
que transibat. nec ullo tempore facilior aut indulgen-
10 tior traditur, eaque momenta domestici ad aliquid peten-
dum magno <o>pere captabant.

Et super cenam autem et semper alias comissimus   **22**
multa ioco transigebat; erat enim dicacitatis plurimae,
etsi scurrilis et sordidae, ut ne praetextatis quidem
15 uerbis abstineret. et tamen nonnulla eius facetissima
extant, in quibus et haec: Mestrium Florum consularem, admonitus ab eo plaustra potius quam plostra
dicenda, postero die Flaurum salutauit. expugnatus
autem a quadam, quasi amore suo deperiret, cum per-
20 ductae pro concubitu sestertia quadringenta donasset,
admonente dispensatore, quem ad modum summam
rationibus uellet inferri: 'Vespasiano,' inquit, 'adamato.'

◌ *Titus and the eruption of Vesuvius, TIT. 8.3–4*

Quaedam sub eo fortuita ac tristia acciderunt, ut   **8.**3
conflagratio Vesuuii montis in Campania, et incendium
Romae per triduum totidemque noctes, item pestilentia
quanta non temere alias. in iis tot aduersis ac talibus
5 non modo principis sollicitudinem sed et parentis affec-
tum unicum praestitit, nunc consolando per edicta,
nunc opitulando quatenus suppeteret facultas. cura-   4
tores restituendae Campaniae e consularium numero
sorte duxit; bona oppressorum in Vesuuio, quorum
10 heredes non extabant, restitutioni afflictarum ciuitatium
attribuit. urbis incendio nihil publice nisi perisse
testatus, cuncta praetoriorum suorum ornamenta operi-
bus ac templis destinauit praeposuitque compluris ex
equestri ordine, quo quaeque maturius peragerentur.
15 medendae ualitudini leniendisque morbis nullam diui-
nam humanamque opem non adhibuit inquisito omni
sacrificiorum remediorumque genere.

◌ *Difficulties for Domitian, DOM. 12*

Exhaustus operum ac munerum inpensis stipen-   **12**
dioque, quod adiecerat, temptauit quidem ad releuan-
dos castrenses sumptus numerum militum deminuere;
sed cum et obnoxium se barbaris per hoc animaduer-
5 teret neque eo setius in explicandis oneribus haereret,
nihil pensi habuit quin praedaretur omni modo. bona
uiuorum ac mortuorum usquequaque quolibet et accu-

satore et crimine corripiebantur. satis erat obici quale-
cumque factum dictum[q]ue aduersus maiestatem prin-
10 cipis. confiscabantur alienissimae hereditates uel uno 2
existente, qui diceret audisse se ex defuncto, cum uiueret,
heredem sibi Caesarem esse. praeter ceteros Iudaicus
fiscus acerbissime actus est; ad quem deferebantur, qui
uel[ut] inprofessi Iudaicam uiuerent uitam uel dissi-
15 mulata origine imposita genti tributa non pependissent.
interfuisse me adulescentulum memini, cum a procuratore frequentissimoque consilio inspiceretur nonage-
narius senex, an circumsectus esset.

Ab iuuenta minime ciuilis animi, confidens etiam et 3
20 cum uerbis tum rebus immodicus, Caenidi patris con-
cubinae ex Histria reuersae osculumque, ut assuerat,
offerenti manum praebuit; generum fratris indigne
ferens albatos et ipsum ministros habere, proclamauit:
<*Hom. Il. 2, 204*>:

25 οὐκ ἀγαθὸν πολυκοιρανίη.

∾ Difficulties for Domitian (continued), Dom. 18

Statura fuit procera, uultu modesto ruborisque **18**
pleno, grandibus oculis, uerum acie hebetiore; praeterea
pulcher ac decens, maxime in iuuenta, et quidem toto
corpore exceptis pedibus, quorum digitos restrictiores
5 habebat; postea caluitio quoque deformis et obesitate
uentris et crurum gracilitate, quae tamen ei ualitudine longa remacruerant. commendari se uerecundia 2

oris adeo sentiebat, ut apud senatum sic quondam iactauerit: 'usque adhoc certe et animum meum
10 probastis et uultum.' caluitio ita offendebatur, ut
in contumeliam suam traheret, si cui alii ioco uel iurgio
obiectaretur; quamuis libello, quem de cura capillorum ad amicum edidit, haec etiam, simul illum seque
consolans, inseruerit <*Hom. Il. 21, 108*>:

15   οὐχ ὁρά<ᾳ>ς, οἷος κἀγὼ καλός τε μέγας τε;
eadem me tamen manent capillorum fata, et
forti animo fero comam in adulescentia senes-
centem. scias nec gratius quicquam decore nec
breuius.'

∾ *Vita Horati*

Q. Horatius Flaccus, Venusinus, pa-
tre ut ipse tradit libertino et exactionum coactore, (ut uero
creditum est salsamentario, cum illi quidam in altercatione
exprobrasset: 'Quotiens ego uidi patrem tuum brachio se
5   emungentem!') bello Philippensi excitus a Marco Bruto im-
peratore, tribunus militum meruit; uictisque partibus uenia
inpetrata scriptum quaestorium comparauit. Ac primo Maecenati, mox Augusto insinuatus non mediocrem in amborum
amicitia locum tenuit. Maecenas quantopere eum dilexerit
10 satis testatur illo epigrammate:

Ni te uisceribus meis, Horati,
Plus iam diligo, tu tuum sodalem
Ninnio uideas strigosiorem:

sed multo magis extremis iudiciis tali ad Augustum elogio:

15 'Horati Flacci ut mei esto memor!' Augustus epistolarum
quoque ei officium optulit <ut> hoc ad Maecenatem scripto
significat: 'Ante ipse sufficiebam scribendis epistolis amicorum, nunc occupatissimus et infirmus Horatium nostrum
a te cupio abducere. Veniet ergo ab ista parasitica mensa
20 ad hanc regiam, et nos in epistolis scribendis iuuabit.' Ac
ne recusanti quidem aut suscensuit quicquam aut amicitiam
suam ingerere desiit. Extant epistolae, e quibus argumenti
gratia pauca subieci: 'Sume tibi aliquid iuris apud me,
tamquam si conuictor mihi fueris; recte enim et non te-
25 mere feceris, quoniam id usus mihi tecum esse uolui, si
per ualitudinem tuam fieri possit.' Et rursus: 'Tui qualem
habeam memoriam, poteris ex Septimio quoque nostro au-
dire; nam incidit ut illo coram fieret a me tui mentio. Neque enim si tu superbus amicitiam nostram spreuisti, ideo
30 nos quoque ἀνθυφερηφανοῦμεν.' Praeterea saepe eum inter alios iocos 'purissimum penem et homuncionem lepidissimum' appellat, unaque et altera liberalitate locupletauit.
Scripta quidem eius usque adeo probauit mansuraque perpetua opinatus est, ut non modo Saeculare carmen compo-
35 nendum iniunxerit sed et Vindelicam uictoriam Tiberii Dru-
sique, priuignorum suorum, eumque coegerit propter hoc
tribus carminum libris ex longo interuallo quartum addere;
post Sermones uero quosdam lectos nullam sui mentionem
habitam ita sit questus: 'Irasci me tibi scito, quod non in
40 plerisque eius modi scriptis mecum potissimum loquaris;
an uereris ne apud posteros infame tibi sit, quod uidearis
familiaris nobis esse?' Expressitque Eclogam ad se, cuius

initium est:

> Cum tot sustineas et tanta negotia solus,
45 > Res Italas armis tuteris, moribus ornes,
> Legibus emendes: in publica commoda peccem,
> Si longo sermone morer tua tempora, Caesar.

Habitu corporis fuit breuis atque obesus, qualis et a
semet ipso in Satiris describitur et ab Augusto hac epistola:
50 'Pertulit ad me Onysius libellum tuum, quem ego †ut
accusantem† quantuluscumque est, boni consulo. Vereri
autem mihi uideris ne maiores libelli tui sint, quam ipse
es; sed tibi statura deest, corpusculum non deest. Itaque licebit in sextariolo scribas, ut circuitus uoluminis
55 tui sit ὀγκωδέστατος, sicut est uentriculi tui.'

Ad res Venerias intemperantior traditur; nam speculato
cubiculo scorta dicitur habuisse disposita, ut quocumque re-
spexisset ibi ei imago coitus referretur. Vixit plurimum in
secessu ruris sui Sabini aut Tiburtini, domusque ostenditur
60 circa Tiburni luculum. Venerunt in manus meas et Elegi
sub titulo eius et epistola prosa oratione quasi commendan-
tis se Maecenati, sed utraque falsa puto; nam Elegi uulga-
res, epistola etiam obscura, quo uitio minime tenebatur.

Natus est VI. Idus Decembris L. Cotta et L. Torquato
65 consulibus, decessit V Kl. Decembris C. Marcio Censorino
et C. Asinio Gallo consulibus post nonum et quinquagesimum annum, herede Augusto palam nuncupato, cum urgente
ui ualitudinis non sufficeret ad obsignandas testamenti tabu-
las. [Humatus et] conditus est extremis Esquiliis iuxta Mae-
70 cenatis tumulum.

Commentary

∾ *The assassination of Julius Caesar, IUL. 81.1–82.3*

Suetonius ends each of his imperial biographies with an account of the subject's death, often accompanied by a list of portents that foretold the death. Belief in portents was widespread in antiquity; in Rome, more sinister signs (e.g., rains of blood), called prodigies, were thought to reflect the anger of the gods and thus signified imminent danger to men. Inclusion of prodigies in the account of Caesar's assassination thus allows Suetonius to ascribe a cosmic significance to the event. Even more crucially, this passage sets up the author's own use of portents in the rest of the *Caesars*. For Suetonius, prodigies are closely intertwined with imperial destiny: clear to those who know to look for them, they give notice of the imminent deaths—and also the accessions—of the Caesars. In failing to heed the portents given to him, Caesar, poised between Republic and Empire, seals not only his own fate, but also Rome's.

A more mundane reality (as Suetonius himself discusses in earlier chapters) was that through his aloofness and highhandedness Caesar offended members of the Senate. A number of them accordingly formed a plan to kill him at a meeting of the Senate, to be held in the Meeting-hall of Pompey, on the 15th of March (the Ides in the Roman calendar) 44 BCE. Suetonius' account of Caesar's assassination can be compared with those found in Plutarch (*Caesar* 62–66), Appian (*Civil Wars* 2.111–17), and Cassius Dio (44.12–22), as well as the contemporary Nicolaus of Damascus's *Life of Augustus*.

2   **paucos ante menses** "a few months before" (see Bennett sec.
     357 for this idiomatic use of *ante*); this is the first of a series
     of temporal expressions that structure the passage (*proximis
     diebus*, 14; *pridie . . . Idus*, 19; *ea . . . nocte*, 22)

2–3 **in colonia Capua** the ancient city of Capua—founded, ac-
     cording to legend, by a companion of Aeneas, Capys—lay in
     some of Italy's most fertile territory, and in 59 BCE legislation
     passed by Caesar as consul (hence called a *lex Iulia*) resulted
     in the settlement of deserving Roman citizens here in a "colo-
     ny" (*colonia*)

3   **ad extruendas uillas** gerundive construction, with *ad* + acc.,
     to express purpose

4   **dis[s]icerent** Square brackets mark text the editor wishes to
     excise, without good manuscript authority; here, the editor
     prefers a spelling of the verb with only one *s*. The mood is
     subjunctive because the clause introduced by *cum* (line 2) de-
     notes the circumstances in which the action of the main verb
     (*reperiebant*, line 6) occurs.

     eo the adv. is used correlatively with *quod* in the following
     line, and the compar. *studiosius* (literally, "the more eagerly
     for this reason, because . . . ")

5   **aliquantum uasculorum** *uasculorum* is a gen. of the whole
     (or partitive gen.), followed by a gen. of description, *operis
     antiqui*

7   **sepultus** the infinitive *esse* (as often with this verb, Bennett
     sec. 116.5) is to be supplied, to form with the pple. a pf. pass.
     infinitive, dependent on *dicebatur*

8   **conscripta** modifies *tabula* (line 6), and followed by an abl.
     of means (*litteris uerbisque Graecis*) and abl. of attendant cir-
     cumstances (*hac sententia*, "to this effect")

9–12 **quandoque . . . uindicaretur** indirect discourse, depend-
     ing on the verb of speaking implied in *sententia*; the infini-
     tive is *fore* (= *futurum esse*), followed by *ut* and a substantive
     clause (with the subjunctives *necaretur* and *uindicaretur*), a

construction Latin uses to get around the lack of a true fut. pass. infinitive (cf. Bennett sec. 270.3a); the plpf. subjunctive in *detecta essent* corresponds to what would be a fut. pf. indicative in direct discourse (i.e., "Whenever the bones of Capys will have been found, a descendant of his will be killed . . . ")

10 **illo prognatus** *illo* is an abl. of source (Bennett sec. 215). The reader can take Capys' descendant to be Caesar, who traced his descent back to Venus and her son Aeneas, a countryman of Capys; the "kinsmen" (*consanguineorum*) who kill Caesar are thus his fellow countrymen. The message of the bronze tablet here overlaps with the curses sometimes found inscribed on ancient tombs, while its mysterious language also resembles that of a prophecy.

12 **cuius** connective rel.

ne quis the indef. *quis* frequently stands with *si*, *nisi*, *num*, and *ne*, in place of *aliquis*; translate: "so that nobody . . . "

13 **Cornelius Balbus** A close friend of Caesar, who superintended affairs in Rome while Caesar was away; he lent crucial assistance to Caesar's great-nephew Octavian—the future emperor Augustus—after the Ides of March, when Octavian took up the cause of avenging Caesar's death. Balbus might have been the source for other portents, which feature in the other extant accounts of Caesar's assassination.

14 **proximis diebus** abl. of time within which, i.e., within a very few days of Caesar's death (see note above on *paucos ante menses*, line 2)

greges acc. subject in the indirect discourse governed by *comperit* (line 16)

14–15 **in traiciendo Rubiconi flumini** with the gerund *traiciendo*, one must understand the acc. object *Rubiconem flumen* from the dat. that follows; *Rubiconi flumini* is itself an indirect object with *consecrarat*. Rivers were typically conceived of as gods in ancient times, and so could be honored with sacrifices or gifts; perhaps Caesar made this particular gift because some of his horses somehow made a favorable sign when he illegally crossed the Rubicon river in 49 BCE, at the outset of the civil war with his rival Pompey.

15 **consecrarat** pf. and plpf. tense forms with -*vi*- or -*ve*- sometimes are syncopated (or shortened) by dropping -*vi*- or -*ve*-; hence *consecrarat* for *consecraverat*. Note that the (implied) subject of this sentence is Caesar—Suetonius frequently omits the name of a life's subject, where in English it must be supplied (see **Introduction, Addendum 1** in the **Introduction**).

17 **immolantem** supply *Caesarem* (see previous note)

17–18 **Spurinna** a famous diviner (*haruspex*) of the day; *haruspices*, who came from Etruria, were used by the Roman Senate to explain prodigies and portents

18 **caueret** the substantive clause following the verb of command, *monuit*, does not require *ut* (see Bennett sec. 295.8)

19 **Martias Idus** "the Ides of March"; on the Roman calendar, see further **Introduction, Addendum 2**

easdem Idus *pridie* may be followed by the acc. (Bennett sec. 144.2)

20 **auem regaliolum** an alternative name for the wren (*trochilus*), chosen here for obvious reasons

Pompeianae curiae A hall where the Senate sometimes convened, in the great theater complex Caesar's rival Pompey dedicated in 55 BCE; murdering Caesar in it had symbolic appeal for the conspirators, a number of whom had fought for Pompey. The dat. here expresses the limit of motion.

23 **et ipse** *et* is adverbial, "even"; *ipse* emphasizes the idea here that Caesar had prior warning of his death

23–24 **per quietem** "in his sleep." Dreams were frequently considered significant, sometimes even prophetic, in Greco-Roman culture; but note the contrast here between Caesar's own dream, which seems to look forward to his deification (cf. *Gai.* 57.3), and Calpurnia's.

24   **alias** N.B.: this is the adv. *alias*

25   **dextram iungere** the clasping of (right) hands was a token of friendship

      Calpurnia Caesar's wife since 59 BCE

26   **fastigium** "pediment," recently added (by vote of the Senate) to Caesar's house in the Forum, giving it the appearance of a temple

28   **simul et** "and also"

29   **cunctatus** governs an indirect question, introduced by *an* ("whether") and employing the subjunctive

30   **Decimo Bruto** A favorite of Caesar, who fought under him in Gaul, Decimus Brutus nonetheless played a key part in luring Caesar to his death, according to a number of ancient authors.

30–31 **adhortante, ne . . .** the pple. *adhortante* governs a substantive clause, in the negative, hence introduced by *ne* (see Bennett sec. 295)

31   **frequentis . . . opperientis** the ending *-is* frequently substitutes for *-es* in the m./f. acc. pl. of the pres. act. pple.

32   **quinta . . . hora** abl. of point of time. Romans divided the period of daylight (regardless of season) into twelve hours; so "around the fifth hour" would be approximately 11 AM.

      libellum a written note; according to Plutarch (*Caes.* 17), Caesar often preferred to communicate by letter, believing it more efficient

34–35 **quasi . . . lecturus** "on the grounds that he was going to read them soon"

35–36 **cum litare non posset** adversative clause with *cum* (Bennett sec. 309)

36–37 **Spurinnamque irridens** the enclitic *-que* here links the idea of *irridens* with the abl. absolute that precedes (*spreta religione*) and almost has the force of "and what is more"

38   **sua noxa** *suus* here is equivalent to an objective gen. (hence *sua noxa* means "harm to himself")

adessent The use of the subjunctive here shows that the reason given in the causal clause introduced by *quod* should be attributed to Caesar, rather than the writer (see Bennett sec. 286.1).

38-39 **quanquam ... diceret** in Latin of the imperial age, *quanquam* regularly takes a subjunctive, as here, often meaning "and yet"

41 **Cimber Tillius** Cimber seems to have participated in the conspiracy out of anger that Caesar had refused to recall Cimber's brother from exile; note that his *cognomen* precedes his *nomen* (see further **Introduction, Addendum 2**).

42-43 **renuenti ... et gestu[m] ... differenti** dat. of reference (Bennett sec. 181.1), denoting the person affected, here Caesar; *gestu* is abl. of means with *differenti* ("putting him off by a gesture")

44-45 **'ista quidem uis est!'** the use of direct speech (as opposed to indirect discourse) adds excitement at a climactic point in the narrative

45 **alter e Cascis** one of two brothers, each named Servilius Casca, who took part in the conspiracy

49 **toga** abl. of means

50 **quo honestius caderet** *quo* frequently introduces purpose clauses, especially when they contain a comparative (Bennett sec. 282.1a); it typically replaces *ut* + *eo*, with *eo* as an abl. of degree of difference (Bennett sec. 223)

53 **sine uoce edito** "without letting out a word"; the pf. pass. pple. with a noun can replace an abstract noun with a dependent gen. (Bennett sec. 337.6)

54 **καὶ σὺ τέκνον;** This Greek phrase, as punctuated here, means "You, too, child?" (On the use of Greek, see **Introduction, Addendum 1**.) Along with Suetonius only the Greek historian Cassius Dio mentions this comment, and he too rejects it. The famous conspirator Marcus Brutus certainly was not Caesar's own son, but the vocative use of τέκνον here need not imply kinship, and suggests that the phrase is a verse quotation, perhaps from a tragedy. Alternatively, it has been suggested (with

less plausibility) that the Greek employs a colloquialism, and means something like: "Go to hell, kid!"

55-57 **donec . . . rettulerunt** *donec* + indicative, to denote an actual event (Bennett sec. 293)

56 **domum** acc. of limit of motion, "home"

๛ *The work habits of Augustus,* AUG. *78*

A long civil war followed the assassination of Julius Caesar, at the end of which Caesar's maniacally ambitious great-nephew, and adopted son, Augustus, emerged supreme. A paltry general, this second Caesar sought to achieve glory instead by establishing a new type of government for Rome, one that would bring lasting peace. Though this government was effectively a monarchy, Augustus was careful not to go by the odious title of king, but rather *princeps*, which meant "leading man." He also formally preserved much of the machinery of the Republican government (e.g., the Senate and Senatorial magistrates such as the consuls).

A key part of Augustus' success lay in establishing the right image for himself and the family who helped him to rule—here he could learn from mistakes made by Caesar and also Marc Antony, who fought Augustus in the civil wars after Caesar's death. Augustus, like many politicians since, wished to be seen as sober, godly, and hard-working. That image is reflected in Suetonius' account here, from the very long and rich life of Augustus, which in many ways provides the model against which later emperors are to be judged. As somebody who worked for later emperors (including Hadrian, who wished to be the new Augustus), Suetonius, it may also be noted, takes special interest in the working habits of his subjects (cf. the selection on **The work habits of Vespasian** below).

1 **cibum meridianum** Romans of high status typically ate a light midday meal and then, in later afternoon or evening, after the day's work was over, a more elaborate meal, the *cena* (line 3); according to Suetonius (*Aug.* 76), Augustus ate lightly

2   **retectis pedibus** abl. absolute; because Augustus remained
      clothed and shoed, he could not cover his feet

3   **lucubratoriam** this word nicely illustrates Latin word for-
      mation; the verb *lucubro* (literally "to work by lamplight") is
      joined with the suffix *-torius* to create an adj. meaning "ap-
      propriate for nighttime study"

4–5   **donec . . . conficeret** *donec* takes a subjunctive to denote an-
      ticipation or expectancy, an indicative to denote an actual
      event (cf. *donec . . . rettulerunt, Iul.* 81.1–82.3, lines 55–57)

5   **ex . . . parte** with adjs. expressing magnitude, this expression
      means "to a . . . degree" (here "to a very large degree")

7   **cum plurimum** "at most"; the *quam* that follows completes
      the compar. *amplius* (line 6)

8–9   **ut . . . expergisceretur** *ut* is used in the sense here "in such a
      manner that" and takes a subjunctive verb (like result clauses
      introduced by *tam, talis*, and so forth)

9–10 **si . . . posset** in Livy and later writers, the subjunctive of the
      historical tenses is used in place of the indicative in the prota-
      sis of a general conditional (Bennett sec. 302.3.a)

11   **resumebat producebatque** these verbs, like *reciperare* (line
      10), take as their object *somnum*

14   **uigilandum esset** for the mood and tense, see note above on *si
      posset* (lines 9–10); the pass. periphrastic is used impersonally
      here

16   **cenaculo** "upstairs apartment," typically fairly modest (see,
      e.g., *Vit.* 7.2)

17   **somni** gen. with an adj. (Bennett sec. 204)

      et dum . . . deportaretur for the subjunctive here, see the note
      on *donec . . . reficeret* (lines 4–5 above); note that in the sec-
      ond part of this phrase *et deposita lectica* Suetonius employs
      instead an abl. absolute

18   **lectica** A litter was a comfortable—and very expensive—way
      to travel in ancient Rome; in one, protected by curtains, it was
      possible for a man of business to work—or sleep (see **Fig. 1**).

Suetonius later notes (*Aug.* 82.1) that Augustus traveled by litter, at nighttime, to the hills outside Rome, where rich Romans went to escape the heat of the City.

Fig. 1. A Roman litter (reconstruction drawing). Curtains could be attached to the rod above the canopy. Photo Fig. 9 in D. C. Munro, *A Sourcebook of Roman History* (Boston, 1904).

∽ *The work habits of Augustus (continued),* AUG. 33

In this earlier chapter of his life of Augustus, Suetonius also draws attention to Augustus' strong worth ethic, as well as Augustus' desire to be *seen* working hard. Here the focus is on the emperor's administration of justice in Rome. In the Republic, jurisdiction lay with the elected magistrates, who might preside over courts with empanelled jurors, hand the matter over to a judge drawn from a larger panel, or themselves hold hearings (called *cognitiones*). While this machinery continued after the Republic, emperors from Augustus onwards also had jurisdiction; sometimes this was primary, but even more often an appeal was made after a judgment had been rendered by another organ of the law. Legal hearings before the emperor were also frequently referred to as *cognitiones*, and (as this passage suggests) could borrow procedures from the courts.

Jurisdiction was therefore a key part of the emperor's job, and throughout his *Caesars* Suetonius shows an interest in it (cf., e.g., *Claud.* 14, *Dom.* 8.1). But the biographer's focus is less on the detailed content of decisions and their legal ramifications than the manner in which decisions were made. The emperor's personality is thereby revealed, but there is also an implication that the success of an appeal might depend on idiosyncratic features of the personality.

1   **ius dixit** "he sat as judge"; this idiomatic expression shows that Augustus is giving judgments here rather than (for instance) simply voting with a jury

3   **pro tribunali** "on the front of the tribunal"; the tribunal was the raised platform on which a Roman magistrate sat in judgment

     domi "at home"; the locative is regular with this noun (Bennett sec. 232.2)

6   **culleo insueretur** the traditional penalty of being sewn up in a sack—along with a dog, a cock, a snake, and a monkey—was still prescribed in Augustus' own lifetime for those who murdered their own fathers

     quod "because" (adverbial)

9   **ageretur** *ago* is used in a technical sense, "to institute legal proceedings"

     lege Cornelia a *lex Cornelia*, passed by the Dictator Sulla in the late 80s BCE, legislated against forging of and tampering with wills

     tenerentur the pass. of *teneo*, in legal contexts, means "to be liable to" and takes an abl.

10   **tabellas** small tablets used to record a vote in the courts of Rome

11   **cognoscentibus** The use of the verb *cognosco* here strongly suggests that this action of Augustus took place during a *cognitio*; that is, he held the inquiry, but he relied on a panel for advice—and had them vote using a procedure familiar from the courts (see note on *tabellas*, line 10).

12   **qua ignosceretur** the verb is subjunctive here, in a rel. clause of purpose

13   **constitisset** plpf. of the impers. *constat* ("it is established," Bennett sec. 128), subjunctive in a rel. clause of characteristic

       appellationes Augustus had a two-pronged strategy for "appeals," depending on whether they were made by parties from Rome, in which case they were referred to the urban praetor, or parties in the provinces, in which case they were referred to men specially designated by the emperor.

15–16   **quos . . . praeposuisset** rel. clause of characteristic

∾ *Tiberius on Capri, TIB. 40–44*

Augustus died in 14 CE, seventy-six years old. As the principate he sought to establish was not to be explicitly a monarchy, he found other formulas to prepare for a succession by Tiberius, the son of Augustus' third wife, the formidable Livia Drusilla. Augustus (1) adopted Tiberius as his own son; (2) shared certain powers with Tiberius; and (3) in his will named Tiberius as his chief heir.

Fifty-six years old when Augustus died, Tiberius from the start found the role of *princeps* a difficult one to play in Rome; it had not been defined legally, and therefore required a great deal of image management, if not dissimulation, as well as constant vigilance against all manner of threats, even from within the emperor's own household. He spent much of the years 21 and 22 CE in Campania, where wealthy Romans customarily spent their holidays. Returning to Campania in 26 CE, he then settled permanently on Capri (ancient Capreae), a small, craggy, and beautiful island in the Bay of Naples (**Fig. 2**). Though he would frequently visit the Italian mainland, he never again saw Rome.

Pondering Tiberius' withdrawal, the historian Tacitus famously proposed that the emperor desired to practice secret vices there (*Ann.* 4.57). But a rather more understandable desire to escape his difficulties in Rome may well have been the real explanation; on Capri, Tiberius could cultivate his interests in Greek literature,

Fig. 2. Panoramic view of the Isle of Capri, c. 1900. Photo Alinari / Art Resource, NY.

astrology, art-collecting, even gardening, while handling important matters through correspondence. Still, Tiberius' absence of
over ten years aroused hostility. Discussions of what Tiberius was
doing could easily slide into dark allegations, not readily verified;
after Tiberius' death these would only multiply and were committed to writing.

So it was that in retrospect the retirement came to be seen as
the turning point of Tiberius' principate, and this is reflected in the
structure of Suetonius' biography. Early chapters cover Tiberius'
ancestry and early life, and then the more positive aspects of his
principate. Next comes a pivotal discussion of Tiberius' residences
(chapters 38–41), and a programmatic statement that Suetonius is
turning now to the vices of Tiberius, since this third Caesar was
able to give free rein to them on Capri (42.1). The discussion of these
vices, including indulgence in drink, sexual perversion, and cruelty,
occupy most of the rest of the life. While many of the remarkably
lurid stories that cropped up about "Tiberius on Capri" cannot be
verified—and could not, in Suetonius' own day, as Suetonius himself

occasionally acknowledges—Suetonius could not resist telling them, in an effort to explain his subject and satisfy his reader's curiosity. Coming after Suetonius' *Augustus*, his *Tiberius* can also be appreciated as a dark inversion of Tiberius' predecessor. Tiberius on Capri is the image of an emperor who neglected his duties to indulge himself—to the detriment of his subjects.

1   **peragrata Campania** abl. absolute, followed by a clause with *cum* (with the subjunctive in *dedicasset*, denoting circumstances), before the main verb *contulit*

        Capuae like *Nolae*, in the locative case, as is regular for the sing. of cities, towns, and small islands of the first and second declensions to denote place in which (Bennett sec. 232); the *Capitolium* was a temple of Jupiter, as at Rome

2   **templum Augusti** After Augustus' death in his father's house in the Campanian town of Nola, the house was turned into a shrine, perhaps the temple mentioned here.

3   **Capreas** for cities, towns, and small islands, the acc. of place to which requires no prep. (Bennett sec. 182). The island of Capri, purchased by Augustus from the city of Naples in 29 BCE, was in the exclusive possession of the imperial family and contained a number of villas and other buildings used by the emperors and their staffs.

3-4   **delectatus insula** the verb *delecto* in the pass. means "to take pleasure in" and takes an abl. of cause (Bennett sec. 219)

4   **adiretur** the subjunctive indicates that the reason given here is to be attributed to Tiberius (Bennett sec. 286)

6   **mari[s]** On square brackets, see the note above on *dis[s]icerent* (*Iul.* 81.1–82.3, line 4). If *profundo* is taken as an adj., the depth of the sea is (appropriately for this passage) emphasized; if, on the other, the noun *profundum* is understood, the expression is less forceful.

        assidua obtestatione abl. of means, within the abl. absolute *reuocante . . . populo* (lines 6–7)

8   **amphitheatri ruina** abl. of cause. According to Tacitus (*Ann.* 4.62–63), the wooden amphitheater in Fidenae (five miles north of Rome) collapsed because its builder, the freedman Atilius, employed shoddy construction to maximize his profits; after the catastrophe, the Senate introduced new regulation of such structures.

10   **adeundi sui** the gerundive construction substitutes for the gerund *adeundi* + direct object; Suetonius regularly uses the verb *adeo* to refer to approaching the emperor, often to make an appeal (see, e.g., *Aug.* 53.2)

     tanto magis, quod the *quod* clause goes with the main verb *fecit* (and for the mood of its verbs *edixerat* and *submouerat*, lines 11–12, see note above on *adiretur* [line 4]); translate: "so much the more (willingly) did he do this, because . . . " (*tanto* is abl. of degree of difference)

11   **ne quis . . . edixerat** the verb *edixerat* is followed by an indirect command introduced by *ne* (Bennett sec. 295.1); *ne* in turn should be taken closely with the indef. pron. *quis* (Bennett sec. 91.5); translate: "he had decreed that nobody . . . "

12   **submouerat** *submoueo* can mean "to clear from the path" (of a magistrate or the emperor)

13–14   **usque adeo . . . ut** *usque adeo* introduces a result clause with *ut* + subjunctive ("to such an extent . . . that"); note the pf. tense of the subjunctive is used here, representing the result as a fact without reference to its continuance (see Bennett sec. 268.6)

14   **decurias equitum** panels of equestrians from whom judges and jurors were selected; membership on a panel—probably enjoyed by Suetonius himself (see **Introduction, Suetonius' career**)—was a distinction granted by the emperor

15   **tribunos militum praefectosque** Military tribunes served as officers of the army legions, while the prefects commanded auxiliary troops; both groups were typically of equestrian rank.

17   **consularibus legatis** Provinces with larger concentrations of troops, including Spain and Syria, were governed by legates (*legatis*) who had served as consuls, appointed directly by the emperor. Tiberius kept his legates of Spain and Syria, Arruntius and Lamia respectively, in Rome, surely not from negligence but rather as an administrative experiment: just as he administered through legates, the legates themselves might too.

18–19   **Armeniam . . . Moesiam . . . Gallias** There is no evidence whatever to support the claim that Tiberius allowed these provinces to be seized by the neighboring peoples of Rome's empire.

20   **dedecore . . . nec . . . discrimine** abls. of attendant circumstances

21–22   **nanctus . . . et quasi . . . oculis remotis** note how Suetonius joins a nom. pple. (agreeing with the implied subject of the sentence, Tiberius) with an abl. absolute

23–24   **singillatim . . . referam** It is typical of Suetonius' manner to break down a topic into individual items: here instances of Tiberius' particular vices (bibulousness, lust, and so forth) are enumerated; the catalogue that follows occupies many chapters—in this selection there is discussion first of indulgence in drink and food (chapter 42) and then sexual perversion (43).

25–26   **Biberius** The name plays on *bibo* ("to drink") and the other two nicknames also suggest bibulousness: *Caldius* plays on the adj. *cal(i)dus* ("warm, hot") but also, likely, the noun *cal(i)dum*, referring to a hot drink of wine and water; Mero plays on the noun *merum* ("unmixed wine"); one might translate the whole name as "Boozer Hot-Strong." Note that at this point Tiberius has neither of the imperial titles, *Caesar* and *Augustus*; for more on Roman names, see **Introduction, Addendum 2**.

27   **ipsa . . . morum correctione** From Augustus onwards emperors were to oversee the community's morals—much as censors had before—although the terms in which this power was couched are debated.

27-28 **Pomponio Flacco et L. Pisone** As Piso was appointed prefect of the City in 13 CE (before Tiberius was *princeps*), and
Flaccus did not leave for Syria until 33 CE, this story is open
to serious objections; clearly it was elaborated over time, to
match other allegations made about Tiberius.

31 **codicillis** letters of appointment written by the emperor,
conferring major offices (such as those mentioned here, lines
29–30)

32 **Cestio Gall[i]o** the text is corrected so as to refer to the consul
of 35 CE

33 **ab Augusto ignominia notato** *notare ignominia* is a technical
term, "to mark the name of a citizen with ignominy," which
resulted in some legal disadvantages; Augustus perhaps as-
signed the *nota* during one of the censuses he conducted

34 **ante paucos dies** for the use of *ante* + acc. meaning "so many
days etc. before" see Bennett sec. 357

increpito note that *increpo* is an example of a first conjugation
verb with a pf. in -*ui* without *a* (i.e., *increpui*); for a list of other
such verbs, see Bennett sec. 120.II

34-35 **cenam ... condixit** *cenam ... condicere* = "to engage oneself
for a meal"; in Rome's hierarchical society, one socially superior might set a stipulation on accepting an invitation

36 **utque** continues the indirect command introduced by the ver-
bal idea in *ea lege* (34–35)

cenaretur the intransitive *ceno* is used impersonally, literally
"there be dining" (Bennett sec. 138.IV)

37 **ignotissimum quaesturae candidatum** The quaestor was
the lowest ranking of the major Senatorial offices; this candidate, unlike his noble opponents, has no magistrates in
his family tree. Pliny the Elder (*Natural History* 14.144–47)
identifies the champion drinker as Novellius Torquatus of
Milan.

nobilissimis dat. with a compound verb (Bennett sec.
187.III)

38 **propinante se** the reflex. in the abl. absolute refers to the subject of the sentence, Tiberius. At a *convivium*, a master of ceremonies (*magister bibendi*) would make a toast with a cup, sip the wine, and then pass the drink to the man toasted, announcing how much was to be consumed.

38-39 **amphoram** An amphora was a large two-handled jar used for storing wine, and was also a measure of capacity (over six gallons!).

sestertia ducenta On the sum, 200,000 sesterces—a large one, considering a soldier was paid 900 sesterces per year in the age of Augustus—see **Introduction, Addendum 2**.

40 **dialogo** a literary work in dialogue form, in which presumably the various delicacies mentioned debated their own merits

42 **a uoluptatibus** the prep. *ab* with a noun in the abl. indicates the post of a slave or officer; such phrases can function as nouns, e.g., *ab epistulis*, "Secretary for Correspondence," the last post Suetonius had in his official career (see **Introduction, Suetonius' career**)

equite R. = *equite Romano*, "Roman knight"

43 **secessu uero Caprensi** *uero* marks the transition back to the time on Capri, where another vice burst forth: sexual perversion

sellaria According to Tacitus (*Ann.* 6.1), the previously unknown terms *sellaria* (or perhaps *sellarii*) and *spintriae* were devised during Tiberius' time on Capri; that Suetonius has straightaway to explain what the *sellaria* was would seem to confirm this. Literally, a *sellarium* was a place where a seat, *sella*, is kept, and might refer to a latrine, or privy, or just a room with seats—on which prostitutes sometimes sat in front of a brothel to solicit, which may be the right context for understanding Tiberius' *sellaria* (a *sellarius* would be a male staffing the *sellaria*). Novel words, or usages, are conspicuous in the rest of this passage, enhancing its monstrous subject: in addition to *spintrias* (line 46), see *Caprineum* (line 56) and *pisciculos* (line 59); and also note *a uoluptatibus* (line 42).

45 **exoletorum** When Greek writers describe male prostitutes they refer to boys hired to play a passive role sexually; Roman writers refer to such "boys" but also have a term for male prostitutes who were fully mature, *exoleti* (literally "grown up"); an *exoletus* might play an active role sexually.

46 **spintrias** The word, apparently deriving from the Greek σφιγκτήρ ("sphincter, bracelet"), is first attested in the mid-first century CE, again evidently confirming Tacitus (see above on *sellaria*, line 43); "squeezers" might be a possible translation.

46–47 **triplici serie** apparently triads were formed, each consisting of a *puella*, an *exoletus*, and a *spintria*

47 **incestarent** The participants debauch themselves by participating in an "impure" arrangement (*incestum*), in which perhaps (male) *spintriae*, as "devisers of unnatural coupling," play a key role by functioning both passively and actively.

ipso forms of *ipse* are frequently used for indirect reflexives (Bennett sec. 249.3)

49 **tabellis ac sigillis** abl. of means with *adornauit*

50 **libris . . . Elephantidis** A sex manual, illustrating positions for intercourse, was attributed to a female author, Elephantis (tellingly, the other known sex manuals from the Greco-Roman world are also attributed to women).

51 **impe[t]ratae** The correction to the text, though lacking good manuscript authority, is easy and attractive.

53 **prost[r]antisque** removing the letter *r* is a necessary correction; *prosto* literally means "to stand in front," and with a notion of soliciting implied, comes to mean "to prostitute oneself"

54–55 **pube Paniscorum et Nympharum habitu** Paniscus was a "little Pan," the Greek deity who was represented as half-man, half-goat and was worshipped in caves. In later Greek and Roman art he was playfully depicted in scenes of erotic struggle (e.g., **Fig. 3**); Tiberius is bringing such scenes to life here on Capri. Also popular in art were nymphs, young female inhabitants of areas with water, mountains, and trees.

Fig. 3. Aphrodite, Pan, and Eros. Athens, National Archeological Museum. This amusing statue group from the Greek island of Delos, dating to c. 100 BCE, shows the goddess of love fending off with a slipper a lecherous Pan. Photo Marie Mauzy / Art Resource, NY.

55   **nomine** abl. with *abutentes* (Bennett sec. 218.1)

56   **'Caprineum'** The place name is derived from the word for goat, *caper*, and the Greek ending *-eum* to denote places (e.g., *Museum* = "place of the Muses"). Goats are an age-old symbol of lewdness; the novel *Caprineum* (otherwise unattested in Latin literature) is a fitting analogue for the *sellaria* (line 43).

57   **infamia flagrauit** *flagro*, with an abl., can mean "to be intensely subjected to (hatred, infamy)"; ostensibly, Suetonius is distancing himself from the allegations that follow—but he still reports them

57–58   **ut . . . fas sit** result clause, with the normal rules for sequence of tense adjusted as logic demands (cf. Bennett sec. 268.7); the expression *fas est* ("it is right, proper") takes a complementary infinitive

58–60   **quasi . . . institueret** the clause, with a subjunctive verb, states a situation hypothesized; here *quasi* = "that" (following *credi*)

59   **primae teneritudinis** gen. of quality

60   **natanti sibi** dat. of reference (where, from English idiom, one might expect a gen.: Bennett sec. 188.1)

     femina n. pl. of *femur* (the first syllable is short, as opposed to that of *femina, -ae,* f.)

61–62   **atque etiam quasi** *quasi* is used as in line 58

62   **lacte** abl. of separation

62–63   **necdum . . . depulsos** the phrase specifies the babies as being almost ready for weaning; inclusion of such precise details adds to vividness of Suetonius' horrific account

64–65   **Parrasi . . . tabulam** Parrasius was a Greek painter of the fifth to fourth century BCE whose works were well known—and highly valued—in imperial Rome. Pliny (*Natural History* 35.67) seems to refer to a different painting by Parrasius—depicting a High Priest of the goddess Cybele—displayed in Tiberius' bedroom, suggesting once again that the anecdote Suetonius retails here could be a fabrication.

65   **Atalanta** Atalanta was a mythical heroine who wished to remain a virgin; known for killing two centaurs who tried to rape her and defeating Peleus in wrestling, she participated in the great hunt for the Calydonian boar, during which her fellow hunter Meleager fell in love with her. The iconography of this painting, therefore, is, to say the least, unexpected, and adds to its salaciousness.

65-66   **ore morigeratur** an arch way of referring to oral sex (*morigeror* can mean "to please [a man]", i.e., sexually)

66   **sub condicione** Bequests to the emperor by prominent Romans—typically in the form of cash—were customary from Augustus onwards, building on a Republican tradition of recognizing friends through one's will; here the nameless testator leaves Tiberius a choice of the painting or one million sesterces (on the sum, see **Introduction, Addendum 2**).

69-70   **ministri acerram praeferentis** Scenes of sacrifice in Roman art often show an officiant (frequently the emperor) standing at the altar, with an attendant holding a box of incense—to be offered at the altar—and one or more flute-players to provide music (cf. *tibicinem*, line 72 below).

70   **abstinere, quin . . .** a verb of hindering, accompanied by a negative, can use *quin* (in place of *ne*) to introduce its substantive clause (Bennett sec. 295.3a)

71   **seductum** the pf. pass. pple. modifies *ministrum* (understood); it is probably better rendered in English in parallel with *constupraret* (lines 71–72), i.e., "abstain from . . . taking aside and debauching . . . "

72-73   **utrique** dat. of reference (see note above on *natanti sibi*, line 60)

73   **quod . . . exprobrarant** for the mood of *exprobrarant*, see note on *adiretur* (line 4); note that *exprobrarant* is a syncopated form

74   **fregisse** take with *fertur* (line 68)

∾ *Tiberius on Capri (continued), TIB. 60*

This chapter comes in the midst of a long discussion of Tiberius' cruel and cold nature (*saeva ac lenta natura*, *Tib.* 57.1), already evident in his youth. Love of cruelty is another of the *uitia male diu dissimulata* (*Tib.* 40–44, line 22) that erupted on Capri, and is the penultimate in the long catalogue Suetonius offers, to be followed only by Tiberius' own hatred of himself. The subject of cruelty—a vice that those in power have unusual opportunity to indulge and display—looms large in Suetonius' imperial biographies.

46   A Suetonius Reader

1   **in paucis diebus** time within which is denoted by an abl., sometimes with a prep. (Bennett sec. 231)

     quam Capreas attigit *quam* here is used in a temporal expression and means "after"

     piscatori dat. of reference (where, by English idiom, one might expect a gen.: Bennett sec. 188.1)

2   **sibi** the reflex., though it stands in a subordinate clause whose subject is the "fisherman," refers to Tiberius, subject of the main clause, and hence is an indirect reflex. (see Bennett sec. 244)

     secretum agenti "keeping himself withdrawn"

2–3 **grandem mullum . . . obtulerat** Red mullets were a delicacy in Rome, with heavier specimens fetching large prices; in presenting the big fish to Tiberius, the fisherman thought he was doing the emperor a favor.

4   **aspera et deuia** the adjs. are used substantively, "steep and trackless places"

5   **gratulanti** with this pple. understand again *piscatori* (from line 1)

6   **praegrandem** a predicate adj. (especially a superl. or the like) belonging to the antecedent may stand in the rel. clause; here the adj. almost = "as it was very large"

7–8 **militem praetorianum** the soldiers of the praetorian guard served as the emperor's bodyguard and helped keep the peace in the City of Rome

8   **pauonem** Peacocks, along with other more or less exotic animals, were kept on the grounds of upper-class Roman villas for decoration and for profit (peacock itself was considered a culinary delicacy: see below *Vit.* 13, lines 12–13).

     capite puniit literally "punished with his head," i.e., "had executed"; the abl. is one of penalty (Bennett sec. 208.2b); on the construction *ob subreptum . . . pauonem*, see note above on *sine uoce edito* (*Iul.* 81.1–82.3, line 53)

9   **lectica** see note on *lectica* (*Aug.* 78, line 18)

10   **exploratorem uiae** The scout is said to be in the "first co-horts" (*primarum cohortium*), and since *primus* can in military contexts mean "highest-ranking," *primae cohortes* may be an (unparalleled) way of referring to the cohorts that made up the praetorian guard that guarded the emperor (see note above on *militem praetorianum*, lines 7–8); it is also possible that in place of *primarum* we should read *praetoriarum*. A centurion of the praetorian guard was a high-ranking officer, a detail that adds to the outrage here.

❧ *Tiberius on Capri (continued), TIB. 62.2*

Another passage from the elaborate treatment of Tiberius' cruelty.

5   **cui** the indef. pron. *quis* typically is used in place of *aliquis* in combination with *si, nisi, num,* and *ne*; the compound verb *inesse* takes the dat. here

    residui spiritus quicquam the n. sing. pron. *quicquam* takes a partitive gen., or gen. of the whole (Bennett sec. 201.2)

8   **fidicularum . . . tormento** a *fidiculae* was a rack with cords; the noun is pl. because it had many strings (cf. the word for "lyre," *fides*, which is the pl. of *fides*, "string," and see further Bennett sec. 56); *tormento* is abl. of means, with *distendo* ("to torture by distention")

❧ *Caligula's capers, GAI. 19*

Suetonius' life of Caligula, the most notorious of the twelve Caesars, shows a similar structure to that of Tiberius: a preliminary section covers background and career up to accession; final sections, personal appearance and habits along with death and portents preceding it; and a central section, actions as *princeps*, first creditable, then disgraceful. Making the transition in that central section, Suetonius famously writes: "So far the discussion has been of the emperor; the rest must tell of the monster" (21). Such a division is a dramatic example of Suetonius' tendency to partition his material neatly, it again

shows the author's preoccupation with vice, and it amply indulges
the reader's curiosity; but one result is to slight political challenges
faced by the emperor.

Gaius Caesar, as he was officially and widely known—"Caligula"
was a childhood nickname—came to power following the death of
Tiberius in March 37 CE. The son of the late, and much lamented,
Germanicus and Agrippina the Elder, he had the blood of Augustus
in his veins and was widely embraced after the last grim years of
Tiberius' rule. But only twenty-four years old when he acceded, and
having spent much of his time with Tiberius in Capri rather than in
the Senate or in army camps, he was in some ways ill-prepared for
rule; keeping the Senate on his side was thus a challenge, especially if
Caligula was as conceited and cruel as the ancient sources indicate.

Writing after his death, they all paint a rather hostile portrait
of him, at times characterizing him as downright erratic, even insane—although, it must be noted, Suetonius can also be more positive. He gives Caligula credit for an astute display at the start of his
principate of piety to deceased family members, including his mother Agrippina, and for repealing repressive measures of Tiberius, for
instance (*Gai.* 15–16). Some modern scholars have largely accepted
the ultimately negative characterization, while others have tried to
rationalize the portrait, even suggesting that much of what is described as Caligula's capriciousness or craziness actually reflected a
concerted attempt to create something more akin to the divine mon-
archies of the Hellenistic East. What might have been serious efforts
to hold on to power, or articulate it in new ways, thereby came to be
passed off as acts of incompetency—or caprice. It is hard to be sure,
for Caligula was assassinated not four years after his accession by
members of his own praetorian guard; his short time in power gave
him less opportunity to develop as a ruler, and after his death the
sensitive political situation made it nearly impossible for there to be
any respect for the slain ruler's memory.

In this selection—from the account of Caligula as *princeps* rather
than monster—Suetonius describes one of Caligula's "capers," the
construction in 39 CE of a bridge of boats across part of the Bay of
Naples, in emulation of the great Persian King Xerxes (see further

below). Caligula's contemporary Seneca gives a scathing account of the episode (*On Benefits* 18.5–6), as does the Greek historian Cassius Dio (59.17), but such a spectacle (as Suetonius classifies the episode) may well have appealed to the tastes of many, beyond Caligula himself. Furthermore, as some modern scholars have emphasized, the inexperienced Caligula may have been trying to pass himself off as a great conqueror, celebrating in particular a recent (diplomatic) settlement with the neighboring Parthian empire, the only major power on the border of the empire. In coming to grips with the episode, though, Suetonius has no space for such an explanation, and instead foregrounds an idiosyncratic tale connected to his favorite theme of imperial destiny.

2–3   **Baiarum medium interuallum †Puteolanas moles** The editor has introduced a dagger to indicate his belief that the exact text—as reconstructed from the available manuscripts—is beyond recovery. Suetonius should be describing the "middle part of the gap" (*medium interuallum*) across the water from the resort town of Baiae to the piers of Puteoli (the major port of the region; see the map, **Fig. 4**); it has been proposed therefore simply to place an *ad* before *Puteolanas moles*, but this is not pleasing stylistically nor does it account for how the text was corrupted.

4–6   **contractis . . . nauibus . . . et . . . conlocatis** in the abl. absolute, *nauibus* takes two pples.; a further abl. absolute follows in *superiectoque terreno ac derecto* (line 6)

5   **ad anc[h]oras** where English would use a sing., Latin more concretely employs a pl., since the reference is to multiple anchors (see Bennett sec. 353.1)

7   **ultro citro** a conj. is sometimes omitted between coordinate words (Bennett sec. 345); cf. the expression *rursum prorsum* ("back and forth")

7–8   **biduo continenti** abl. of time within which, i.e., most likely Caligula crossed the bridge and came back over a space of two days altogether (see *primo die* and *postridie* below)

Fig. 4. Map of the Bay of Naples. Mapping Specialists, Ltd. © 2011 Bolchazy-Carducci Publishers, Inc.

8 **phalerato equo** *phalerae* were metal disks that decorated war horses, and the other insignia here are military: the crown of oak leaves (*quercea corona*, lines 8–9) was traditionally awarded to a citizen who had saved the life of a fellow citizen and the *chlamys* (line 9) was a short cloak worn by a general

10 **quadrigario habitu** On the second day, Caligula staged a variation on the triumph (the parade in which a general processed through Rome in a chariot accompanied by his soldiers and officers, along with captives): he here wears a charioteer's tunic, uses his famous race-horses, displays a Parthian hostage, and is accompanied by members of his praetorian guard and friends.

11 **Dareum** son of the Parthian king Artabanus III, he had been sent to Rome after a diplomatic settlement with Parthia was reached at the start of Caligula's principate

11–12 **ex Parthorum obsidibus** the partitive expression with *ex* ("from among") shows that there was more than one hostage; the *obses* was not an unwilling captive as such, but typically a young man sent to Rome for education, as a means of fostering goodwill

14–16 **qui . . . contabulauerit** the subjunctive in the rel. clause implies that this is the thought of the *plerosque* rather than the writer (see Bennett sec. 314); the Persian king Xerxes crossed the Hellespont dividing Asia from Europe on the eve of his invasion of Greece, in an operation memorably described by Herodotus (*Histories* 7.33–37)

16–18 **ut . . . territaret** the purpose clause states the motive others (*alios*) assign for Caligula's construction of the bridge; Caligula departed for the north in September 39 CE, apparently to campaign there (see further *Gai.* 45–46 below)

18 **fama** abl. of means

puer the noun is in apposition with the subject of the sentence (implied by *audiebam*) and literally means "as a boy" but might better be rendered "in my childhood"; only occasionally does Suetonius so explicitly include such personal knowledge, and in doing so here, he foregrounds the claim being made

19   **causam** direct object of *narrantem*, modified by *proditam*

20–21   **quod . . . affirmasset** the substantive clause with *quod* ("that")
           stands in apposition with *causam*; the subjunctive shows that
           the reason stated is that of the courtiers

           Thrasyl\<l\>us mathematicus Thrasyllus was Tiberius' trust-
           ed astrologer, with him through his final days on Capri; the
           report of his prophecy reflects Suetonius' fascination with the
           theme of imperial destiny (also prominent in **The assassina-
           tion of Julius Caesar** above).

21   **uerum nepotem** Tiberius' "true grandson" was Tiberius
           Gemellus (son of Tiberius' son Drusus); Caligula was only
           Tiberius' grandson through adoption. Both were men-
           tioned in Tiberius' will, but Gemellus was killed soon after
           Caligula's accession.

∾ *Caligula's capers (continued), GAI. 55*

In this chapter, Suetonius turns to what he deems Caligula's excessive
fondness for various entertainers, including his beloved racehorse,
Incitatus. Public games (*ludi*) and shows (*spectacula*)—including
horse races in the circus, gladiatorial combat and beast hunts in the
amphitheater, and all manner of dramatic productions in the theater—were a fundamental aspect of life in imperial Rome, provid-
ing not just entertainment, but a way for their imperial sponsors to
cultivate relations with the people. Suetonius takes great interest in
games—he wrote a separate scholarly work, now lost, *On Games*—
and it should be noted that Caligula is not faulted here for putting
on games as such. Rather, Suetonius considers it inappropriate for an
emperor to consort too closely with entertainers, who were not traditionally accorded a high social status in Rome—even though they
could be extraordinarily popular. This paradox comes to the fore in
the career of Nero (see the selection on **Nero the artist** below).

1   **ad insaniam** "to the point of insanity"; what starts as devotion
           (*studium*) to individuals Caligula takes to irrational extremes

1–2   **omnibus . . . fauit** verbs of favoring take the dat. (Bennett sec. 187.III)

2   **Mnesterem** a famed dancer (*pantomimus*) in early imperial Rome, he has already been mentioned in Suetonius' life of Caligula (36.1) as a sexual partner of the emperor

3   **si qui . . . obstreperet** in combination with *si, nisi, num,* or *ne, qui* (and *quis*) may stand as a substantive, "anyone" (Bennett sec. 91.4); *si* here introduces the protasis of a general conditional in past time, which uses a subjunctive, while the apodosis uses the indicative (see Bennett sec. 302.3.a)

5   **denuntiauit, abiret . . .** the order following *denuntiauit* is given in a substantive clause with a subjunctive verb (see Bennett sec. 295.8)

6   **Ostiam** for the lack of prep., see note above on *Capreas* (*Tib.* 40–44, line 3); Ostia was situated at the mouth of the Tiber and functioned as the main port of Rome

   Ptolemaeum regem king of Mauretania, in western Africa, he was summoned to Rome by Caligula and was ultimately killed. The key for understanding this anecdote is the old tradition of a messenger carrying the order for his own death; the knight was to be kept in suspense until Ptolemy opened the (sealed) message.

8   **boni quicquam** gen. of the whole (or partitive gen.)

9   **feceris** take with the negatives *neque . . . neque* as a prohibitive subjunctive (see Bennett sec. 276)

   Thr<a>eces gladiators armed with sabers and small shields, appointed by Caligula to command the German guards who were to protect the emperor's life—a security force separate from the praetorians. Caligula in turn reduces the arms of the Thracians' opponents (*murmillonum*, line 10). N.B.: the angle brackets indicate text the editor believes must be restored to the manuscripts.

11   **Columbo** evidently a *murmillo*, Columbus has still won his match; the name (meaning "dove") was a term of endearment—fitting, since gladiators were not infrequently considered heartthrobs, or else ironic

12   **Columbinum** since the adj. can mean "dove-colored" (i.e., light gray) and was applied to natural substances, it could be that a poison already existed by this name, which was then (incorrectly) explained as deriving from Caligula's victim

13   **sic certe . . . scriptum** supply *uenenum*; translate: "at least, a poisoned labeled thus . . . "

       uenena Suetonius earlier explains (*Gai.* 49.3) that after Caligula's death, a box of the emperor's poisons was found in a search through the imperial palace.

14   **prasinae factioni** The "Greens" were one of the four main groups (all named for colors) that participated in the chariot races of Rome, an extraordinarily popular entertainment: the great Circus Maximus could hold perhaps a quarter of a million spectators.

       addictus et deditus supply *est*; auxiliary forms of *esse* are sometimes thus omitted (Bennett sec. 166.3)

16   **Eutycho** the Greek name means "Lucky," suitable for a charioteer (to whom Caligula was devoted)

       comisatione quadam abl. of time when; the *comisatio* was an after-dinner drinking session

       apophoretis This Greek word refers to "party favors" (literally "things to be taken away"), sometimes quite substantial, but two million sesterces (*uicies sestertium*) is beyond the pale (for the sum, see **Introduction, Addendum 2**).

17   **Incitato equo** the racehorse's name means "Speedy"

17–18 **pridie circenses** *circenses* were games in the Circus, i.e., chariot races; *pridie*, normally an adv., can also function as a prep. that takes the acc. (Bennett sec. 144.2)

19   **indicere** make sure to distinguish this verb from *indicare* (1); the infinitive here introduces a substantive clause (*ne inquietaretur*, line 18)

21   **e gemmis** "of precious stones"

22-23   **quo . . . acciperentur** *quo* can be used to introduce a purpose clause that contains a compar., in place of *ut + eo*; see note above on *quo honestius caderet* (*Iul.* 82.2)

23   **consulatum quoque traditur destinasse** supply *Incitato* (from line 17); Suetonius saves the most outrageous detail for a powerful conclusion, even though he does not actually state as a fact that Caligula planned to make his horse consul

ꙮ *Caligula's capers (continued)*, GAI. 45–46

In the fall of 39 CE Caligula traveled north, spending time in Gaul and on the German frontier, before returning to Rome in the spring. Historians have had trouble piecing together his activities—no full and reliable account might ever have been committed to writing, given that Caligula was killed so soon after his return to Rome. Many believe, as Suetonius seems to, that Caligula was ultimately contemplating an invasion of Britain, with the securing of the German frontier a necessary preliminary (certainly, Caligula's successor Claudius launched an invasion of the island in 43 CE, to much fanfare). The son of a prominent British ruler defected to Caligula, and Caligula made it as far as the Channel coast, but then returned to Rome. Some have thought that his troops nearly mutinied, forcing the return; others have suggested that the journey to the Channel was from the start intended only for display purposes. But whatever the truth, these two chapters—beginning with sham operations on the German frontier—form a brilliant contrast to the traditionally elaborate reporting of military affairs in Roman historiography. As a hard-nosed biographer, Suetonius is interested in what his subjects personally contribute to their campaigns (see also, e.g., *Iul.* 57–70 and *Claud.* 17).

1   **deficiente . . . materia** abl. absolute

3   **post prandium** an especially deflationary touch

    quam tumultuosissime *quam* strengthens the superl., with the force of "as possible" (Bennett sec. 240.3)

    adesse hostem indirect statement following the infinitive *nuntiari*, which itself depends on *iussit*

4   **quo facto** in the abl. absolute, *quo* functions as a connective rel. (= *et eo*; cf. Bennett sec. 251.6)

5   **equitum praetorianorum** each cohort of the emperor's praetorian guard had an attachment of perhaps ninety praetorian cavalrymen

6   **in modum tropaeorum** Romans set up victory monuments on the sites of battles, called trophies (*tropaea*), sometimes in the form of tree trunks clad in enemy armor, meant to resemble the defeated; trophies in this form appear frequently in Roman art too.

7   **ad lumina** "by lamplight"; Latin often uses a pl. in this manner (Bennett sec.353.1)

7–8 **qui secuti . . . essent** rel. clause of characteristic, which conveys a causal force ("since they did not follow")

9   **nouo genere ac nomine** hendiadys (Bennett sec. 344.4), "with a new type of crown with a new name"

9–10 **coronarum** a variety of crowns, including the "civic crown" (fashioned from oak leaves), served as military decorations in Rome (cf. above *quercea corona*, *Gai.* 19, lines 8–9)

11   **exploratorias** the adj. means "scouting" and is formed from the noun *explorator* and the suffix *-ius* (see Bennett sec. 151.2); the cosmic imagery of these crowns may seem overblown, although heavenly bodies were used to determine directions

    obsides for hostages, see note above on *ex Parthorum obsidibus* (*Gai.* 19, lines 11–12); those in question here might be envisioned as the sons of German chieftains recently taken, their Roman education already underway in a school that would teach the rudiments of reading and writing

13 **deserto . . . conuiuio** cf. above *post prandium* (line 3); similar details in both stories suggest that they might be what historiographers call "doublets" (i.e., Suetonius reports two different versions of what had originally been one incident)

insecutus supply *est* (see note above on *addictus et deditus, Gai.* 55, line 14)

15 **mimo** the mime was a dramatic entertainment, often highly ribald; here Suetonius uses the term to mean a "farce"

16 **renuntiantis** m. acc. pl. of the pres. act. pple.

coactum agmen indirect statement after *renuntiantis*: supply *esse* with *coactum*; the expression *agmen cogere* = "to bring up the rear" (i.e., to have completed the task at hand)

17 **ad discumbendum** "to take their places at the table"; gerund + *ad* to express purpose (Bennett sec. 338.3)

18 **Vergili uersu** The line of Vergil's *Aeneid* that follows is a recasting (into a substantive clause following *monuit*) of the last line of a speech in which the hero Aeneas tells his followers to be brave and look to better times: *durate, et vosmet rebus servate secundis*. So familiar was the *Aeneid*, lines from it were frequently quoted, in life and in literature; here the quotation serves once again to underscore the gap between Caligula's phony military success and the deeds of epic heroes.

20 **inter haec** "in the meantime"

21 **grauissimo . . . edicto** emperors from Augustus onwards regularly issued edicts—as Republican magistrates had before— and they came to have the force of law

21–24 **quod . . . celebrarent** for the subjunctive, see note above on *adessent* (*Iul.* 81.1–82.3, line 38)

22–23 **tempestiua conuiuia** "luxurious parties" (literally "starting at an early hour")

24 **quasi perpetraturus** "as if he intended to carry out a war"; the fut. act. pple. is used, especially in later prose writers, to express intention. Suetonius is (from a historian's perspective)

maddeningly vague, but the war anticipated seems to have
been an invasion of Britain (cf. the account in Cassius Dio
59.25.1–3).

26–27 **quidnam coepturus esset** indirect question, employing the
act. periphrastic conjugation (Bennett sec. 115)

28 **spolia Oceani** Various efforts have been made to rationalize
this notorious story which, at least on the surface, makes Caligula look capricious, if not unstable. The shells mentioned
would be thought to contain pearls, an appropriate spoil for a
triumphant general to bring back to Rome, and so, if Caligula
gave such an order, perhaps it was to accumulate props for an
anticipated triumph, in the event never celebrated.

28–29 **Capitolio Palatioque** "to the Capitoline and Palatine tem-
ples"; spoils were often dedicated to the gods, and Julius Caesar is said to have dedicated a breastplate of pearls to Venus
after his return from Britain (Pliny, *Natural History* 9.116)

29–30 **altissimam turrem** Suetonius envisions the lighthouse as a
sort of victory monument but if Caligula actually built it, it
might have been part of real preparations for a war. Certainly in ancient times a functional lighthouse did stand on the
Channel coast at Boulogne, the main point of embarkation
for Britain.

30–31 **ex qua . . . emicarent** rel. clause of purpose

30 **Pharo** Pharus was the island off Alexandria in Egypt, where
stood the famous lighthouse (also called Pharus), one of the
seven wonders of the ancient world.

32 **militi** "to the army"; the noun is used (as often) collectively

donatiuo Soldiers were given rewards in excess of their regular salary, to mark special occasions (although it had not hap-
pened on campaign since the time of Augustus); the sum here
is nearly half the soldier's normal yearly pay—large, but by no
means so large as those attested for other occasions.

∾ *Claudius the scholar,* CLAUD. *41–42*

Though he was the brother of the beloved Germanicus, Claudius, born in 10 BCE, was never expected to become emperor of Rome. Suffering from a nervous disorder—the symptoms mentioned included irregular motor movements, a stammer, and drooling—he was deemed unsuitable for public life; even his own mother, Suetonius claims, liked to call him "a freak of a man, not finished by Nature, but only begun" (*Claud.* 3.2). She along with the rest of rest of the family finally decided, when Germanicus was consul in 12 CE, that Claudius was not to serve in any magistracy or to join the Senate. "The public," as Augustus wrote to his wife Livia at the time, "must not be given a chance of mocking him—and us" (*Claud.* 4.2). Claudius was given no experience of warfare, oratory, and the law, the three staples of a Roman noble's education. Instead, he filled his days writing voluminous histories, in Latin and in Greek—described in the selection here.

According to Suetonius' memorable account (*Claud.* 10), after Caligula was murdered, a terrified Claudius fled to a corner of the imperial palace and hid behind a set of curtains. A soldier, noticing a pair of feet protruding, pulled out their owner, recognized Claudius, and acclaimed him emperor. Claudius was then taken to the camp of the praetorian guard, who swore allegiance to him, even as he promised every man there 15,000 sesterces. Some scholars have doubted whether it all came to pass exactly this way; but certainly the praetorians had effectively chosen a new emperor, and in doing so perpetuated the rule of the Caesars. A number of Senators could never forgive Claudius for this, and his principate was marred by strained relations with them.

Literature, long an enthusiasm of the ruling classes of Rome, naturally occupied an important place in the imperial court; a post developed, that of *a studiis*, to superintend such matters, and was held by Suetonius (see **Introduction, Suetonius' career**). Emperors might wish to be entertained by works, would commission them, and would also sometimes write themselves. Not surprisingly, then, Suetonius regularly discusses the literary proclivities and accomplishments of his subjects (e.g., *Iul.* 55–56, *Aug.* 84–89, *Tib.* 70–1). One question of particular importance, as this selection from the life of Claudius exemplifies, was the extent to which emperors chose to immerse themselves in Greek language and literature. While Suetonius, who produced some of his own scholarship in Greek, evidently admired Greek learning, as did many others, some Romans felt distrustful of certain aspects of Greek culture—which, it should be remembered, was quite alive and well in the eastern half of the empire.

1   **Historiam** only a few quotations from the history survive, in Pliny the Elder's work *Natural History*

      hortante T. Liuio abl. absolute; Titius Livius, more commonly known as Livy, was the greatest historical writer in the Rome of Augustus, ultimately producing a work of 142 books!

1–2   **Sulpicio uero Flauo** the identity of Sulpicius Flavus is unknown; the adversative *uero* prepares for *adiuuante*: Flavus gave greater support

3   **cum . . . commisisset** *cum*, when referring to the past, takes the subjunctive to denote the circumstances under which something took place (Bennett sec. 288.1); the verb is followed by an indirect object ("when . . . he had brought it before a full audience"). Public readings (*recitationes*) were a way authors disseminated their works and counted as entertainment, especially among high-ranking Romans.

4   **a semet ipso** the phrasing here is emphatic

5–6   **cum . . . exortus esset** see note above on *cum . . . commisisset* (line 3)

6–7   **ne sedato quidem tumultu** abl. absolute; *ne . . . quidem* = "not even," with the emphatic word always between

7–8   **quin . . . reminisceretur** the negative force of *ne . . . quidem*, taken with *temperare*, a verb of hindering ("to refrain"), introduces a substantive clause with *quin* + subjunctive (Bennett sec. 295.3)

8   **facti** gen. with the verb of remembering *reminiscor* (see Bennett sec. 206)

10   **per lectorem** as emperor, Claudius relied on a reader

10–11 **initium autem . . . historiae** the history began in 44 BCE, with the months of confusion that followed the Ides of March (see **The assassination of Julius Caesar** above)

11   **sed et** *et* here likely means "also": Claudius' history in a sense has two starting places

12   **a pace ciuili** "from the civil peace (i.e., peace between citizens)"; Claudius perhaps resumed his narrative with the year 27 BCE, in which the second Caesar took the name *Augustus*

12–13 **cum sentiret . . .** causal clause with *cum* + subjunctive

13   **de superioribus** supply *temporibus* (cf. *inferiora tempora*, line 12)

14–15 **et a matre et ab auia** Claudius was rebuked by his mother, Antonia, the daughter of Marc Antony, and by Livia, Augustus' wife and mother of Claudius' father Drusus; to treat the period candidly would throw Augustus in a bad light

16–17 **de uita sua** Like Augustus and Tiberius—and earlier Republican politicians—Claudius wrote an autobiography, perhaps drawn on by Suetonius (see *Claud.* 2.2 for a possible reference). Such writing furnished a way for emperors to try to control the historical record about themselves.

18   **Ciceronis defensionem** This was a response to a work by C. Asinius Gallus, son of the renowned (and cantankerous) orator, Asinius Pollio; in Gallus' work, which compared his father to Cicero, Pollio came off better. After his gruesome death, Cicero was the touchstone against which all orators were judged, and his style in particular was a subject of ongoing debate throughout the early imperial period.

19–20 **nouas . . . litteras tres** Claudius' three new letters (**Fig. 5**) were (1) an anti-sigma or crossed X, representing the consonant combination *BS* as distinguished from *PS*; (2) an inverted digamma representing consonantal V; (3) half-H, a vowel, likely representing the Greek upsilon. Inscriptions survive with the second and third only.

Fig. 5. Claudius' new letters (reconstructing drawing). From left to right these are the anti-sigma; the inverted digamma; the half-H. Photo Wikimedia Commons.

21–22   **cum priuatus . . . edidisset** the contrast between *priuatus* and *princeps* (line 22) indicates that the clause with *cum* + subjunctive is adversative in force (*cum* = "although") (see Bennett sec. 309); Suetonius is with a characteristically light touch commenting on the prerogatives afforded by imperial rule though as a scholar he took interest in orthography, while, as secretary of correspondence, the matter was more than academic (cf. *Aug.* 88)

23   **optinuit ut . . . essent** *optinuit* introduces a substantive clause of result (Bennett sec. 297)

24–25   **diurnis titulisque operum** the *acta diurna* were public records of the state's affairs; *tituli* were inscribed plaques attached to public buildings (*opera*)

26   **Graeca studia** Suetonius transitions (with *nec minore*) to the subject of Claudius' skill with Greek, on which see introductory note above.

27   **linguae** take with both *amorem* (as objective gen.) and *praestantiam* (as subjective gen.)

28   **barbaro** the word can mean simply "foreigner," especially one who speaks neither Latin nor Greek natively

28–29   **'cum . . . sis paratus'** Suetonius only quotes a fragment of Claudius' comment, a causal *cum* clause

utroque . . . sermone nostro The point here is that normally Latin would be viewed by Romans as "our" language, but Claudius views "both languages" (*utroque . . . sermone*), i.e., Latin and Greek, as "ours."

30   **Achaia** Claudius returned control of the province of Achaia (Greece) to proconsuls chosen by lot from among the Senators (*patres conscripti*).

gratam supply *esse*

32   **legatis** ambassadors, who might seek from the Senate privileged treatment (e.g., tax immunity); Claudius responds to them in a sustained speech (*perpetua oratione*) in Greek

33   **pro tribunali** "from the (front of the) tribunal" (i.e., the elevated platform on which Roman magistrates, and later the emperor, sat in judgment)

33–34   **Homericis . . . uersibus** Homer was so familiar to educated Romans that they might quote apposite lines from him, expecting (if not always receiving) instant recognition; according to Suetonius, other emperors quoted Homer (e.g., *Aug.* 65.4, *Tib.* 21.6; *Dom.* 18.2, included below).

34–35   **quotiens . . . ultus esset** the impf. and plpf. subjunctive are frequently used in imperial writers to denote a repeated action (Bennett sec. 287.2)

35   **excubitori tribuno** "the tribune on sentry duty." It was customary (*de more*, line 35–6) for the tribune who commanded the praetorian cohorts on duty in the palace to request the watchword (*signum*) from the emperor personally. Here the line of Homer given by Claudius ("defend against the man, whosoever becomes angry unprovoked"), which appears both in the *Iliad* and the *Odyssey*, ostensibly would cast its Roman speaker as an innocent victim; but in the context of avenging an enemy (*hostem*) as distinguished from a plotter (*insidiatorem*), it is pleasingly ironic: Claudius might be the one "angry unprovoked." On Suetonius' inclusion of Greek, see **Introduction, Addendum 1**.

36   **non temere aliud . . . quam** "nothing more readily, easily . . . than"

38   **Graecas . . . historias** Suetonius reaches his final topic in this section (note *denique*), two histories that Claudius also (*et*) wrote, in Greek, concerning the Etruscans and the Carthaginians. Note that the titles *Tyrrhenicon* (*Etruscan Matters*) and *Carchedoniacon* (*Carthaginian Matters*) are actually Greek forms in the gen. pl. (cf. the Greek title of Petronius' novel, *Satyricon*).

39–40   **ueteri Alexandriae Musio** A shrine for the Muses (*Musium*, or *Museum*) was established in Alexandria by the Ptolemaic kings as a center of literary activity; it was close to the famous library, and continued to function as a center of learning after Egypt's annexation by Rome.

40   **additum** supply *est*

         <nouum> understand *Musium*, "a new Museum"; it is necessary to supply an adj. here to distinguish this second *Musium* (called the "Claudium") from the old one, and *novum* is a good choice, since it could easily have fallen out of the manuscripts because of its similarity to *nomine*

41   **institutumque** again, supply *est*; a substantive result clause follows

41–42   **in altero . . . in altero** understand *Musio* here with each *altero*

∾ Nero the artist, NER. 20–21

Claudius' successor Nero, who became emperor at the remarkably young age of sixteen, attempted to fashion a new model for the principate by devoting himself to artistic endeavors—especially singing—and refining the taste of Romans in the process. This passage directly confronts Nero's bold experiment, while also illustrating Suetonius' own interest in Greek culture and his preoccupation with the games emperors staged. This is also the pivotal passage of the whole life, the structure of which may be compared to those of Tiberius and Caligula in particular. After treating Nero's ancestry and early life, Suetonius next covers (ostensibly) blameless and even praiseworthy acts of the principate—an important perspective for modern students of Nero—and then turns to "follies and crimes" (19.3), the first part of which is this account of Nero's musical aspirations. (An unusually lengthy narrative of Nero's final days follows, along with a description of his more personal characteristics and an account of the reaction to his death.)

1–2   **imbutus et musica** "having been instructed also in music." Music was not typically part of the education of a Roman aristocrat, which was to prepare for a career in warfare, law, and, oratory; and yet, orators trained their voices much as singers might, and it is possible that Nero's interest in music was sparked by such exercises.

2   **statim ut** "the moment that" (*ut* is used temporally)

Terpnum a citharoedist (*citharoedus*) whose Greek name means "Delightful"; these performers, wearing long-flowing robes and elevated boots (see **Fig. 6**), sang, to their own accompaniment on the lyre (*cithara*), arias with tragic themes (for an example, see below *Niobam*, line 43)

Fig. 6. Coin of Nero, dating to c. 62–68 CE. Nero is depicted, and on the reverse a lyre-player (*citharoedus*) with characteristic flowing robes, usually identified as Apollo, god of music. Suetonius (*Ner.* 25.2) knew such coins, and took the figure of the lyre-player to be Nero himself. Photo © The Trustees of the British Museum / Art Resource, NY.

4   **canenti** dat. with the compound verb *assidens* (see Bennett sec. 187.III)

     in multam noctem "long into the night" (*multa nox* = "a late time of night")

5   **et ipse** "he too"

7   **conseruandae uocis causa** a gerundive construction with *causa* + gen., to express purpose

8   **factitarent** subjunctive in a rel. clause of characteristic (translate: "which artists of this kind . . . might make a habit of doing")

     sed et "but even"

9   **sustinere . . . purgari et abstinere** the infinitives are parallel with *omittere* (line 6), and depend on *coepit* (line 5)

10   **pomis cibisque** abl. of separation, with *abstinere* (see Bennett sec. 214.2)

10–12 **donec . . . concupiit** *donec* + indicative, to denote an actual event (Bennett sec. 293.III)

11   **exiguae uocis et fuscae** gen. of quality

12   **Graecum prouerbium** It is highly appropriate for Nero to invoke a *Greek* saying to justify his desire for public performance; for a Roman of high status to appear on the stage was, at least according to traditional Roman morality, degrading. The *prouerbium* is given in indirect discourse.

13   **occultae musicae** dat. of reference ("for music hidden, there is no regard")

14   **Neapoli** locative; it is appropriate that Nero's public debut should be in the city of Naples, an old Greek colony that still had a Greek character; Tacitus dates the appearance to 64 CE (*Ann.* 15.33)

15   **motu terrae** abl. of means, within the abl. absolute *concusso . . . theatro*; Tacitus mentions no earthquake (*motus terrae*), and instead reports that after the audience left the theater, it collapsed

16   **absolueret** *ante . . . quam* takes the subjunctive to denote an act as anticipated, but the notion of anticipation can be quite weak (Bennett sec. 292)

nomon a Latin rendering of the Greek noun for "song," with the Greek acc. ending here (Bennett sec. 27); it adds to the Greek flavor of the scene

18 **secreti** gen. with the adj. *impatiens*; in marked contrast to Suetonius' Tiberius, Nero requires an audience for his disgraceful behavior

19-20 **frequente populo** abl. absolute, with an adj. in place of the pple.

20-21 **si paulum subbibisset . . . se . . . tinniturum** a fut. more vivid conditional, rendered in indirect discourse (governed by *promisit*); with *tinniturum*, supply *esse*

aliquid . . . sufferi acc. of result produced, after *tinniturum* (see Bennett sec. 176); *sufferi* is a gen. of the whole (partitive), with sing. n. pron. ("he promised that he would ring out something rather fierce")

22 **modulatis . . . laudationibus** Such "rhythmical cheers" (which could be accompanied by clapping) were a specialty of the inhabitants of Alexandria in Egypt (compare *Aug.* 98.2); as the recent convoy (*nouo commeatu*) must be that of the Egyptian grain ships that docked in Puteoli, the Alexandrians in Naples should have been sailors.

23 **Neapolim** for the lack of prep., see note above on *Capreas* (*Tib.* 40–44, line 3); similarly, *Alexandria*, abl. of place from which, requires no prep.

24 **neque eo segnius** "and no less actively by this much," i.e., "and just as enthusiastically"; *eo* is by origin abl. of degree of difference, but has almost a causal meaning

25 **quinque amplius milia** *amplius* = *amplius quam* (Bennett sec. 217.2). According to Tacitus, Nero organized a claque of equestrians for the "Juvenile Games" he staged in Rome in 59 CE (*Ann.* 14.15); here, for the emperor's own debut as a performer, the claque is suitably enlarged.

27 **plausuum genera** The three types of applause mentioned here ("bees, roof-tiles, and bricks") appear to be named for the sound they made through humming or clapping.

condiscerent subjunctive in rel. clause of purpose

29 **sibi** indirect reflex., referring to Nero

coma abl. of respect, as are *cultu* and *laeuis*; the youths' thick hair likely should be envisioned as pomaded with scented oil

30 **pu[e]ris ac sine anulo laeuis** equestrians normally wore gold rings as an insignia of their status; on square brackets, see note above on *dis[s]icerent* (*Iul.* 81.1–82.3, line 4)

32 **magni** gen. of value

32-33 **Neroneum agona** Earlier in this life (*Ner.* 12.3–4), Suetonius describes how Nero introduced Greek-style games in Rome, with contests in music, gymnastics, and riding, to be held every four (or perhaps five) years and called *Neronia*; fitting, then, is the use of *agon*, a third declension Greek noun, here in the acc. case (see Bennett sec. 47). First held in 60 CE, a second Neronia was evidently embarked on in 64 CE, perhaps with its date moved forward slightly in the year (hence *ante praestitutam diem*); but midway through, Nero then postponed most of the contests, apparently to 65 CE, when Tacitus dates the event (*Ann.* 16.2–5; and see further below). Whatever the exact timing, both authors agree that at this second Neronia, Nero not only performed publicly in Rome but also ostensibly competed with other performers.

34-35 **in hortis** *horti* (pl.) was an estate on the periphery of Rome, used for market gardening as well as being a pleasure park for the wealthy

36 **statione militum** the cohorts of the praetorian guard on duty

38-39 **citharoedorum** see note above on *Terpnum* (line 2)

39-40 **sorticula . . . demissa** abl. absolute

41 **tribuni militum** officers, presumably of the praetorian cohorts

42 **utque constitit** "when he took up his position"; *ut* is used temporally here

42-43 **peracto principio** the "opening phase" (*principium*) perhaps was an address by Nero to the judges (cf. *Ner.* 23.3)

43-44 **Niobam se cantaturum . . . pronuntiauit** "he announced that he would sing the role of Niobe"; a figure of Greek myth, Niobe was the mother of a large number of children (fourteen according to Ovid), who boasted that she was more prolific than Leto, mother only of two, Apollo and Artemis. In revenge, Apollo and Artemis killed all of Niobe's children; her tale was a most suitable subject for an emotional aria.

Cluuium Rufum a consular, and part of Nero's entourage, he wrote a historical work often thought to be a major source used by later writers for the Neronian period

44-45 **in horam . . . decimam** i.e., until late in the afternoon (see note above on *quinta . . . hora, Iul.* 81.1–82.3, line 32)

46 **in annum sequentem** see note above on *Neroneum agona* (lines 32–33)

saepius "more than was specified"

47 **quod cum tardum uideretur** *quod* is a connective rel. (= *et id*), which introduces a causal clause with *cum*

49 **priuatis spectaculis** "non-imperial shows," i.e., those given by the magistrates

daret subjunctive in an indirect question

50 **sestertium decies** for the sum (one million sesterces), see **Introduction, Addendum 2**

50-51 **tragoedias** The "tragedies" Nero sung were not those of the classic authors such as Sophocles, but once again dramatic solos; the mythological subjects mentioned here are all notable for their extreme states of anguish, presenting special opportunities for the performer: (1) Canace committed incest with her brother; (2) Orestes killed his mother Clytemnestra and was driven mad by the Furies; (3) Oedipus blinded himself after discovering that he had killed his father and married his own mother; (4) Hercules was driven mad by the goddess Hera, who caused him to kill his wife and children. What is more, there are clear links between these stories and events of Nero's own life, such as the murder of his mother Agrippina in 59 CE and his alleged amorous relationship with her.

51   **heroum** *heros*, like *herois* (see *heroidum*, line 52), is a Greek noun; the gen. depends on *tragoedias*

53   **prout quamque diligeret** "according to as much as he loved each one"; i.e., Nero's female masks reflect his latest love interest

56   **tirunculum** the suffix -*culus* creates a dimunitive noun (Bennett sec. 148)

59   **ferendae opis gratia** a gerundive construction with *gratia* + gen., to express purpose (cf. *conseruandae uocis causa*, line 7 above)

∾ *Galba's family*, GALB. 2–3

In the face of rebellion by his provincial commanders and loss of support by the praetorian guard and the Senate, Nero killed himself in 68 CE. The dynasty established by Augustus was thus extinct, full civil war broke out, and Rome saw three emperors in quick succession, Galba, Otho, and Vitellius, before Vespasian emerged supreme and established the new Flavian dynasty. Mirroring the events in question, Suetonius devotes three short biographies to Galba, Otho, and Vitellius: there was little compass to analyze the characters of these emperors, as there had been for their predecessors. Suetonius does, however, devote some space to their family background. This is typical of all his lives (cf. **The life of Horace** below), and of ancient biographical method more generally. But in the context of 68 CE, there is added point, as this selection from the life of Galba makes clear.

But Suetonius was not just emphasizing that Ser. Sulpicius Galba was not from the house of the Caesars; he was also suggesting that Galba's parading of his illustrious lineage was ultimately a worthless strategy for political survival. What really counted, as Tacitus shows in his *Histories* (the major account of the war), was winning the support of the soldiers, along the frontiers and in Rome. At the start of 69, the Rhine legions revolted and proclaimed Vitellius emperor; and meanwhile, in Rome, Otho won over the praetorian guard (they were disgruntled by Galba's stinginess) and overthrew Galba in a *coup*. "He was killed beside the Lake of Curtius," Suetonius memorably writes, "and was left just as he was, until an ordinary soldier, returning from a distribution of grain, threw down his load and cut off Galba's head" (*Galb.* 20.2). The soldier first tucked the head under his robe, then stuck his thumb into its mouth, and carried it to Otho.

1   **gradu** used in the technical sense "degree of relationship" (and *domus*, line 2, means "house" in the sense of "family")

2   **nobilissimus** the adj. refers here not to moral quality but an illustrious family background; even Republican Rome had a concept of hereditary nobility: *nobiles* were descendants of consuls

3   **prosapia** abl. of source; the archaic word is well suited to the context

3–4   **ut qui . . . ascripserit** the rel. clause of characteristic, accompanied by *ut*, has a notion of cause (Bennett sec. 283.3), here complementing *haud dubie*: "seeing as he . . . added"; the pf. subjunctive emphasizes the historicity of the act (Bennett sec. 268.7)

3   **titulis** dat. with compound verb *ascripserit*

        pronepotem supply *esse* and take as predicate after *se* (line 4), all in indirect statement after *ascripserit*

4   **Quinti Catuli Capitolini** A very distinguished Senator in the late Republic, Quintus Lutatius Catulus was in charge of rebuilding the Temple of Jupiter on the Capitoline after it burned down in 83 BCE (hence his extra *cognomen*).

5   **stemma** In the entrance-hall (*atrium*) of a noble's house, images of the ancestors (*imagines*, line 8) would be joined by painted lines to form such a family tree; epitaphs (*elogia*) identified members' honors and accomplishments.

6   **Pasiphaam** the wife of King Minos of Crete, she was the daughter of the Sun; noble families liked to trace their ancestry back to gods and goddesses—the Julians claimed to be descended from Venus—but the exact connection claimed between Galba's mother Mummia Achaica (see below) and Pasiphae is uncertain

7   **referret** subjunctive in a causal rel. clause

8   **uniuersi generis** The Sulpicii were a large clan (or *gens*), with many lines, each with its own *cognomen*; Suetonius will treat only the Sulpicii Galbae.

8–9   **longum est** Latin idiom uses the indicative to express a potential: "it would be tedious" (Bennett sec. 271.1b)

9   **familiae** gen., with *imagines et elogia* understood; the coordinate phrasing (*universi generis / familiae*) allows Suetonius to omit an expected adversative (see Bennett sec. 346)

9–10 **qui . . . traxerit** before *qui* supply *is*: "the man who was the first of the Sulpicii to take the *cognomen* of Galba" (on this use of *primus*, see Bennett sec. 241.2); the whole phrase forms the subject for the verb *traxerit*, subjunctive in an indirect question introduced by *cur aut unde*. The discussion that follows reflects Suetonius' lexicographical interests: study of words was central to much of his scholarship (see **Introduction, Suetonius the scholar**).

12–13 **succenderit** the implied subject is the first Sulpicius Galba

14   **uteretur** for the subject, see the previous note; notice that Suetonius uses an impf. subjunctive here to express a repeated action, even though by the normal rules for sequence of tenses he should use a pf.

15   **uisus** must be a noun here

     uocent subjunctive, because this is part of the explanation offered by *nonnulli* (contrast *sunt . . . nascuntur appellanturque*, line 17), rather than the author Suetonius; the explanation that the name Galba derived from a Celtic word, referring to obesity, may well be correct. Roman *cognomina* often denoted physical characteristics (e.g., Naso, Crassus), and one of the Sulpicii could have earned the name fighting the Gauls, Rome's Celtic neighbors.

16   **tam ... quam ...** correlative

18   **Seruius Galba** Romans frequently referred to distinguished men only by *praenomen* and *cognomen* (cf. *Quinti Catuli*, line 4 above and **Introduction, Addendum 2**); this Galba was consul in 144 BCE, and hence became *consularis*, "of consular rank."

19   †**et eloquentissimus** *et* does not make sense here; a simple correction is *vel* (*vel*, with a superl., means "altogether"), but it is also perfectly possible that an adj. (e.g., *ditissimus*, "richest") dropped out before *et eloquentissimus*

19–20   **ex praetura** "following on his praetorship" (held in 151 BCE)

20–21   **triginta Lusitanorum milibus . . . trucidatis** abl. absolute; *perfidia* is abl. of manner. According to other sources, as governor Galba invaded Lusitania (modern Portugal), suffered a defeat, pretended to make peace with the Lusitanians, and then massacred and enslaved them; his eloquence helped him to escape conviction back in Rome in 149 BCE, but one of the Lusitanian survivors, Viriathus, launched a campaign against the Romans that took a decade to put down.

21   **nepos** This Servius Galba was an officer (*legatus*) of Julius Caesar during the Gallic War (58–50 BCE), but was disappointed in his hopes of a consulship and joined the conspiracy to murder Caesar, for which he was condemned by the Pedian law (*Pedia lege*, line 24) of 43 BCE that provided for the prosecution of Caesar's murderers; his son, the emperor Galba's grandfather (*auus*, line 25) stayed out of the limelight.

22   **Iulio Caesari** dat., with an adj. signifying unfriendliness, *infensus* (see Bennett. sec. 192.1)

26   **enim** the particle is often used in a parenthetical explanation

28   **pater** Galba's father, Servius Galba, probably was consul in 5 BCE

consulatu abl. with *fungor* (see Bennett sec. 218.1)

29   **modicaeque . . . facultatis** gen. of quality, whereas *breui corpore* (line 28) is abl. of quality: physical qualities more typically are expressed in the abl.

30   **Mummiam Achaicam** Mummia, as Suetonius explains, was the great-granddaughter of the Lucius Mummius who conquered Greece in 146 BCE, for which he won the honorary *agnomen Achaicus* ("Victor over Achaia, i.e., Greece"; see **Introduction, Addendum 2**). In the Augustan period a number of families dusted off these old titles and paraded them for distinction.

32   **Liuiam Ocellinam** Galba's rich stepmother was at best only very distantly related to Augustus' (far more distinguished) wife Livia.

35   **uitium** direct object of *detexit*; *instanti*, "to her pressing," serves as the indirect object

37   **Seruium** the future emperor; Gaius, his brother, was consul in 22 CE

38   **urbe** the "City," as often, is Rome; abl. of place from which

39   **sortiri . . . proconsulatum** *sortior* ("to obtain by lot") takes a direct object. Five years after serving as consul former consuls were eligible to draw the lot for a province, normally Asia or Africa; but in the year in which he was first eligible (this is the meaning of *suus annus*), Gaius Galba was blocked by Tiberius.

∾ Otho's youth, OTH. 2–3

Suetonius typically recounts an emperor's life before accession with an eye on what was to follow. Evidence of qualities that were to manifest themselves more fully later interests him (e.g., Caligula's cruel nature, *Gai.* 11); so too do any significant achievements (e.g., Vespasian's exploits as an officer in Britain, *Vesp.* 4). And while this tendency was in keeping with ancient biographical practice—it is really only in the modern period that childhood has earned a significant place in biography—a more distinctive feature of Suetonius' accounts is his effort to trace one emperor's encounters with his predecessors. Of course, this was inevitable when treating an explicitly designated successor such as Nero, but Suetonius takes it further, looking closely, for instance, at Tiberius' treatment of Claudius (*Claud.* 5), or Augustus pinching the young Galba's cheeks and saying "You, too, child, will have a taste of my power" (*Galb.* 4.1), or Caligula being flattered by a young Vitellius (*Gai.* 4). Such scenes underscore the sense of imperial destiny, and its sometimes strange workings, so prominent in Suetonius.

This passage from the life of Otho well illustrates Suetonius' technique. Otho's close relationship with Nero is explored in unflattering detail, preparing for discussions of Otho's revival of Nero's memory after its condemnation by Galba (*Oth.* 7.1) and Otho's personal habits (12.1). But what is also notable here is that Suetonius devotes less space to Otho's principate than to his early life. To be sure, the principate was brief: proclaimed emperor on 15 January 69 CE, by mid-March Otho left Rome to fight the forces of Vitellius. Defeated, he committed suicide on 16 April.

1   **IIII. Kal. Mai.** on the date (28 April) and the year (32 CE), see **Introduction, Addendum 2**

3–4 **obiurgaretur** subjunctive, in a result clause; floggings were, at least in principle, more typically given to slaves than highborn youths

4   **noctibus** "at nighttime"

     solitus supply *esse*; the infinitive depends on *ferebatur*, and itself governs *uagari*, *corripere*, and *iactare*

5   **potulentum** the adj. is formed from the pple. of *poto* ("to drink") and the suffix *-ulentus*, which denotes fullness ("full of")

7   **libertinam aulicam** Emperors relied on their own slaves and freedpersons (i.e., manumitted slaves, who legally owed their former owners various services) in carrying out the administrative tasks necessary to run the empire; and so, through

their proximity to the emperor, the slaves and freedmen could exercise a great deal of influence. A famous example is the freedwoman Caenis, mistress of the emperor Vespasian, mentioned below (*Vesp.* 21–22, line 7).

8   **quo** introduces a purpose clause containing a compar. (Bennett sec. 282.1.a), replacing *ut* + *eo*, *eo* being abl. of degree of difference (Bennett sec. 223)

9   **insinuatus** *insinuo*, in the pass., means "to become intimate (with)" and takes a dat.

10   **congruentia** abl. of cause (as is *consuetudine*, line 11)

11   **uero** here must be used in a conjunctive sense ("moreover"), but the position of the phrase as a whole is odd

11–12   **consuetudine . . . stupri** *stuprum* was an illicit sexual act, typically the violation of a freeborn Roman, either male or female; since the *stuprum* is *mutuum*, the implication is that Otho and Nero took turns penetrating each other; *consuetudine* here has a sexual meaning, "intercourse"

12   **tantum** prepares for the result clause (*ut . . . dubitaret*, lines 12–14)

        potentia "influence" (as opposed to official power, *potestas*); abl. of specification (Bennett sec. 226) with *ualuit*

12–13   **repetundis** the abl. gives the crime, "extortion"; the expression derives from the phrase *pecuniae repetundae*, "money to be recovered" (i.e., from the corrupt official)

13   **pactus** m. sing. pf. pass. pple. of *paciscor*, "having agreed on"

14   **restitutionem** reinstatement into one's former status, following a legal disqualification (e.g., loss of citizenship or, as here, membership in the Senate)

17   **necandae matri** the dat. of purpose in the gerundive construction is commonly used in imperial Latin (Bennett sec. 191.3). Tacitus (*Ann.* 14.1–13) gives an elaborate account of Nero's plans to kill his mother, all set in the year 59 CE, after Otho had left Rome to govern Lusitania (*Ann.* 13.46); this tale, then, may only be a later fabrication.

destinarat on the syncopated form, see note above on *consecrarat* (*Iul.* 81.1–82.3, line 15)

exquisitissimae comitatis gen. of quality

19 **Poppaeam Sabinam** Described as beautiful, charming, and witty, Poppaea Sabina was destined to marry Nero, to whom she bore a daughter. Her first husband was the praetorian prefect, Rufrius Crispinus, and according to the version of the tale given here, she was divorced from him to marry Otho, simply to allow Nero easier access to her (other accounts give different versions of this *ménage*, and so once again we must hesitate to accept Suetonius' account as historical).

tunc adhuc amicam eius "then still his (i.e., Nero's) mistress"; the word *amica* in this period usally corresponds to the English "mistress," the lover of a man who is neither his wife nor a professional prostitute

20 **demandatam** "handed over"

nuptiarum the noun is used in the pl. only (for a list of other such nouns, see Bennett sec. 56)

21 **nec** the negative force applies to *contentus*

corrupisse the pf. infinitive, after a verb of feeling (here *contentus*), denotes a completed action; *contentus* does not require a subject acc.; *corrumpo* means "seduce" (i.e., entice to sexual intercourse), and forms a contrast here to *dilexit*

22 **ne . . . quidem** see note above on *ne sedato quidem tumultu* (*Claud.* 41–42, lines 6–7)

tulerit as often, Suetonius uses a pf. subjunctive in the result clause to represent the result as a fact without reference to its continuance (see Bennett sec. 268.6); cf. above *Tib.* 40–44, lines 15–20

23 **missos** the pple. functions substantively, "men sent"

ad arcessandam supply *eam* (i.e., Poppaea)

24 **ipsum** i.e., Nero himself

26 **depositum reposcentem** a business metaphor

27   **per causam** "on the pretext of" (+ gen.)

      legationis governorship of a province controlled directly by
      the emperor, Lusitania

28   **uisum** supply *est*

      ne . . . diuulgaret negative purpose clause

      mimum a similar metaphorical use at *Gai.* 45–46, line 15, but
      here with added point because the concealment of adulterous
      loves was a standard theme of mime

29   **sic quoque** "even so, even as it was"

      disticho Lampoons in verse frequently made the rounds in
      Rome, and Suetonius enjoys quoting them (e.g., *Iul.* 20.2, *Aug.*
      70.1–2, *Tib.* 59). The poem here is an elegiac couplet, a stan-
      dard verse form in which the first line is a dactylic hexameter,
      the second a pentameter; note how the key word *suae* is dex-
      terously saved for the ending, a common device in epigrams.

33   **quaestorius** Normally a province such as Lusitania was gov-
      erned by a man of praetorian rank, but the twenty-six-year-
      old Otho had held no rank higher than the quaestorship.

34   **moderatione atque abstinentia** abls. of manner

∽ *Vitellius the glutton,* VIT. *13*

A Caesar's dining habits are often noted by Suetonius (e.g., *Iul.* 53,
Aug. 74–77, *Claud.* 32–33; cf. *Tib.* 41, above), but nowhere more
amusingly than here. But as so often with the images of excess found
in Roman literature, this account of Vitellius' gluttony need not
be taken as objective: it may reflect instead a tradition of invective
against Vitellius, which took shape during the civil war and was then
crystallized after the Flavian dynasty consolidated its victory. The
image of Vitellius' inability to control himself mapped on to that of
the emperor unable to control Rome itself (cf. *Vit.* 11–12; and for a
more elaborate sketch, see Tacitus, *Hist.* 2.87–99).

But invective, to be effective, must have some credibility. It does
seem that Vitellius liked to eat—an ancient cookbook attributed to the
gourmet Apicius named several (fairly modest) recipes after Vitellius.

And coins depict the emperor with fleshy cheeks and a double chin (see, e.g., **Fig. 7**). Such imagery may, at least in part, have been designed to recall the later portraiture of Nero, to whose memory Vitellius paid some respect. But it ultimately helped to provide a basis for the less flattering portrait of Vitellius we find here in Suetonius' words.

Fig. 7. Coin of Vitellius, dating to 69 CE. Vitellius is depicted, and on the reverse the goddess Vesta, seated on a throne, with the legend PONT MAX (abbreviating *pontifex maximus*, the chief priesthood held by Roman emperors). Photo © The Trustees of the British Museum / Art Resource, NY.

1   **uel praecipue** "in particular"; *uel* strengthens superls. and also (frequently in Suetonius) *praecipue*; of the two topics mentioned here, *luxuria* ("high living") is treated in chapter 13, *saeuitia* in chapter 14

2   **trifariam** the suffix *-fariam* forms multiplicative advs. (here "three times"); normally one would have a feast (*epulae*) at most once a day, and certainly not for breakfast (*iantaculum*) or at a dedicated drinking party (*comisatio*)

4   **uomitandi consuetudine** the practice is elsewhere attested, with Seneca even famously claiming of the Romans: *uomunt ut edant, edunt ut uomant* (*To Helvia* 10.3)

5   **indicebat** make sure to distinguish *indicere* from *indicare*; it is the first used here ("to impose an obligation of")

     aliud alii "different meals to different individuals" (for the construction, see Bennett sec. 253)

cuiquam dat. of reference, "for any one" with the verb *con-sto*, "to cost"; take closely with *singuli apparatus* ("individual preparations")

6   **quadringenis milibus nummum** *milibus* is abl. of comparison (after the adverbial *minus*), while *nummum* preserves an archaic form of the gen. pl. (Bennett 25.6), used here partitively. The *nummus* was equivalent to the *sestertius*, and 400,000 sesterces—the property requirement for an equestrian—was a stereotypically large sum (just as, say, one million dollars is today); see further **Introduction, Addendum 2.**

8   **aduenticia** take with *cena*: "a feast to celebrate an arrival"

9   **septem** supply *milia* (from line 8)

   apposita supply *esse*

   quoque "even"

10 **ipse** i.e., Vitellius

   patinae A large earthen-ware dish used for both cooking and serving; Vitellius jokingly calls it the "shield of Minerva," perhaps thinking in particular of the colossal statue of Athena the Warrior on the Acropolis in Athens.

11 **πολιούχου** The Greek word means "Defender of the city" but plays on a similar word meaning "of large capacity." Untranslated words of Greek frequently were employed in Roman conversation, and Suetonius in a sense is quoting Vitellius here.

12 **scarorum** Though not certainly identified, this sea-fish was highly prized. It and the other exotic ingredients that follow (brains of pheasants and peacocks, tongues of flamingoes, small intestines of lampreys) calculatedly convey the breadth of Rome's empire—Vitellius' dish is a microcosm; but there is also implicitly a rebuke here, in that the emperor uses warships (*triremes*), commanded by senior captains (*nauarchos*).

14 **lactes** "small intestines"; the noun is apparently related to, but not the same as, *lac* ("milk"); it occurs only in the pl.

   a Parthia usque "all the way from Parthia"; when combined with a noun and prep., *usque* sometimes follows the noun

freto . . . Hispanico "the Spanish strait," i.e., the strait of Gibraltar

15   **petitarum** f., agreeing with the nearest antecedent *murenarum*, but also modifying *scarorum*, *phasianarum*, *pauonum*, and *phoenicopterum*

15–16   **ut . . . homo** "as is natural for a man"

16   **non . . . modo sed . . . quoque** "not only . . . but also . . . "

17   **ne . . . quidem** The expression brackets *in sacrificio* ("not even in sacrificing"); *aut itinere ullo* prepares for the last part of the sentence (beginning *circaque uiarum popinas*). Compare the story of Tiberius' inappropriate behavior at the sacrifice (*Tib.* 44.2 above): both tales reek of impiety.

18   **temperauit quin . . .** a verb of hindering, accompanied by a negative, can use *quin* (in place of *ne*) to introduce its substantive clause (Bennett sec. 295.3a)

19   **uiscus et farris †paene** During a sacrifice, food was placed on the altar and/or burned; *uiscus* (usually in the pl. *uiscera*) refers to inner organs or "flesh," while *far* was a kind of wheat used to make sacrificial cakes. The dagger indicates that the text as recovered from the manuscripts defies easy restoration: the gen. *farris* is dangling, and perhaps should be completed with *frustra* ("scraps"); but then again, *paene* might be a corruption for either *panem* or *panes* ("cake[s]").

∾ *The work habits of Vespasian,* VESP. 21–22

On 1 July 69 CE, the two legions of Egypt proclaimed Ti. Flavius Vespasianus emperor; the legions of Judea and then Syria followed. The plan was for Vespasian to stay in the east, cutting off the Egyptian and African grain ships that fed Rome, thereby undermining Vitellius' position, while a separate force went by land to Italy. But the Balkan legions, who had fought for Otho, transferred loyalty to Vespasian and decided themselves to invade Italy, ahead of the eastern forces. They prevailed over Vitellius' forces and ultimately marched on Rome, entering the city in December 69 CE. Vitellius was dragged half-naked through the streets, taunted, and then killed. Vespasian was recognized as emperor in Rome, and would remain emperor until his death in 79 CE. As part of his (quite successful) effort to restore order, he promoted his family as a new ruling dynasty, called "Flavian" (after his *nomen*). In particular, he shared some key powers and offices with his elder son Titus, who succeeded him (his younger son, Domitian, was kept more in the background).

Suetonius' final three Flavian lives are surprisingly short and as a result (most would agree) inferior in quality when compared to those of the early emperors: while many of the same rubrics are used, there is simply less information than one would expect, especially in the lives of Vespasian and Domitian. (One change to the patterning, however, did make sense: most of the information on family background is placed, quite logically, in the first chapter of the life of Vespasian.) It may be that Suetonius was simply more interested in the period of Caesar and Augustus (see **Introduction, Suetonius' career**).

As in his biography of Augustus, Suetonius, after considering the background to Vespasian's principate, looks first to public life (chapters 8–19), then private (20–23), before finally turning to the death and omens preceding it. And this selection, coming from the analysis of Vespasian's private life, should be compared in particular to **The work habits of Augustus** (*Aug.* 78) above (and cf. also the selections **Tiberius on Capri**). By returning to the same topics in his biographies, Suetonius facilitates such comparisons—and implicitly reflects a notion of what the ideal emperor was. This passage also suggests, once again, how crucial the management of *image* was to imperial success: note, for instance, how Vespasian puts on his shoes himself (rather than relying on slaves), and only after his entourage has been admitted—suggesting that they take precedence over all else. After the perceived excesses of Rome's first dynasty, Vespasian's deliberately bluff manner worked admirably for him.

2   **de nocte** "when it was still night"; the preceding *ac* ("and in fact") corrects *maturius*

3   **officiorum . . . breuiariis** summary reports submitted by gov-
       ernment officials (*officium*, in the sing. or pl. can by metonymy
       mean "body of officials"); emperors had a great deal of paper-
       work to get through, as Suetonius, secretary for correspondence
       (*ab epistulis*) under Hadrian, knew

4   **salutabatur** In Roman Republican society it was customary for
       a powerful man to be greeted by his clients and friends at dawn;
       the custom, not surprisingly, was taken over by the emperors.

       calciabat ipse se "he put on his shoes himself"; *ipse* corresponds
       to the intensive "himself" of English; normally, a high-ranking
       Roman would have help from slaves in getting dressed

5   **decisa** a pf. pass. pple. in combination with a noun (here *ne-
       gotia*) can stand in for an abstract noun with dependent gen.
       (e.g., *Quinctius defensus* = "the defense of Quinctius"; Bennett
       sec. 337.6); note that Vespasian's *amici* arrive first, because
       emperors typically consulted with a group of advisors (called
       "friends") before making a decision

6   **gestationi** being carried in a litter counted as a form of recre-
       ation; cf. note above on *lectica* (*Aug.* 78, line 18)

7   **pallacarum** gen. of the whole; this Greek word means "concu-
       bine," a woman with whom a man might sleep with regularly
       but who was of lower social status, perhaps legally ineligible for
       marriage to him. Vespasian's most famous concubine was the
       secretary and freedwoman Caenis, on whom see note above on
       libertinam aulicam (*Oth.* 2–3, line 7) and see also below *Dom.*
       12, lines 20–22; the exact date of her death is unknown.

8   **plurimas** "in very great numbers"; predicate adjs. (especially
       superls.) belonging to the antecedent may stand in the rel.
       clause

       secreto the private part of the palace

8–9   **balineum tricliniumque** Romans typically went to the baths
       in early afternoon, after lunch, but one could also bathe before
       lunch.

10   **traditur** supply *esse*

domestici members of Vespasian's household, including in particular the imperial slaves and freedpersons

12 **Et ... et** "both ... and" almost with the sense of "not only ... but also"

super cenam "over dinner"; Suetonius is trying to make a neat transition by means of the dinner, the last meal of the day, to the subject of Vespasian's sense of humor

alias N.B.: this is the adv. *alias*

comissimus m. sing. nom. superl. of the adj. *comis*

13 **dicacitatis** gen. of quality

14 **praetextatis** the *toga praetexta* was that worn by boys up to their formal entry into manhood, and so something *praetextatus* is typical of youths, i.e., unseemly or obscene

15 **uerbis** abl. of separation

16 **in quibus et haec** "among which in particular are the following"; *sunt* is supplied

17 **plaustra ... plostra** in ordinary speech, the diphthong -*au*- was turned into a long *o* (the demagogic aristocrat, Publius Claudius, preferred to refer to himself as Clodius); the point of this anecdote seems to be that Vespasian deliberately cultivated the vulgar pronunciation.

18 **Flaurum** Vespasian's new pronunciation of *Florus* is a bilingual pun, for it gives the Greek word "worthless"; on familiarity with Greek see **Introduction, Addendum 1**.

19 **quasi ... deperiret** *quasi* with the subjunctive expresses the grounds of action; the anonymous woman claims that she was dying of love for Vesapsian (*amore suo*)

20 **pro concubitu** "for sexual intercourse"

donasset subjunctive, in a *cum* clause denoting the circumstances in which the main action of the sentence took place

21 **dispensatore** a slave in charge of disbursing payments; 400,000 sesterces is a stereotypically large sum (see also *Vit.* 13.1 above); the pres. pple. *admonente*, where one might

expect a pf. pple., is fairly commonly used when setting up a question and its response

22   **uellet** subjunctive in an indirect question

Vespasiano . . . adamato render here: "To a passion for Vespasian"; for the construction, see note on *decisa*, line 5 above

∽ *Titus and the eruption of Vesuvius, TIT. 8.3–4*

Suetonius' life of Titus has been said to be that of a "fairy prince." Handsome, charming, and talented, Titus, because of the raucous parties he gave as a young man, was believed to be profligate and cruel, but as emperor he put all such fears to rest, and through his virtuous rule became the "delight and darling of the human race" (*Tit.* 1). His premature death, at the age of forty-one, was felt as a great loss to Rome, Suetonius writes (11)—but of course, had Titus ruled longer, there might have been more opportunity to disappoint. The discussion of the principate itself (chapters 7–9) is organized as a panegyric of Titus' virtues of restraint, generosity, benevolence, and clemency.

This brief selection, illustrating some of those virtues, also exemplifies other interests of Suetonius, in particular how the emperor handled the physical maintenance of the sprawling city of Rome and also how he handled finances. The selection also mentions what for modern readers is one of the most famous events in Roman history, the eruption of the volcanic Mt. Vesuvius in August of 79 CE, which destroyed Pompeii, Stabiae, and Herculaneum, towns on the Bay of Naples where wealthy Romans had vacation houses. (For an eyewitness account, see the two letters of Pliny the Younger, *Epistles* 6.16 and 20.)

1   **ac tristia** "and dreadful ones at that"

eo the reference is to Titus

ut "such as"

2–3   **incendium Romae** According to the Greek historian Cassius Dio (66.24.1–3), in 80 CE, while Titus was overseeing reconstruction efforts in the area of Vesuvius, a terrible fire broke out in Rome, destroying a number of important buildings, including the Temple of Jupiter on the Capitoline. Titus began restorations, but so short was his principate that much was left to be completed by his brother Domitian (see below *Dom.* 12, line 1).

3   **pestilentia** epidemics occurred not infrequently in Rome, unsurprisingly given that perhaps as many as a million souls were packed into the city; other authors refer to a terrible outbreak under Titus (e.g., Cassius Dio 66.23.5)

4   **quanta non temere alias** "of a size hardly occurring at any other time"; the verb is best supplied from *acciderunt* (line 1)

6   **per edicta** on imperial edicts, see note above on *grauissimo . . . edicto* (*Gai.* 45–46, line 21); they furnished the emperor a means of managing public relations

7   **quatenus . . . facultas** a variant on the rel. clause of characteristic (see Bennett sec. 283.5)

7–8   **curatores restituendae Campaniae** the dat. of the gerundive construction is commonly used after nouns meaning officers, offices, and the like, to indicate the function or scope of the office; according to Cassius Dio (66.24.3), two ex-consuls were appointed to the office of "restoring Campania," and there is also epigraphic evidence for Titus' restoration of damaged buildings

10   **restitutioni** see previous note

11   **urbis** as so often, the reference is to Rome, "the City"

        perisse infinitive (syncopated for *periise*, from *pereo*) in indirect statement after *testatus*; understand *se* as the subject of the infinitive; in direct speech, Titus' cry would have been *perii!* ("I am ruined!")

12   **praetoriorum** "the imperial properties," filled with valuable paintings, statues, furniture, and the like

13   **compluris** m. pl. acc.; this adj. exists only in the pl., and shows
      i-stem forms

14   **quo . . . peragerentur** *quo* introduces a purpose clause with
      a compar., replacing *ut + eo*; see note above on *quo hones-*
      tius caderent (*Iul.* 82.2); a fitting comment for Suetonius, the
      equestrian administrator, to make!

15   **medendae ualitudini** dat. with the gerundive construction to
      express purpose

17   **sacrificiorum** since plagues could be viewed as punish-
      ments by the gods, sacrifices could be performed in hope of
      appeasement

⌘ Difficulties for Domitian, DOM. 12

After the premature death of Titus in 81 CE, Titus' younger brother,
the capable but ultimately very oppressive Domitian, succeeded.
Writing after Domitian's assassination (at the hands of members of
his own household, including possibly his wife), the Senators Tacitus
and Pliny the Younger immediately condemned his memory. Certainly, relations with the Senate had been strained, especially after
a failed uprising of two Rhine legions under Antonius Saturninus
at the start of 89 CE. But as part of the condemnation of Domitian's
memory, more creditable achievements might have been distorted,
or misconstrued, too. Some scholars have suggested, for instance,
that Suetonius is wrong to suggest in this passage that Domitian,
desperately in need of money, took to confiscating the estates of "living and dead"; the "confiscations" rather arose from a political situation—the estates of those condemned passed to the emperor. Indeed,
it has even been suggested that Domitian was a very careful manager
of the imperial finances, leaving a surplus that helped his immediate
successors, Nerva and Trajan.

     Managing the finances was a difficult part of the emperor's job.
With no ability to issue bonds, or to print money (coin was, in theory
anyway, to be worth its precious metal content), the emperor had to
reconcile a stream of outgoing expenses with an incoming flow of

revenues, both personal and public at once. To increase expenditure, therefore, was likely to lead to resentment in some segment of the society, as it would have to be met through immediate new taxes, stricter enforcement of existing rules, or confiscation. Suetonius is keenly interested in the emperor's financial affairs (see, e.g., *Aug.* 29 and 41–43; *Tib.* 46–49; *Cal.* 17.2–21 and 38–42). But rather than analyzing the budget systematically or objectively, he prefers to pass judgment on whether he deems expenditures worthy or not. This is largely a consequence of his aim in the *Caesars* to look at the virtues, and vices, of his subjects; but it also reflects more general attitudes to wealth in Roman society, as well as the particular resentment some emperors caused through their financial practices.

1 **operum ac munerum impensis** the gens. are objective, after *impensis*; Domitian spent heavily on public works (not least because of the terrible fire of 80 CE) and on shows (see *Dom.* 4), as did other emperors, but the notion that he was seriously strapped by these expenditures has been questioned by modern scholars (see introduction above)

1–2 **stipendio** payment of the soldiers, increased by Domitian from 900 to 1,200 sesterces per year (*Dom.* 7), a 33% increase in the budget

3 **deminuere** There is little evidence to support Suetonius' claim here, although one legion likely was destroyed after an invasion of Pannonia by the Sarmatians who lived north of the Danube.

4 **obnoxium** supply *esse*

barbaris the principate of Domitian saw considerable military activity on the Rhine and especially the Danube (see note above on *deminuere*, line 3)

5 **neque eo setius** "and nonetheless"; the adv. *setius* occurs only in this compar. form

6 **nihil pensi habuit** "he had no scruples" (*pensi*, pf. pass. pple. from *pendo*, is a gen. of the whole); the expression takes a clause of prevention with *quin* (see Bennett sec. 295.3)

praedaretur a strong verb, usually referring to wartime activity

7   **quolibet** take with *accusatore* and *crimine*

9–10   **maiestatem principis** In the Republican period to diminish the majesty (*maiestas*) of the Roman People was prosecutable, and under Augustus the scope of the law expanded to include offenses against the emperor, including conspiracies but also libel; the charge offered emperors a way to eliminate those whom they feared, whether legitimately or not.

10   **confiscabantur** the verb is first found in Suetonius and means literally "to seize for the *fiscus* (i.e., the emperor's treasury)"

        alienissimae hereditates estates of those not in any way connected to Domitian

11   **qui diceret** rel. clause of characteristic; *diceret* introduced an indirect statement with *se* and *audisse*, and *audisse* in turn introduces another indirect statement with *Caesarem* and *esse*

12   **sibi** indirect reflex., referring to the deceased

        ceteros supply *fiscos* (from *fiscus*, line 13)

12–13   **Iudaicus fiscus** "The Jewish treasury," established by Vespasian after the Great Rebellion of the Jews (66–70 CE), received a special poll tax of 8 sesterces a year paid by all Jews, in place of the tax they had paid to the Temple in Jerusalem. As a tax levied on longstanding inhabitants of the empire, this was a unique penalty, but probably to be explained by a desire of the Flavians to play up their successful destruction of the rebels; also, it was ostensibly used for the rebuilding of the Temple of Jupiter in Rome, adding to its political value. Domitian's enforcing of it too, then, might not have arisen from financial straits.

14   **inprofessi** Suetonius refers to two groups, (1) those who were not officially registered but who lived a Jewish life (including perhaps sympathizers), and (2) those who were by origin Jewish but did not pay the tax (including possibly some Christians).

14-15   **dissimulata origine** abl. absolute

16   **me adulescentulum** a rare explicit intrusion into the text of
        Suetonius' own experience (see **Introduction, Suetonius the
        scholar**)

16-17   **procuratore** Procurators (either of equestrian status or freed-
        men) administered the emperor's financial affairs; the procu-
        rator here is assisted by a group of advisors (*consilium*).

19   **minime ciuilis animi** Suetonius turns to Domitian's lack of
        civility, a quality in emperors deemed important by Suetonius
        (cf. *Vesp.* 12, *civilis et clemens*); *animi* is gen. of quality

20   **Caenidi** on Caenis, see note above on *libertinam aulicam*
        (*Oth.* 2–3, line 7)

21   **osculum** It was customary for a woman to kiss her own rela-
        tives, and those of her husband, but since Vespasian was not
        actually Caenis' husband, Domitian snubs her here by hold-
        ing out his hand, normally a way to greet an inferior.

        assuerat syncopated form of *assueuerat*; see note above on
        consecrarat (*Iul.* 81.1–82.3, line 15)

22   **generum fratris** Flavius Sabinus, who was married to Ti-
        tus' daughter Julia; when he appears with his attendants clad
        in imperial white, Domitian takes umbrage—even though
        Domitian's attendants also are in white, although Domitian
        is not yet emperor! *generum* functions as the acc. subject in
        indirect statement after *indigne ferens*, with *habere* as its verb.

23   **et ipsum** "as well as he" (i.e., Domitian); the implication is
        that to have table attendants dressed in white was a special
        imperial prerogative

25   **οὐκ ἀγαθὸν πολυκοιρανίη** "A multiplicity of rulers is not
        a good thing." The phrase is from a speech of Odysseus in
        Homer's *Iliad*. On the use of Greek here, see **Introduction,
        Addendum 1.**

◌◦ *Difficulties for Domitian (continued)*, *DOM. 18*

Description of physical appearance is a regular feature of Suetonius' imperial biographies (e.g., *Aug.* 79–80, *Tib.* 68, *Oth.* 12) and at times reflects the author's interest in physiognomy, a widely accepted "science" in Rome according to which one's outer appearance reflected inner character (note Domitian's own comment to the Senate in this passage). For Suetonius, physiognomy also might reveal in particular how worthy one was to be an emperor (cf. *Tit.* 2–3). Domitian's deteriorating appearance can thus be seen as mirroring his deteriorating rule.

1 **statura** abl. of description, as are the nouns that follow, *uultu, oculis,* and *acie* (lines 1–2); the (implied) subject of *fuit* is Domitian

2 **praeterea** in this clause, a second *fuit* is supplied on the basis of the first

4–5 **quorum . . . habebat** "the toes of which were rather short"

5 **postea** in this clause, a third *fuit* is supplied, with *deformis* functioning as predicate adj.

6 **tamen** the word does not mean "nevertheless" here but marks the rel. clause as a parenthesis

 ei: dat. of reference; by English idiom we would expect a gen. after *crurum* instead

6–7 **ualitudine longa** abl. of cause

7 **uerecundia** abl. of means

8–9 **iactauerit** note the pf. tense of the subjunctive is used here in the result clause in secondary sequence, representing the result as a fact without reference to its continuance (see Bennett sec. 268.6)

10 **probastis** syncopated form of *probavistis*

 caluitio Early portraits of Domitian depict him with a full head of curls, while in later types, although the coiffure is still elaborate, there seem to be hints of a receding hairline (**Fig. 8**).

Fig. 8. Bust of Domitian. Capitoline Museums, Rome. This portrait, dating c. 88 CE, shows the emperor with less hair than earlier examples. Photo Scala / Art Resource, NY.

11   **in contumeliam suam traheret** *trahere* with *in* here means "to take as"; the use of *suus* here is equivalent to an objective gen. (hence *contumeliam suam* means "insult against himself" or "personal insult")

cui alii *cui* is a form of the indef. pron. *quis* commonly used (instead of *aliquis*) with *si*, *nisi*, *num*, and *ne*; the adj. *alius* makes clear that the "someone" is definitely not Domitian himself

ioco uel iurgio dats. of purpose

12 **obiectaretur** the implied subject is *calvitium*; the impf. subjunctive is used in the *si* clause to represent a past repeated action (see Bennett sec. 302.3a); the main verb, *traheret*, would normally be impf. indicative, but is subjunctive here because it is in a result clause introduced by *ut* (line 10) and signaled by *ita* (line 10)

libello The book *On Hair Care* was, to judge by *adulescentia*, a product of Domitian's youth, when he is known to have composed other works, including poetry. Suetonius' interest in it reflects the biographer's ongoing interest in the emperor's own literary activities (see further above **Claudius the scholar**).

13 **haec** "the following"; the quotation begins with a line of Homer and ends with *breuius* (line 19)

14 **inseruerit** *quamuis* (line 12), even when introducing a statement of fact, can take the subjunctive in imperial Latin prose (Bennett sec. 309.6)

15 **οὐχ ὁρά<ᾳ>ς, οἷος κἀγὼ καλός τε μέγας τε;** The line of Greek quoted by Domitian, "Do you not see, what a man I am, how huge, how splendid?," is from Homer, *Iliad* 21.108, part of a speech in which the Greek warrior Achilles refuses to spare the Trojan Lycaon, pointing out that all mortals face the same fate of death, even Achilles himself, despite Achilles' strength and beauty. On the use of Greek, see **Introduction, Addendum 1** and also the note on *Homericis . . . uersibus* (*Claud.* 41–42, lines 33–34).

18 **scias** optative subjunctive, followed by an indirect statement in which *quicquam* is the acc. subject and the infinitive of *esse* (as often with this verb) must be supplied

∾ *Vita Horati*

Quintus Horatius Flaccus—or "Horace," as he is more commonly known to speakers of English—was one of Rome's most distinguished poets, remarkable for his versatility and generic innovation. Early works of his included a book of often scurrilous *Epodes*, inspired by the archaic Greek poet Archilochus and deploying the iambic meter; and also two books of *Satires*, this time modeled on an earlier Latin poet, Lucilius, and written in dactylic hexameters (also the meter of Greek and Roman epic). Horace later turned to lyric, claiming the Greek poets Sappho and Alcaeus as his models (Pindar was also important), and produced altogether four virtuoso books of *Odes* (*Carmina* in Latin), composed in a variety of meters and frequently addressed to distinguished men of the Rome of Augustus; he also put out a book of verse letters (*Epistulae*), in hexameters like the *Satires*, again addressed to various distinguished men, but reflecting on moral themes. Two further, longer *Epistulae* followed, one addressed to Augustus himself, the other to Florus, both concerned with literature. Also preserved in the poet's manuscripts is a hymn commissioned by Augustus for the Centennial Games of 17 BCE (see further below); and the *Ars Poetica*, another verse epistle concerned with literature.

Horace lived through the momentous transition from Republican to imperial government in Rome—and as a leading poet of the age, himself contributed to the cultural efflorescence, and change, that was so distinctive of this era, when other great poets such as Vergil, Propertius, and then Ovid were at work. Horace's work was influential for later Latin poets (including the satirists Persius and Juvenal, as well as Statius, who wrote lyric poetry); and it was regularly used as a school text. In the first century CE, the grammarian Valerius Probus addressed questions pertaining to the text.

The life of Horace that follows is preserved in several manuscripts of his poems, as a guide for readers. Modern scholars believe that it represents substantially the life of Horace composed by Suetonius (see further below), since Suetonius is elsewhere cited as the source for one of the letters of Augustus that is quoted in this *Vita Horati*.

The life would have been just one of Suetonius' serial *Lives of Poets*, part of his larger work, *On Famous Men*, a collection of biographies of men of letters. (On this work see **Introduction, Suetonius the scholar**). In writing his lives of poets, Suetonius would have drawn on earlier research, as well as his own reading of the poets' works. His particular interest, though, was not literary criticism as we understand it, but the biographical quest for each poet—where was he born, what did he look like, and so forth, interests also very much on display in *Lives of the Caesars*.

A particular interest, showcased in this life of Horace and in other remnants of *On Famous Men*, is the literary men's relations with Augustus and his successors; the letters from Augustus cited here may indeed be the result of Suetonius' own original research. If, as seems likely, *On Famous Men* preceded *Lives of the Caesars*, Suetonius' interest in the Caesars in his literary lives was an interesting anticipation of what was to come—while perhaps also reflecting Suetonius' own ascent towards a post in the imperial government. The literary scene of imperial Rome had, by Suetonius' day, become quite dependent on the emperors themselves.

1   **Q. Horatius Flaccus** on Roman names see **Introduction, Addendum 2**

    Venusinus Horace came from Venusia, a town of Apulia in southern Italy, located on the Appian Way; it is a curious fact that virtually all of the famous writers of Latin literature did not come from the city of Rome itself

1–2 **patre . . . libertino et exactionum coactore** *patre* is abl. of source (see Bennett sec. 215), with *coactore* as an appositive; Horace's father had at one point been enslaved, and he functioned as a "collector" (*coactor*) in auctions, i.e., the agent who transferred funds between buyer and seller; it has been suggested that when Venusia rebelled against Rome during the Social War (91–88 BCE), Horace's father—perhaps a man of some wealth—was enslaved with his other townsmen as punishment, and then, though freed, had to work to repair his fortunes

2   **ut ipse tradit** in the sixth poem of Horace's first book of *Satires*

2-3   **ut uero creditum est** *uero* ("but on the other hand") puts this
      clause in sharp contrast with what came before (*ut ipse tradit*);
      according to this second view, Horace's father was believed to
      have had the lowlier occupation of seller of salt fish (*salsamen-
      tarius*), so uncouthly did he behave

3   **salsamentario** again, abl. of source

3-4   **cum . . . exprobrasset** causal clause with *cum*

5   **bello Philippensi** Horace himself writes (*Epist.* 2.2.41–52) that
      he was studying in Athens when he got swept into the terrible
      civil war that broke out after the assassination of Julius Caesar.
      Brutus came to the Greek city in 44 BCE and from among the
      Roman youths studying there recruited officers who fought
      with him against Caesar's heir, Gaius Octavius (the future em-
      peror Augustus) and Antony. The final showdown took place
      at two battles on the plains near the Macedonian city of Philip-
      pi, after which Cassius and Brutus committed suicide. In one
      of his *Odes* (2.7), Horace writes that he fled the battle.

6   **tribunus militum** Each legion had six military tribunes as of-
      ficers, normally men of high status, rather than the son of a
      freedman; but in civil war social hierarchies were relaxed, and
      Horace's father might not have been a typical freedman (see
      above note on *patre . . . libertino et exactionum coactore*, lines
      1–2). With this appointment, Horace almost certainly gained
      equestrian status.

6-7   **uictisque partibus uenia inpetrata** two abl. absolutes

7   **scriptum quaestorium** "office of treasury clerk" (note that
      here *scriptum* comes from *scriptus, -us*). This was no lowly
      position, but a senior civil service post, tenable for life, that
      could lead to financial enrichment; its occupants handled
      official documents (e.g., decrees of the Senate), but would
      have delegated most of the work to underlings. As Suetonius'
      wording here shows, it could be purchased; but how Hor-
      ace repaired his fortunes directly after Philippi remains a

mystery—perhaps some of his father's fortune was intact, or perhaps he received help from powerful friends, such as the aristocrat Valerius Messalla Corvinus.

8   **insinuatus** on this verb, see note above on *insinuatus* (*Oth.* 2–3, line 9). Maecenas was one of the future Augustus' earliest and most important supporters; never holding official office, he operated from behind the scenes, handling secret negotiations, managing affairs in Italy in Augustus' absence. Wealthy and a lover of fine living, Maecenas cultivated a group of poets, including Vergil as well as Horace, who dedicated works to him that also helped articulate the ideology of the new Augustan regime. According to Horace himself, he was introduced to Maecenas by Vergil (see *Satires* 1.6), and the relationship rested on respect for one another's integrity; but the reality—reflected neither by Suetonius' *insinuatus* nor Horace's account—must surely have been that Maecenas was first drawn to Horace by the latter's poetry.

9   **quantopere . . . dilexerit** indirect question

10   **illo epigrammate** *ille* = "the following"; the short poem recalls lines from Catullus 14.1–2

11   **uisceribus meis** abl. of comparison after *plus*; translate the pl. noun literally as "vital organs" or more loosely as "life"

13   **Ninnio** text and interpretation are uncertain here; *ninnius* could mean "rag doll" or it might be a proper name; but other emendations for the *nimium* of the manuscripts have been proposed

      uideas optative subjunctive

14   **multo magis** supply *testatur* (line 10); *multo* is abl. of degree of difference

      extremis iudiciis this phrase (literally "the last tokens of one's esteem") is regularly used in Latin to refer to a will; Suetonius goes on to quote a codicil (*elogium*) from Maecenas' will, telling his heir Augustus to show regard for Horace

      elogio abl. of means

15   **Horati Flacci . . . mei** gen. with an adj. signifying memory
        (see Bennett sec. 204.1)

        esto the fut. imperative is commonly used in laws, wills, trea-
        ties, etc. (Bennett sec. 281.1)

15–16   **epistolarum . . . officium** Suetonius' phrasing here may be
        somewhat anachronistic, reflecting the later post of *ab epistu-
        lis* in which he served under Hadrian. According to the letter
        that follows, Augustus was looking for help primarily with
        writing letters to friends (Augustus was from early in his life
        an avid correspondent). N.B.: *epistula* and *epistola* were both
        accepted spellings, even in the same period (like *gray* and *grey*
        in English)

16   **Hoc . . . scripto** the pple. is functioning substantively; parts
        of Augustus' vast correspondence were published after his
        death, but Suetonius also seems to have had access to previ-
        ously unpublished letters of the first emperor, from which he
        made ample quotation in his earlier imperial biographies (see,
        e.g., *Aug.* 71, *Tib.* 21, *Claud.* 4)

17   **scribendis epistolis** dat. use of the gerundive construction
        following *sufficiebam*

19   **ista parasitica mensa** joking language drawn from Roman
        comedy; Maecenas' table is that of a "sponger" (*parasitus*),
        Augustus' that of the wealthy patron (one meaning of *rex*)

21   **recusanti** from the next quotation, it emerges that Horace's
        excuse for declining was ill health

        suscensuit the subject is Augustus

        quicquam "at all"; the n. acc. of the pron. is used adverbially
        here (Bennett sec. 176.3)

22   **epistolae** "a letter"; the pl. can refer to a single letter

23   **aliquid iuris** "any privilege" (gen. of the whole)

24   **tamquam si conuictor mihi fueris** "as if you had been
        one who lived with me on intimate terms"; the conditional
        clause of comparison, expressing something hypothetical,
        takes a subjunctive, typically following normal rules for

the sequence of tense (Bennett sec. 307); hence *fueris* is pf. subjunctive

25   **feceris** fut. pf. indicative, emphasizing the completion of the action in future time

        id usus "that degree of familiarity"; this use of a gen. with *id* is not uncommon (e.g., *id furoris*, "that degree of madness"); the phrase is functioning as the acc. subject in indirect discourse introduced by *uolui*

25–26   **si ... possit** the pres. subjunctive here suggests that Augustus has still not ruled out the fulfillment of this condition: "if it should be possible through your health"

26–27   **Tui qualem habeam memoriam** indirect question; on the case of *tui*, compare the note on **Horati Flacci ... mei** above (line 14)

27   **habeam memoriam** *habere memoriam* = "to remember, be mindful," just as, e.g., *habere fidem* = "to trust"

28–29   **Neque enim** "nor in truth": the negative force in *neque* applies to the main verb ἀνθυφερηφανοῦμεν (translate the whole phrase: "nor, in truth, will we, if you haughtily spurned our friendship, for that reason return your disdain"). On the use of Greek in Roman conversation and thought, see **Introduction, Addendum 1**; the Greek verb is not otherwise attested, and could be a coinage of Augustus.

31–32   **purissimum penem et homuncionem lepidissimum** *penis*, originally meaning "tail" but a standard word for "penis" could also evidently be used affectionately; *homuncio* is a playful diminutive

32   **unaque et altera liberalitate** *unus et alter* = "one or two"

33   **mansura** supply *esse*

34   **Saeculare carmen** a hymn written by Horace for performance at a great festival held by Augustus in 17 BCE, the "Centennial Games" (*Ludi Saeculares*) that marked the beginning of a new era (*saeculum*); according to the official record of the event, a chorus of 27 boys and 27 girls sang Horace's hymn, the words of which are still extant

34–35   **componendum** certain verbs, including *iniungo* here, can take an acc. with a gerundive to denote purpose (Bennett sec. 337.8.b)

35   **iniunxerit** subjunctive in a result clause (anticipated by *usque adeo*, line 33); the pf. subjunctive, in secondary sequence, emphasizes the finality of the result (Bennett 268.6); *coegerit* (line 36) and *sit questus* (line 39) are also part of the result clause

   Vindelicam uictoriam Probably a gerundive has dropped out of the manuscripts here, and we should add a word such as *illustrandam* (supplying *componendam* does not yield particularly good sense). Augustus' stepsons Tiberius (the future emperor) and Tiberius' younger brother Drusus were sent in 15 BCE on a successful campaign against the Vindelici of northern Europe— part of Augustus' campaign to pacify the Alpine regions, and also an effort to bring glory to his family members.

37   **carminum** Horace's first three book of *Odes* (*Carmina*) were published as a collection in 23 BCE, while the fourth book may not have been released until 11 BCE

38   **post Sermones uero quosdam lectos** "but after a reading of some of the *Sermones*" (on the construction, see note above on *Vespasiano . . . adamato* [*Vesp.* 21–22, line 22]); the reference here is not to Horace's satires but rather the verse epistles that he wrote, addressed to a variety of individuals; the first book of them was completed in 20 BCE, and another "letter" to Florus was finished, before Horace wrote the letter to Augustus quoted from here (the full poem is still extant, preserved in the second book of the poet's *Epistles*)

39   **habitam** supply *esse*; the infinitive is part of indirect discourse, dependent on *sit questus*

   scito for the imperative of *scio*, the fut. *scito* is always used in the sing.

41   **infame tibi sit, quod uidearis** *sit* is subjunctive in a fear clause; *infame* is completed with a substantive clause with *quod* ("the fact that . . . "), which employs the subjunctive (*uidearis*) to indicate that this would be Horace's possible thought, rather than that of the writer Augustus

42   **Eclogam** an *ecloga* is a selection from a work or a short poem
        of any kind (the title *Eclogues* is famously given to Vergil's
        pastoral poems, which more properly should be called *Bucoli-
        ca*); the "selection" addressed to Augustus survives as the first
        poem in the second book of Horace's *Epistles*, and concerns
        the contemporary literary scene

46–47   **peccem . . . si . . . morer** a "should-would" condition (Bennett
        sec. 303)

49   **Satiris** especially at *Satires* 2.3.308–9, but note also *Epistulae*
        1.20.24 and 1.4.15; *Satiris* evidently can refer to both works

        hac epistola on the letters of Augustus, see above on *Hoc . . .
        scripto*, line 16

50   **Onysius** the name of the messenger may not be accurately
        preserved in the manuscripts

50–51   †**ut accusantem**† if this text were accepted, the meaning
        would be: "your small work, of which—like the one finding
        fault, however small it is—I approve"; *ut excusantem* has been
        proposed, and at least makes better sense

51   **boni consulo** "I think well of, am satisfied with"; the defining
        gen. is used predicatively, and is paralleled in other expres-
        sions, e.g., *lucri facere* = "to make a profit"

52   **libelli** Horace's publication would take the form of scrolls, a
        necessary point for understanding the humor that follows

54   **licebit** followed by a subjunctive (*scribas*): "And so you may
        write on a pint pot, so that the circumference of your volume
        may be very well-rounded out, like that of your own belly"
        (the idea is that Horace will produce a poem filling a short but
        very thick scroll)

55   **ὀγκωδέστατος** "very well-rounded out"

56   **intemperantior** supply *esse*; the sentence that follows was
        obelized (i.e., marked as spurious) by prior editors, including
        Roth, but for no reason other than modern prudery! I have
        modified the text accordingly. And note: Suetonius only re-
        ports hearsay (*dicitur*).

58   **plurimum** adverbial acc.

59   **ruris** "country estate"; Horace refers to both of the locales mentioned here by Suetonius in his poetry—Tibur (modern Tivoli) and the hilly Sabine country beyond

60   **Tiburni** the legendary founder of Tibur

      Venerunt Suetonius starts a discussion here of works falsely attributed to Horace; almost certainly, he would have begun with a listing of Horace's books (*Epodes*, *Satires*, *Odes*, and *Epistles*), but when Suetonius' life was attached to the copy of Horace's poems (see introductory note) this could easily be excised

      Elegi poems written in elegiac couplets, very often of an erotic nature

62   **falsa** fakes might be produced to fill in, or exploit, gaps in a well-known author's career; the *Culex* attributed to Vergil, dedicated to the very young Octavius (the future Augustus) is a good example

63   **quo uitio** the antecedent is incorporated into the rel. clause because it is appositive: "the letter also (was) obscure—a fault to which he was in no way prone"

64–65 **VI. Idus Decembris L. Cotta et L. Torquato consulibus** 8 December 65 BCE (see **Introduction, Addendum 2**)

65–66 **V Kl. Decembris C. Marcio Censorino et C. Asinio Gallo consulibus** 27 November 8 BCE

66–67 **post nonum et quinquagesimum annum** The text as printed here gives Horace 59 years of life, when in fact he only had 57 (see previous two notes). Scholars have proposed adding after *quinquagesimum* and before *annum* the following line: *diem quam Maecenas obierat, aetatis agens septimum et quinquagesimum*; the assumption is that this line fell out, owing to similarity of the two numbers involved.

67   **palam** Normally a will was written on waxed wooden tablets (*tabulae*) that were closed shut, and sealed (in the presence of witnesses), notionally to prevent tampering; but if

the testator was incapable of signing a will, he might declare an heir openly—again, in the presence of witnesses. Horace made Augustus his heir, just as Maecenas did (see above lines 14–15).

69 **conditus est** "he was laid to rest." In Horace's day, the corpse of the deceased typically was cremated on a pyre, the remains were gathered, placed in a receptacle of some sort, and then interred in a final resting place. Failure to conduct a proper interment was thought to result in eternal unrest for the deceased's soul. *humatus* is not a word typically used by Suetonius (or other classical writers) to refer to the normal funerary practice, and it is likely that it was added later as an explanation of the word *conditus*; *humatus et* therefore is probably best deleted.

extremis Esquiliis "at the edge of the Esquiline," one of Rome's hills, where Maecenas built a splendid house and grounds; in death Horace would be close to his friend and patron, as in life

Vocabulary

ā *or* **ab**, *prep.* + *abl.*, from, away
from; by; since, on, in

abdūcō, -ere, -duxī, -ductus,
to lead away, take away; to
withdraw; to seduce

abeō, -īre, -iī, -itus, to go away,
depart; to disappear

abiciō, -ere, -iēcī, -iectus, to
throw away, throw down; to
slight

absens, -entis, *adj.*, absent;
missing

absoluō, -ere, -uī, -ūtus,
to release; to acquit; to
complete, finish

absolūtōrius, -a, -um, *adj.*,
granting acquittal

abstinentia, -ae, *f.*, restraint;
integrity

abstineō, -ēre, -tinuī, -tentus,
to withhold, keep away; to
refrain from

abūtor, -ūtī, -ūsus sum, to use
up; to misuse, abuse

ac *or* **atque,** *conj.*, and, and also,
and what is more, and in
fact; as; than

accēdō, -ere, -cessī, -cessum, to
come up to, approach

accidō, -ere, -cidī, to happen,
occur, come to pass

accipiō, -ere, -cēpī, -ceptus,
to take, receive, accept; to
incur; to entertain

accubō (1), to lie, recline (at
table or in bed); to lie near

accurrō, -ere, -currī *or*
-cucurrī, -cursum, to run
up

accūsātor, -ōris, *m.*, accuser;
prosecutor; informer

accūsō (1), to reproach, blame;
to charge with a crime

ācer, -cris, -cre, *adj.*, sharp,
pointed; energetic; fierce;
biting; drastic

acerbus, -a, -um, *adj.*, bitter,
harsh, sour; cruel, hostile;
rough; strict

acerra, -ae, *f.*, box for incense

Achāia, -ae, *f.*, Achaia, a
district in northern part of
Peloponnese in Greece or all
of Peloponnese

Achāicus, -a, -um, *adj.*, of or
concerned with Achaia

aciēs, -ēī, *f.*, sharpness, sharp
edge; keenness of vision;
eyesight; battle line, battle

actitō (1), to do repeatedly,
act often; to plead a case
frequently

actus, -ūs, *m.*, act, transaction; performance; business

ad, *prep.* + *acc.*, to, toward, at, near; for the purpose of; according to

adamō (1), to love deeply; to fall in love with, conceive a sexual passion for

addictus, -a, -um, *adj.*, addicted to; a slave of

addō, -ere, -didī, -ditus, to add; to insert; to increase; to impart

adeō, *adv.*, to such a degree, so

adeō, -īre, -iī *or* **-īuī, -itus,** to approach; to attack; to visit; to go to for help; to undertake

adficiō, -ere, -fēcī, -fectus, to treat, handle; to influence; to visit with (death etc.)

adgredior, -ī, -gressus sum, to approach; to attack; to undertake, set about (a task)

adhibeō, -ēre, -uī, -itus, to stretch out; to introduce, bring in; to apply; to administer

adhōc *or* **adhūc,** *adv.*, thus far; till now; already; besides, moreover; still further

adhortor, -ārī, -ātus sum, to encourage, cheer on; to urge

adiciō, -ere, -iēcī, -iectus, to add, increase; to throw at or towards; to attach

adipiscor, -ī, -eptus sum, to get, obtain; to arrive at; to inherit; to win

aditus, -ūs, *m.*, access; doorway, entrance; arrival; admittance; attack

adiuuō, -āre, -iūuī, -iūtus, to help; to encourage, promote

administrō (1), to administer, direct, manage; to rule; to conduct

admīrātiō, -ōnis, *f.*, admiration; wonder; surprise

admittō, -ere, -mīsī, -mīssus, to admit, receive (visitors); to permit

admodum, *adv.*, to the limit; very; quite

admoneō, -ēre, -uī, -itus, to admonish, suggest; to warn; to raise the question

admoueō, -ēre, -mōuī, -mōtus, to move up, bring near; to apply to

adornō (1), to adorn; to equip, get ready

adpetō, -ere, -īuī *or* **-iī, -ītus,** to try to reach; to lay hold of; to make for; to attack

adprehendō, -ere, -endī, -sus, to grasp, seize, take hold of

adsum, -esse, -fuī, to be present; to appear; to exist; to give support

aduentīcius, -a, -um, *adj.*, foreign; imported; extraneous; **cēna aduentīca,** reception

aduersum, -ī, *n.*, difficulty, trouble, adversity

aduersus, *prep* + *acc.*, facing; against; compared with

adulescentia, -ae, *f.,* youth; young people

adulescentulus, -ī, *m.,* boy

aegrē, *adv.,* painfully; with difficulty; reluctantly; hardly

aemulātiō, -ōnis, *f.,* emulation, imitation, rivalry

aēnus, -a, -um, *adj.,* of bronze; of copper

aequus, -a, -um, *adj.,* level, even; fair-minded; calm

aesculus, -ī, *f.,* variety of oak tree

aestimō (1), to appraise, rate, value; to esteem highly

aetās, -ātis, *f.,* lifetime, age; period of life

affectus, -ūs, *m.,* disposition, mood; feeling; affection

affirmō (1), to strengthen; to encourage; to assert

afflīgō, -ere, -flixī, -flictus, to knock down; to injure, damage

agitātor, -ōris, *m.,* driver, charioteer

agmen, -inis, *n.,* mass; crowd; body (of armed men); army, column; escort

agō, -ere, ēgī, actus, to drive, lead; to administer; to conduct; to speak about; to institute legal proceedings

agōn, -ōnos, *m.,* contest

albātus, -a, -um, *adj.,* dressed in white

album, -ī, *n.,* record; list; register; white tablet

Alexandrīa, -ae, *f.,* Alexandria, a city in Egypt

Alexandrīnus, -a, -um, *adj.,* Alexandrine; of Alexandria

aliās, *adv.,* at another time, at other times; subsequently; in other circumstances

aliēnus, -a, -um, *adj.,* another's; unconnected, separate; belonging to a stranger

aliquamdiū, *adv.,* for some time; for a considerable distance

aliquantum, -ī, *n.,* a little, some, something

aliquī -qua, -quod, *adj.,* some

aliquis, -qua, -quid, *pron.,* someone, somebody, anyone; some, something

aliquot, *adj.,* some, several

alius, -a, -ud, *adj.,* another, other, different

altāria, -ium, *n. pl.,* altar; altars; burnt offerings

alter, -era, -erum, *adj.,* one (of two); the other; the second

altercātiō, -ōnis, *f.,* altercation, dispute, argument

altitūdō, -inis, *f.,* height; depth; profundity

altus, -a, -um, *adj.,* high, tall; deep, profound; loud; thick; high-born

ambigō, -ere, to dispute, contend; to be uncertain; to argue about

ambō, -ae, -ō, *pl. adj.,* both, two

amīca, -ae, *f.,* girlfriend; mistress

amiciō, -īre, -icuī *or* **-ixī, -ictus,** to wrap around; to cover, cloth, wrap

amīcitia, -ae, *f.,* friendship; ties of friendship; alliance

amīcus, -a, -um, *adj.,* friendly; supportive

amīcus, -ī, *m.,* loved one, friend; patron, protector

amoenus, -a, -um, *adj.,* charming, pleasant

amphitheātrum, -ī, *n.,* amphitheater

amphora, -ae, *f.* amphora (large earthenware jar for holding wine, oil, etc.)

amplius, *n. and adv.,* any further, any more; more, longer

amplus, -a, -um, *adj.,* ample, large, wide; strong; eminent; illustrious

an, *particle,* can it be that...?; or, or whether; whether, if

ancora, -ae, *f.,* anchor

angustus, -a, -um, *adj.,* narrow; close, short; brief

animaduertō, -ere, -tī, -sus, to pay attention to, notice; to observe; to criticize

animal, -ālis, *n.,* animal; living creature

animus, -ī, *m.,* intellect; mind; state of mind; thought, reason; sense; heart, feelings; spirit, courage; will, purpose, desire

annus, -ī, *m.,* year, season; age, time of life; year of office; year's produce

ante, *prep. + acc.,* before, in front of; (*adv.*) before

antepōnō, -ere, -posuī, -positus, to place or station in front; to prefer; to esteem more highly

antīquus, -a, -um, *adj.,* ancient, former, of old times

antrum, -ī, *n.,* cave, cavern, grotto

ānulus, -ī, *m.,* ring

anus, -ūs, *f.,* old woman; hag; (*adj.*) old

anxius, -a, -um, *adj.,* worried, uneasy; meticulous

apophorēta, -ōrum, *n. pl.,* presents for guests to take away

apparātus, -ūs, *m.,* equipment, apparatus; stock; pomp, display, magnificence

appellātiō, -ōnis, *f.,* name, title; naming; addressing; appeal

appellō (1), to speak to, address, accost; to beseech; to name, call

Appius, -a, -um, *adj.,* Appius, a Roman *nomen*; Appian; **uia Appia,** road between Rome and Capua built by Appius Claudius Caecus

appōnō, -ere, -posuī, -positus, to serve, to put or lay near, at; to appoint

apud, *prep. + acc.,* at, by, near; at the house of; before; in the possession of

arbor, -oris, *f.,* tree; mast, oar; gallows

arcānus, -a, -um, *adj.,* secret, concealed; private; trustworthy

arcessō, -ere, -īuī *or* **-iī, -ītus,** to send for, summon

argūmentum, -ī, *n.,* evidence, proof; theme; topic; motif

arguō, -ere, -uī, -ūtus, to prove; to reveal, betray; to accuse, charge

arma, -ōrum, *n. pl.,* arms; armor; war; camp life; troops; equipment, tools

armātūra, -ae, *f.,* arms, armament

Armenia, -ae, *f.,* Armenia, a country of Asia north of Persia

arripiō, -ere, -ripuī, -reptus, to snatch, get a hold of; to obtain

artifex, -icis, *m.,* craftsman, artist, master; performer; musician

ascrībō, -ere, -psī, -ptus, to add in writing, insert; to enroll; to assign

aspectus, -ūs, *m.,* look, sight, glance; appearance

asper, -era, -erum, *adj.,* rough, uneven; wild; cruel

assideō, -ēre, -sēdī, -sessus, to sit near

assiduē, *adv.,* assiduously, continually

assiduus, -a, -um, *adj.,* constantly present, persistent, tireless; busy

assuescō, -ere, -ēuī, -ētus, to accustom to, make familiar with; to become used to

astō, -āre, -itī, to stand erect, stand up; to stand nearby

Atalanta, -ae, *f.,* Atalanta

atque. *See* **ac**

ātrium, -ī, *n.,* atrium, first main room in a Roman house; hall

atterō, -ere, -trīuī, -trītus, to rub against, wear away; to reduce, diminish; to weaken

attingō, -ere, -tigī, -tactus, to come into contact with; to touch (on); to strike

attribuō, -ere, -uī, -ūtus, to allot, assign; to appoint; to put under the command of

auctor, -ōris, *m.,* originator, founder; source; authority

audeō, -ēre, ausus sum, to dare, risk; to be bold

audiō, -īre, -īuī *or* **-iī, -ītus,** to hear, listen to; to learn from; to obey; to be called

audītōrium, -ī, *n.,* lecture hall; audience

āuersus, -a, -um, *adj.,* turned back, in the rear, reversed; remote; alienated; hostile

āuertō, -ere, -uertī, uersus, to turn away, avert; to misappropriate; to distract

augeō, -ēre, -xī, -ctus, to increase, augment; to magnify; to emphasize; to reinforce

Augustus, -ī, *m.*, Augustus, name of Rome's first emperor and a title for later emperors

auia, -ae, *f.*, grandmother

auiditās, -ātis, *f.*, eagerness, longing; avarice

auis, -is, *f.*, bird, sign, omen

aulicus, -a, -um, *adj.*, of or belonging to the imperial household; (*m.*), courtier

aureus, -a, -um, *adj.*, of gold, golden

aut, *conj.*, or, or rather; or at least; **aut . . . aut,** either . . . or

autem, *particle*, but; on the other hand; however; now; moreover, also

auus, -ī, *m.*, grandfather

Bāiae, -ārum, *f. pl.*, Baiae, a resort town at north end of the Bay of Naples

Bāiānus, -a, -um, *adj.*, of or belonging to Baiae

Balbus, -ī, *m.*, Balbus, a *cognomen*

balineum, -ī, *n.*, bath

ballista, -ae, *f.*, artillery piece

barbarus, -a, -um, *adj.*, foreign; barbarous

barbarus, -ī, *m.*, foreigner; barbarian

bellum, -ī, *n.*, war; warfare

bīduum, -ī, *n.*, two-day period; two days

biiugis, -is, -e, *adj.*, two-horse

blandior, -īrī, -ītus, to flatter; to coax; to allure, charm

bōlētus, -ī, *m.*, mushroom

bombus, -ī, *m.*, booming; buzzing; humming

bonum, -ī, *n.*, good thing, good; (*pl.*) property, estate

bonus, -a, -um, *adj.*, good; sound, valid; pretty

brāchium, -ī, *n.* arm, lower arm; branch

breuiārium, -ī, *n.*, abridgement, summary statement

breuis, -is, -e, *adj.*, short, little; shallow; brief; compressed; narrow

breuiter, *adv.*, briefly; quickly; only a short distance

Britannia, -ae, *f.*, Britannia, Britain

Brūtus, -ī, *m.*, Brutus, a *cognomen*; especially of Marcus Brutus, an assassin of Caesar

cachinnus, -ī, *m.*, loud laugh; rippling

cadāuer, -eris, *n.*, dead body, corpse

cadō, -ere, cecidī, cāsum, to fall, sink; to die; to happen, occur; to decline, decay

caedēs, -is, *f.*, killing, slaughter, assassination

caedō, -ere, cecīdī, caesus, to strike, beat; to cut off; to kill

caelestis, -is, -e, *adj.*, heavenly, celestial; supernatural, divine

Caenis, -idis, *f.*, Caenis, the concubine of Vespasian

Caesar, -aris, *m.*, Caesar, a *cognomen* in the Julian *gens* and inherited by all emperors; an emperor

caetra, -ae, *f.*, small light shield

calciō (1), to put shoes on

Calpurnius, -a, -um, *adj,* Calpurnius, a Roman *nomen*; Calpurnian; (*f.*) Calpurnia, wife of Julius Caesar

caluitium, -iī, *n.*, baldness

Campānia, -ae, *f.*, Campania, a region of Italy south of Latium

Canacē, -ēs, *f.*, Canace, the daughter of Aeolus

candidātus, -ī, *m.*, candidate

canō, -ere, cecinī, cantus, to sing, sing of; to prophesy, predict; to sound

cantō (1), to sing; to sing of; to celebrate; to predict; to warble

capillus, -ī, *m.*, hair

capiō, -ere, cēpī, captus, to take hold of, grasp; to captivate, seduce; to defeat

Capitōlīnus, -a, -um, *adj.*, of or connected with the Capitol

Capitōlium, -ī, *n.*, the Capitoline Hill (in Rome); citadel (of any city)

Capreae, -ārum, *f. pl.* Capreae, an island of coast of Campania (now Capri)

captō (1), to try to catch; to chase after; to strive after; to watch for

Capua, -ae, *f.*, Capua, the chief city of Campania

caput, -itis, *n.*, head, top, summit; principal point; leader

Capys, -yis, *m.*, Capys, the companion of Aeneas and founder of Capua

Carchēdoniacos, -ē, -on, *adj.*, Carthaginian

carmen, -inis, *n.*, song, tune, hymn; poem; lyric poetry; incantation; oracular utterance

carnificīna, -ae, *f.*, work of an executioner; execution; torture

cārus, -a, -um, *adj.*, dear, expensive; loving

Casca, -ae, *m.*, Casca, a *cognomen*

Cassius, -a, -um, *adj.*, Cassius, a *nomen*; especially of Cassius, an assassin of Caesar

castra, -ōrum, *n. pl.*, camp, military; service, army life

castrensis, -is, -e, *adj.*, military; characteristic of soldiers

catēna, -ae, *f.*, chain; curb, restraint; (*pl.*), chains, fetters

caueō, -ēre, cāuī, cautus, to beware of, guard against

causa, -ae, *f.*, cause, grounds, reason; business, concern; legal case

causor, -ārī, -ātus sum, to plead, plead as an excuse

cēdō, -ere, cessī, cessus, to grant, concede, yield; to go, move; to depart

celebrō (1), to frequent, crowd; to fill; to celebrate; to honor; to attend

cēna, -ae, *f.,* dinner, dish, course

cēnāculum, -ī, *n.,* garret, attic; upstairs apartment

cēnō (1), to dine on, eat; to dine

centēnī, -ae, -a, *adj.,* one hundred each

centuriō, -ōnis, *f.,* centurion

cerebellum, -ī, *n.,* brain

certāmen, -inis, *n.,* contest; rivalry, discussion; debate

certē, *adv.,* surely, certainly; at least

cessō (1), to cease; to let up; to become remiss; to fail; to hesitate to

cēterum, *adv.,* but, still; otherwise; however that may be; moreover

cēterus, -a, -um, *adj.,* the other, the remaining, the rest

ceu, *particle,* as, just as; as if, just as if

charta, -ae, *f.,* sheet of papyrus, paper; thin sheet of metal

chlamys, -ydis, *f.,* Greek military cape

cibus, -ī, *m.,* food, feed; meal

Cicerō, -ōnis, *m.,* Cicero, a *cognomen* in the Tullian *gens*; especially of the orator Cicero

Cimber, -brī, *m.,* Cimber, a *cognomen*

circā, *prep.+ acc.,* around, surrounding; near; through; (*adv.*) around; round about; in the vicinity

circensēs, -ium, *m. pl.,* games held in the Circus

circuitus, -ūs, *m.,* circuit; going around; detour

circumsecō, -āre, -uī, -tus, to circumcise

circumstō, -āre, -stetī, to surround; to stand around

circus, -ī, *m.,* circus; circus games

cithara, -ae, *f.,* lyre

citharoedus, -ī, *m.,* citharoedist, singer who accompanies himself on the lyre

citrō, *adv.,* to this side; **ultrō (et) citrō,** to and fro

cīuīlis, -is, -e, *adj.,* civil; civic; civilian

cīuitās, -tātis, *f.,* state, community; city; citizenship

clādēs, -is, *f.,* destruction, harm, loss, calamity

clam, *adv.,* secretly; privately; stealthily

clāmō (1), to shout, yell; to proclaim

clārus, -a, -um, *adj.,* loud; clear; bright; famous

classiārius, -a, -um, *adj.,* naval; (*m. pl.*) marines

Claudius, -a, -um, *adj.,* Claudius, a Roman *nomen*; especially of the emperor Claudius

clipeum, -ī, *n.*, round bronze shield; disc

clystēr, -ēris, *m.*, syringe; injection; enema

coactor, -ōris, *m.*, collector (of money, taxes, etc.)

cōdicillī, -ōrum, *m. pl.*, set of writing tablets; petition to the emperor; letter from the emperor; supplement to a will

coepī, -isse, -tus, to begin

cognōmen, -inis, *n.*, surname, family name; nickname

cognōscō, -ere, -nōuī, -nitus, to become acquainted with; to recognize; to inquire into, investigate, hear or try

cōgō, -ere, coēgī, coactus, to gather together, collect; to force, compel

cohors, -tis, *f.*, retinue, escort; cohort; **cohors praetōria,** body guard of general or emperor

coitus, -ūs, *m.*, meeting; junction, meeting place; sexual intercourse

collocō (1), to place; to put in order; to give in marriage; to occupy; to spend

colō, -ere, coluī, cultus, to cultivate; to inhabit; to care for; to honor; to observe; to live, experience; to adorn; to court the favor of

colōnia, -ae, *f.*, colony, colonial town, settlement

colōnus, -ī, *m.*, settler, colonist; husbandman, farmer

coma, -ae, *f.*, hair; mane; fleece; foliage

comes, -itis, *m./f.*, companion; fellow traveler; partner; staff member

cōmis(s)ātiō, -ōnis, *f.*, drinking party, revelry

cōmis, -is, -e, *adj.*, kind; polite; friendly

cōmitās, -ātis, *f.*, politeness; courtesy

comitor, -ārī, -ātus sum, to accompany; to escort; to share; to attend

commeātus, -ūs, *m.*, passage; traffic; convoy

commendō (1), to entrust; to commit, to commend

commentīcius, -a, -um, *adj.*, imaginary, fictitious

commeō (1), to come and go; to go back and forth; to travel repeatedly

commercium, -ī, *n.*, trade, commerce; communication; exchange; goods

comminiscor, -ī, -mentus sum, to think up, contrive; to fabricate; to state falsely

commisceō, -ēre, -scuī, -xtus, to mix together; to confuse; to unite, bring together

committō, -ere, -mīsī, -missus, to bring together; to begin, commence; to undertake; to bring about; to take before someone else for a verdict or decision

commodum, -ī, *n.*, convenience, profit; opportunity; advantage

commūnis, -is, -e, *adj.*, common, joint; ordinary; universal; familiar

comparō (1), to prepare; to purchase; to plan; to put together; to get, collect

comperiō, -īre, -ī, -tus, to find out, discover, learn

complūrēs, -ēs, -a, *adj.*, several, a fair number of

compōnō, -ere, -posuī, -positus, to put together, join; to store up; to settle; to write

concha, ae, *f.*, mollusk, shellfish; sea-shell, pearl, conch

concubīna, -ae, *f.*, concubine

concubitus, -ūs, *m.*, reclining together; sexual intercourse

concupiscō, -ere, -īuī *or* **-iī, -ītus,** to long for, desire; to strive for

concutiō, -ere, -ssī, -ssus, to bang together; to convulse; to shake; to stir up

condiciō, -ōnis, *f.*, contract, arrangement; stipulation, terms, condition

condīcō, -ere, -xī, -ctus, to talk over, arrange together; to engage oneself for

condiscō, -ere, -didicī, to learn thoroughly

conditor, -ōris, *m.* maker, builder, establisher, founder

condō, -ere, -didī, -ditus, to build, found; to write; to store up, preserve; to lay to rest

condormiō, -īre, -īuī *or* **-iī,** to sleep soundly

cōnectō, -ere, -xuī, -xus, to tie, connect; to join, link

conferō, -ferre, -tulī, -lātus, to bring together; to ascribe; to offer; **sē conferō,** to go

confessus, -a, -um, *adj.*, acknowledged; admitted, confessed

confestim, *adv.*, immediately, suddenly

conficiō, -ere, -fēcī, -fectus, to make, do, perform, carry out, complete

confīdō, -ere, -sus sum, to have confidence in, be confident

confiscō (1), to confiscate, seize

confiteor, -ērī, -fessus sum, to confess, acknowledge, admit; to reveal

conflagrātiō, -ōnis, *f.*, conflagration; eruption

confluō, -ere, -xī, to flow together; to flock together, come in crowds

confodiō, -ere, -fōdī, -fossus, to dig up; to stab; to harm

congruentia, -ae, *f.*, consistency; similarity

coniungō, -ere, -xī, -ctus, to join together; to unite

conlābor, -ī, -psus sum, to fall down, collapse

conlaudō (1), to praise highly

conlocō. *See* **collocō**

cōnōr, -ārī, -ātus sum, to try

conquiescō, -ere, -ēuī, to rest, take a rest; to go to sleep

conquīsītus, -a, -um, *adj.*,
  select, choice

consanguineus, -a, -um, *adj.*,
  of the same blood, kindred,
  fraternal

conscrībō, -ere, -ipsī, -iptus, to
  compose, write, draw up; to
  enlist

conscriptus, -ī, *m.*, senator;
  patrēs conscriptī, Senators

consecrō (1), to consecrate; to
  dedicate to the gods below;
  to deify

conseruō (1), to keep safe,
  preserve, maintain

consilium, -ī, *n.*, consultation;
  advice; plan; stratagem;
  decision; council (of
  advisors)

consōlor, -ārī, -ātus sum, to
  console, comfort

conspīrō (1), to act in harmony;
  to conspire

constituō, -ere, -uī, -ūtus, to
  set up; to settle, to arrange;
  to appoint; to decide, decree

constō, -āre, -itī, to stand
  together; to exist; to be
  manifest, evident, apparent;
  to cost

constuprō, (1), to rape

consuētūdō, -inis, *f.*, custom,
  habit; usage; idiom;
  intimacy, sexual intercourse

consul, -sulis, *m.*, consul

consulāris, -is, -e, of or proper
  to a consul; having been
  consul, of consular rank

consulātus, -ūs, *m.*, consulship

consulō, -ere, -uī, -tus, to
  consult; to consider; to
  advise; to offer as advice;
  bonī consulere, to think
  well of

consūmō, -ere, -psī, -ptus, to
  consume, use up; to devour;
  to waste

contabulō (1), to cover with
  boards; to construct with
  multiple stories; to bridge,
  span

contentus, -a, -um, *adj.*,
  content; satisfied

continens, -entis, *adj.*,
  continuous, unbroken; close;
  next; *f.* interior, mainland

contineō, -ēre, uī, -tentus,
  to keep within bounds,
  confine, control, repress

contingō, -ere, -igī, -actum, to
  touch; to be connected (by
  relationship); to arrive at

continuus, -a, -um, *adj.*,
  continuous, unbroken,
  successive

contrā, *prep + acc.*, opposite,
  toward; against; in defiance
  of; (*adv.*) in opposition; in
  turn; on the other hand

contrahō, -ere, -traxī, -tractus,
  to draw together; to
  contract; to shorten; to cause

contumēlia, -ae, *f.*, mistreatment;
  outrage; insult, affront

contus, -ī, *m.*, pole

conuictor, -ōris, *m.*, bosom pal

conuīuium, -ī, *n.*, banquet,
  dinner party; party

cōpia, -ae, *f.,* abundance; supply; opportunity, means; command of language

cōram, *prep.*+ *abl.,* before, in the presence of; (*adv.*) in person; publicly

Corinthus, -ī, *f.,* Corinth, a city in Greece

Cornēlius, -a, -um, *adj.,* Cornelius, a *nomen*; Cornelian; **lex Cornēlia,** Cornelian law, a law of Sulla

corōna, -ae, *f.,* crown, garland; circle of bystanders; ring of defense

corpus, -oris, *n.,* body; matter, substance

corpusculum, -ī, *n.,* puny body; (playfully) plumpness; small object

correctiō, -ōnis, *f.,* correction, improvement

corripiō, -ere, -ripuī, -reptus, to take hold of, seize; to enrapture; to rush; to reproach

corrumpō, -ere, -rūpī, -ruptum, to spoil, ruin; to seduce, allure

crēdō, -ere, -idī, -itus, to lend, loan; to entrust; to believe; to think, suppose; to put faith in

crīmen, -inis, *n.,* indictment; reproach; guilt; crime

cruciātus, -ūs, *m.,* torture; mental torment; instrument of torture

crūs, crūris, *n.,* leg, shin

cubiculum, -ī, *n.,* bedroom, room

cubō (1), to lie, lie down

culleus, -ī, *m.,* leather bag; leather sack

cultus, -ūs, *m.,* tilling; care; culture; style of dress; fancy clothes

cum, *conj.,* when; although; after; since; **cum . . . tum . . . :** not only . . . but also . . . ; (*prep. + abl.*) with

cunctor, -ārī, -ātus sum, to delay, hesitate, linger; to be in doubt

cunctus, -a, -um, *adj.,* all, entire; all together, the whole

cupiō, -ere, -īuī *or* **-iī, -ītus,** to wish, be eager for, long for, desire

cūr, *interr. and adv.,* why

cūra, -ae, *f.,* care, concern, worry; administration

cūrātor, -ōris, *m.,* superintendent, manager; guardian

cūria, -ae, *f.,* meeting place of the Roman Senate

curriculum, -ī, *n.,* race; lap; racetrack; racing chariot; career

cursus, -ūs, *m.,* running, speeding, speed; trip; direction; course

custōdia, -ae, *f.,* protection; safekeeping; defense; custody

custōs, -ōdis, *m.,* guard, guardian, watchman

Dācus, -a, -um, Dacian; *m. pl.,* the Dacians

damnātōrius, -a, -um, *adj.,* that involves or indicates condemnation

damnō (1), to find guilty, convict; sentence, condemn; to pass judgment on

Dārēus *or* **Dārīus, -ī,** *m.,* Darius, a name of Persian and Parthian kings and princes

dē, *prep.* + *abl.,* down from, from; of, out of; about, concerning; after

dea, -ae, *f.* goddess

dēbeō, -ēre, -uī, -itus, to owe; to be responsible for; to have to

dēcēdō, -ere, -cessī, -cessum, to withdraw, depart, clear out; to retreat; to die, cease

December, -bris, -bre, *adj.,* of December, December; *m.,* December

decens, -entis, *adj.,* decent, proper; becoming, handsome

dēcīdō, -ere, -cīdī, -cīsus, to cut off, cut away; to settle, decide

deciē(n)s, *adv.,* ten times; many times, often

decimus, -a, -um, *adj.,* the tenth

Decimus, -ī, *m.,* Decimus, a *praenomen*

decor, -ōris, *m.,* beauty, grace, elegance

dēcrepitus, -a, -um, *adj.,* decrepit, worn out

decuria, -ae, *f.,* group of ten; jury panel; social club

dēdecus, -oris, *n.,* disgrace, dishonor, shame; crime, outrage

dēdicātiō, -ōnis, *f.,* dedication; consecration

dēdicō (1), to dedicate, consecrate

dēditus, -a, -um, *adj.,* given to, devoted to; addicted to

dēdūcō, -ere, -xī, -ctus, to lead away, draw out; to lead forth, conduct; to settle

dēfectiō, -ōnis, *f.,* failure; defection; desertion; weakening

dēfensiō, -ōnis, *f.,* defense

dēferō, -ferre, -tulī, -latus, to bring or carry down; to offer, grant; to announce; to report, denounce; to recommend

dēficiō, -ere, -fēcī, -fectus, to fail, disappoint; to desert; to die out

dēformis, -is, -e, *adj.,* shapeless; disfigured; ugly

dēfringō, -ere, -frēgī, -fractus, to break off, break to pieces

dēfunctus, -a, -um, *adj.,* dead; finished

dēfungor, -ī, dēfunctus sum, to perform, carry out; to finish; to get rid of

dein *or* **deinde,** *adv.,* from that place; thereafter, then; secondly

dēlectō (1), to delight; to amuse, charm

dēlēgō (1), to assign, appoint; to ascribe; to transfer

dēligō (1), to tie up, fasten; to bandage

dēmandō (1), to hand over, entrust

dēminuō, -ere, -uī, -ūtus, to make smaller, lessen, diminish

dēmittō, -ere, -mīsī, -missus, to drop, let drop; to lower; to let down

dēmō, -ere, -psī, -ptus, to take away, remove; to withdraw; to remove from

dēmum, *adv.,* at last, finally; not till then; precisely; in fact

dēnārius, -iī, *m.,* denarius, Roman silver coin

dēnique, *adv.,* finally, at last; in short; just; of course

dēnuntiō (1), to intimate; to announce officially; to warn, threaten

dēpellō, -ere, -pulī, -pulsus, to drive off, drive away; to wean from

dēpendeō, -ēre, -ī, to hang down

dēpereō, -īre, -iī, to be hopelessly in love with; to go to ruin, perish

dēpōnō, -ere, -posuī, -positus, to put down, put aside

dēportō (1), to carry down, carry away; to bring home; to transport

dērigō, -ere, dērexī, dērectus, to direct; to put in order; to level; to construct

dēscrībō, -ere, -psī, -ptus, to write out, transcribe, copy; to describe, design, sketch

dēserō, -ere, -uī, -tus, to desert, abandon, forsake; to forfeit

dēsinō, -ere, -sīuī *or* **-siī, -situs,** to give up, abandon, finish with, stop

destituō, -ere, uī, -ūtus, to set down; to abandon, desert

dēsum, -esse, -fuī, -futūrus, to fall short, fail; to be absent; to be missing

dētegō, -ere, -exī, -ectus, to uncover, expose, lay bare; to reveal

dētrahō, -ere, -traxī, -tractus, to drag down, drag away, pull down; to remove

dēuius, -a, -um, *adj.,* out of the way; off the beaten track, remote

deus, -ī, *m.,* god, deity

dextra, -ae, *f.,* right hand

dialogus, -ī, *m.,* discussion; literary composition in the form of a dialogue

dicācitās, -ātis, *f.,* biting wit

dīcō, -ere, dixī, dictus, to say, speak, utter, tell, declare, assert

dictātor, -ōris, *m.,* dictator

dictitō (1), to keep saying, to state emphatically

dictum, -ī, *n.,* saying, word, statement; maxim; order; promise dīdūcō, -ere, -xī, -ctus, to draw apart, open; to part, sever; to separate

diēs, -ēī, *m. (or f.)*, day, time; period, space of time; light of day

differrō, differre, distulī, dīlātus, to scatter; to postpone, put off

difficulter, *adv.*, with difficulty; barely

diffugiō, -ere, -fūgī, to disperse, disappear

digitus, -ī, *m.*, finger; inch; toe

dignitās, -ātis, *f.*, worth; worthiness; dignity; authority; reputation; self-respect

dīligentia, -ae, *f.*, care, diligence; economy, frugality

dīligō, -ere, -lexī, -lectus, to esteem; to like, to value; to appreciate; to love

dīmittō, -ere, -mīsī, -missus, to send away, let go, release, set free

dīs, dītis, *adj.*, rich; fertile; generous; expensive

discerpō, -ere, -sī, -tus, to mangle, mutilate

disciplīna, -ae, *f.*, instruction, training; learning; science; subject

discrīmen, -inis, *n.*, dividing line; interval; separation; critical moment; danger; risk

discumbō, -ere, discubuī, discubitum, to recline at table; to go to bed

discurrō, -ere, -cucurrī, -cursum, to run in different directions, scamper about

disiciō, -ere, -iēcī, -iectus, to scatter, disperse; to break up

dispensātor, -ōris, *m.*, household manager; steward; treasurer, cashier

dispertiō, -īre, -īuī *or* -iī, -ītus, to distribute, divide

dispōnō, -ere, -posuī, -positus, to place here and there; to arrange; to administer

disserō, -ere, -uī, -tus, to discuss; to talk; to examine

dissimulō (1), to conceal, disguise; to keep secret

distendō, -ere, -dī, -tus, to stretch apart, stretch out; to cause to swell; to distend

distichon, -ī, *n.*, couplet

distinctus, -a, -um, *adj.*, distinct, separate; studded; adorned; diversified; eminent

diū, *adv.*, for a long time; still further

dīuidō, -ere, -uīsī, -uīsus, to divide, separate; to distribute, share; to arrange

dīuīnus, -a, -um, *adj.*, divine, heavenly; godlike; gorgeous, excellent

diurnus, -a, -um, *adj.*, of the day; daily

diuturnus, -a, -um, *adv.*, long, long-lasting; chronic

dīuulgō (1), to divulge, spread among the people; to publish; to publicize

dō, dare, dedī, datus, to give, offer; to dedicate; to permit; to ascribe

domesticī, -ōrum, *m. pl.*, members of the household, one's staff

domesticus, -a, -um, *adj.*, of the house; familiar; private, personal

domus, -ūs *or* **-ī,** *f.*, house, home, family, household

dōnātīuum, -ī, *n.*, bonus

dōnec, *conj.*, while, as long as, until

dōnō (1), to present, grant; to condone; to let off

dormiō, -īre, -īuī *or* **-iī, -ītum,** to sleep, fall asleep; to be idle

dubiē, *adv.*, doubtfully, hesitatingly

dubitō (1), to be in doubt; to consider, ponder

ducentī, -ae, -a, *adj.*, two hundred

dūcō, -ere, duxī, ductus, to lead, guide, direct, conduct; to draw, pull; to command

dūdum, *adv.*, a short time ago, just now; once, formerly; for a long time

dum, *conj.*, while, as long as, until; provided that, if only

duo, -ae, -o, *adj.*, two

duplex, -icis, *adj.*, twofold, double; in double rows

dūrō (1), to harden, solidify; to be tough; to endure, last, hold out

dux, ducis, *m.*, general; guide; leader, head; driver; commander

ē. *See* **ex**

eburneus, -a, -um, *adj.*, ivory

ecloga, -ae, *f.*, short passage from a longer work; poem

ēdīcō, -ere, -dixī, -dictus, to proclaim, publish, decree

ēdictum, -ī, *n.*, edict, proclamation

ēdō, -ere, -idī, -itus, to give out; to publish; to tell, announce; to show

efficax, -ācis, *adj.*, effective, valid

efficiō, -ere, -fēcī, -fectus, to bring about, effect, cause; to make, produce; to show

ego, *pron.*, I, me, myself

ēgredior, -ī, -gressus sum, to go beyond; to go out

elegī, -ōrum, *m. pl.*, elegiac verses

Elephantis, -idis, *f.*, Elephantis, a Greek erotic writer

ēlīdō, -ere, -sī, -sus, to knock out, strike out; to shatter, smash; to stamp out

ēligō, -ere, -lēgī, -lectus, to pluck out; to pick out, choose

ēlogium, -ī, *n.*, inscription, epitaph; codicil

ēloquens, -entis, *adj.*, eloquent

ēmendō (1), to emend, correct; to reform, improve; to atone for

ēmicō, -āre, -uī, -ātum, to dart out, dash out; to shoot out

ēmungō, -ere, -xī, -ctus, to wipe the nose; **sē ēmungō,** to wipe one's nose

enim, *particle,* namely, for instance; indeed; for, because

ēnixē, *adv.,* with strenuous effort

ēnotō (1), to write down, note

eō, *adv.,* there, to that place; to that end; on that account, for that reason

epigramma, -atis, *n.,* inscription, epitaph; short poem; epigram

epistola *or* **epistula, -ae,** *f.,* letter; (*pl.*) letter

ēpōtō, -āre, -āuī, ēpōtum, to swallow, drink down, drink out

epulae, -ārum, *f. pl.,* sumptuous meal, feast; delicacies

epulor, -ārī, -ātus sum, to feast on; to banquet, dine

eques, -itis, *m.,* horseman; cavalryman; a member of the equestrian order ("knight")

equester, -tris, -tre, *adj.,* mounted on a horse; equestrian

equīle, -is, *n.,* a stable for horses

equitātus, -ūs, *m.,* cavalry

equus, -ī, *m.,* horse

ērēpō, -ere, -sī, to crawl through; to crawl up

ergō, *adv.,* therefore, consequently; well then, I say

error, -ōris, *m.,* wandering; wavering; uncertainty; error

ērudītus, -a, -um, *adj.,* learned, educated; accomplished

Esquiliae, -ārum, *f. pl.,* Esquiline Hill

essedum, -ī, *n.,* Gallic war chariot; light traveling carriage

et, *conj.,* and; (*adv.*) besides, also, even; **et . . . et,** both . . . and, not only . . . but also

etiam, *conj.,* and also; *adv.,* also

etsī, *adv.,* even if, although

ēueniō, -īre, -uēnī, -uentus, to come out; to come to pass, happen

ēuidens, -entis, *adj.,* obvious, apparent, manifest

ēuocō (1), to call out, summon; to challenge; to evoke, excite

ex *or* **ē,** *prep.* + *abl.,* out of, down from, up from, by, from, of, after

exāctiō, -ōnis, *f.,* driving out, expulsion; exaction

exanimis, -is, -e, *adj.,* breathless; terrified; lifeless

excaecō (1), to blind; to block up

excellens, -entis, *adj.,* excellent, superior

excīdō, -ere, -cīdī, -cīsus, to cut out, cut off; to raze, demolish

exciō, -īre, -īuī *or* **-iī, -ītus,** to call out, summon; to awaken; to disturb, frighten

excipiō, -ere, -cēpī, -ceptus, to take out, remove; to exempt; to except

excitō (1), to wake up, rouse; to raise; to stimulate; to erect, construct

exclūdō, -ere, -sī, -sus, to exclude, shut out; to remove, separate

excōgitō (1), to think up; to devise, contrive

excubitor, -ōris, *m.,* watchman; member of the Emperor's bodyguard

excubō, -āre, -uī, -itum, to keep watch or guard; to be vigilant

exemplar, -āris, *n.,* copy; transcript; likeness, pattern

exemplum, -ī, *n.,* example, sample; pattern; typical instance; copy

exequor, -ī, -cūtus sum, to follow out; to investigate; to say; to describe, go through

exerceō, -ēre, -uī, -itus, to exercise, train; to keep busy; to cultivate; to practice

exhauriō, -īre, -sī, -stus, to draw out, empty; to exhaust; to deplete; to drain dry

exiguus, -a, -um, *adj.,* slight, small, meager; scanty, poor

exīlis, -is, -e, *adj.,* thin, small, meager; worthless; poor

existimō, -āre, -āuī, -ātus, to form an opinion of, to judge; to consider; to value

existō, -ere, -istitī, -istitum, to come out, come forth; to appear, emerge; to exist

exolētus, -ī, *m.,* male prostitute

exordium, -ī, *n.,* beginning, start; origin

exorior, -īrī, -tus sum, to come out, come forth, rise, appear; to begin, be produced

expergiscor, -ī, -rectus sum, to wake up

explicō (1), to unfold, unroll; to loosen; to arrange; to settle

explōrātor, -ōris, *m.,* scout, spy

explōrātōrius, -a, -um, *adj.,* of or belonging to scouts

exprimō, -ere, pressī, -pressus, to press out, squeeze out; to extract, elicit, extort

exprobrō (1), to bring up as a reproach, charge someone with

expugnō (1), to assault, storm; to plunder; to defeat

exquīsītus, -a, -um, *adj.,* carefully considered; choice

extō, -āre, exstitī, to stand out; to be prominent; to exist

extraordinārius, -a, -um, *adj.,* extraordinary

extrēmus, -a, -um, *adj.,* situated at the edge, the edge of; hindmost; occurring at the end, last

extruō, -ere, -uxī, -uctus, to pile, heap up; to build up, raise, construct

exul, -ulis, *m./f.*, exile, refugee
exuperō *or* **exsuperō** (1), to surmount; to exceed, outdo

fābula, -ae, *f.*, story; talk, conversation; gossip; myth; legend; play
fābulātor, -ōris, *m.*, story-teller; writer of fables
fābulōsus, -a, -um, *adj.*, incredible, legendary, fictitious
facētus, -a, -um, *adj.*, witty, clever; elegant; brilliant
faciēs, -ēī, *f.*, face, look, facial expression; appearance
facile, *adv.*, easily, without trouble; by far; generally; quite; willingly
faciō, -ere, fēcī, factus, to make, do, produce, perform
factiō, -ōnis, *f.*, party, faction; band, group; partisanship
factitō (1), to keep doing; to practice
factum, -ī, *n.*, deed, act; misdeed
facultās, -ātis, *f.*, opportunity; feasibility; ability; skill; (*pl.*) resources
fallācia, -ae, *f.*, deception, deceit, trick
fallō, -ere, fefellī, falsus, to cause to fall, trip; to mislead; to deceive
falsus, -a, -um, *adj.*, false, wrong; groundless; deceitful, spurious
fāma, -ae, *f.*, talk; rumor; report; news; fame; infamy

familia, -ae, *f.*, household slaves; gang of slaves; house; estate
familiāris, -is, -e, *adj.*, domestic, intimate, personal; (*m.*) close friend
fāmōsus, -a, -um, *adj.*, much talked of, famous, renowned; infamous; slanderous
far, farris, *n.*, kind of wheat, emmer; grain from this plant
fās (*indecl. n.*), divine law; sacred duty; divine will, fate
fastīgium, -ī, *n.*, gable, roof, ceiling; main point
fātum, -ī, *n.*, divine utterance, oracle; fate, destiny; (*pl.*) future
faueō, -ēre, fāuī, fautum, to be favorable to; favor, support
fax, facis, *f.*, torch; funeral torch; comet; fire
fēmina, -ae, *f.*, woman; wife
femur, -oris *or* **-inis,** *n.*, thigh
ferē, *adv.*, approximately, nearly, almost; generally, as a rule
ferō, ferre, tulī, lātus, to bear, carry; to endure; to lead, drive; to bring, offer; make known, report
fīcēdula, -ae, *f.*, fig-pecker (small bird eaten as delicacy)
Fīdēnae, -ārum, *f. pl.*, Fidenae, a town of Latium
fidicula, -ae, *f.*, small lyre; (*pl.*) torture rack

figūra, -ae, *f.*, figure, shape, form; nature, kind

fīlia, -ae, *f.*, daughter

fīlius, -ī, *m.*, son

fīō, fierī, factus sum, to come into being; to arise; to be made; to become; to happen

firmus, -a, -um, *adj.*, firm, strong, stable; hardy, sound; trusty

fiscus, -ī, *m.*, basket; money box; imperial treasury, account

Flaccus, -ī, *m.*, Flaccus, a *cognomen*; especially of the poet Horace

flagellō (1), to whip

flāgitium, -ī, *n.*, shame, disgrace, scandal; rascal

flāgitō (1), to demand; to press; to ask repeatedly

flagrō, -āre, -āuī, to blaze, be on fire; to glow with; to be subject to

flagrum, -ī, *n.*, whip; whipping

fleō, -ēre, -ēuī, -ētus, to cry for; cry

flūmen, -inis, *n.*, river, stream

focus, -ī, *m.*, hearth, fireplace; brazier; funeral pyre; altar

foris, -is, *f.*, door, entrance, opening

forma, -ae, *f.*, form, shape; sort; design; plan

fortis, -is, -e, *adj.*, brave, courageous; strong, mighty, powerful

fortuītus, -a, -um, *adj.*, fortuitous, accidental; (*n.*) chance occurrence; misfortune

frangō, -ere, frēgī, fractus, to break to pieces, shatter, crush

frāter, -tris, *m.*, brother

fraus, -dis, *f.*, fraud, deception; error, delusion; offense

frequens, -entis, *adj.*, crowded, packed; usual, common, numerous

fretum, -ī, *n.*, strait, channel; sea; waters

frustrā, *adv.*, in vain, uselessly, for nothing; without reason

fūmō (1), to smoke, fume; to steam; to reek

fungor, -ī, functus sum, to perform, execute; to busy oneself with; to finish

fuscus, -a, -um, *adj.*, dark; dim; husky, hoarse

futūrus, -a, -um, *adj.*, that is to be, coming, future

Gāius, -ī, *m.*, Gaius, a *praenomen* (abbreviated **G.**); especially of the emperor Gaius

Galba, -ae, *m.*, Galba, a *cognomen* in the Sulpician *gens*; especially of the emperor Galba

galba, -ae, *f.*, a small worm

galbanum, -ī, *n.*, galbanum, gum resin

galbeus, -ī, *m.*, armband

galea, -ae, *f.*, helmet

Gallia, -ae, *f.*, Gaul

Gallus, -ī, *m.,* inhabitant of Gaul, a Gaul

gemitus, -ūs, *m.,* groan, sigh

gemma, -ae, *f.,* jewel; signet ring; bud

gener, -rī, *m.,* son-in-law

gens, -tis, *f.* clan, extended family; stock; tribe; nation; people

genus, -eris, *n.,* race, descent, breed, kind, sort, class, fashion

Germānī, -ōrum, *m. pl.,* the Germans

gestātiō, -ōnis, *f.,* action of riding or being carried on horseback, or in a litter

gestus, -ūs, *m.,* gesture, gesticulation; posture, bearing

gibber, -era, -erum, *adj.,* hump-backed

gladiātōrius, -a, -um, *adj.,* gladiatorial

gladius, -ī, *m.,* sword; gladiatorial profession

gnārus, -a, -um, *adj.,* having knowledge or experience

gracilitās, -ātis, *f.,* slenderness; thinness

gradus, -ūs, *m.,* step, pace; degree; stage; rank

Graecus, -a, -um, *adj.,* Greek

grandis, -is, -e, *adj.,* large, great; full-grown; tall

graphium, -ī, *n.,* stylus

grātia, -ae, *f.,* grace, charm; prestige; favor; cause, reason; (*pl.*) thanks

grātiōsus, -a, -um, *adj.,* popular; influential; obliging

grātulor, -ārī, -ātus sum, to be glad, rejoice

grātus, -a, -um, *adj.,* pleasing, pleasant, agreeable, welcome

grauis, -is, -e, *adj.,* heavy, weighty; burdensome; serious; harsh; unpleasant

gremium, -ī, *n.,* lap, bosom, womb

grex, -gis, *m.,* flock, herd; group

gula, -ae, *f.,* throat, gullet; appetite; gluttony

habeō, -ēre, -uī, -itus, to have; to hold, to possess; to keep, retain; to afford

habitus, -ūs, *m.,* condition, physical make-up, build; style, style of dress, "get-up"

haereō, -ēre, -sī, -sum, to cling; to linger; to hesitate; to be at a loss; to waste time in

haruspex, -icis, *m.,* soothsayer

haud, *particle,* hardly; not, not at all, by no means

hebes, -etis, *adj.,* blunt, dull, dim, stupid

Hellespontus, -ī, *m.,* Hellespont

hērēditās, -ātis, *f.,* inheritance; hereditary succession

hērēs, -ēdis, *m.,* heir

hērōis, -idos, *f.,* demigoddess; heroine

hērōs, -ōos, *m.,* hero

hic, haec, hoc, *pron.,* this, these

Hispānia, -ae, *f.,* Hispania, Spain

Hispānicus, -a, -um, *adj.,* of
    Hispania, Spanish
Histria, -ae, *f.,* Histria, a
    peninsula at the head of the
    Adriatic
historia, -ae, *f.,* history;
    account; story, theme
Homēricus, -a, -um, *adj.,*
    of Homer or his poems;
    Homeric
homō, -inis, *m.,* human being,
    man, person, mortal;
    mankind
homunciō, -ōnis, *f.,* mere man;
    poor guy
honestus, -a, -um, *adj.,*
    honored, respected, decent
honōs *or* **honor, -ōris,** *m.,*
    honor, esteem; high position,
    office, post; reward, prize
hōra, -ae, *f.,* hour; time; season
Horātius, -a, -um, *adj.,*
    Horatius, a *nomen;*
    especially of the poet Horace
hortor, -ārī, -ātus sum, to
    encourage, cheer, incite; to
    give a pep talk to
hortus, -ī, *m.,* garden; (*pl.*) estate
hostia, -ae, *f.,* victim, sacrificial
    animal
hostis, -is, *m./f.,* (public) enemy;
    stranger
hūmānus, -a, -um, *adj.,* of
    a human being, human;
    humane, kind; courteous;
    refined
humō (1), to bury
humus, -ī, *f.,* ground, earth,
    soil; land; country

iaceō, -ēre, -uī, -itum, to lie, lie
    down; to lie dead; to lie idle
iactō (1), to throw, hurl; to shake;
    to disturb, stir up; to throw
    out, mention; to brag about
iam, *adv.,* now, already, by then,
    by that time, very soon;
    moreover; actually
iantāculum, -ī, *n.,* breakfast
ibi, *adv.,* there; then
ibidem, *adv.,* in the same
    place, just there, at that very
    moment, there and then
ictus, -ūs, *m.,* strike, blow, hit
īdem, eadem, idem, *pron.,* the
    same, the very same, exactly
    this
identidem, *adv.,* over and over
    again; again and again;
    continually
ideō, *adv.,* therefore
Īdūs, -uum, *f. pl.,* Ides (15th
    day of March, May, July,
    October, and 13th day of
    other months)
ignārus, -a, -um, *adj.,* ignorant,
    unaware, inexperienced;
    strange
ignāuia, -ae, *f.,* idleness;
    cowardice
ignis, -is, *m.,* fire; watch fire,
    fire signal; torch; lightning
ignōminia, -ae, *f.,* ignominy,
    dishonor, disgrace;
    dishonorable discharge
ignoscō, -ere, -nōuī, -nōtus, to
    pardon, forgive, excuse
ignōtus, -a, -um, *adj.,* strange;
    unknown; low-born; ignoble

īlicō, *adv.*, on the spot; right then and there, immediately

ille, illa, illud, *pron.*, that; that famous; the following

illustrō (1), to light up, illuminate; to make clear; to embellish; to make famous

imāginor, -ārī, -ātus sum, to imagine

imāgō, -inis, *f.*, likeness; reflection in a mirror; portrait (of an ancestor)

imbrex, -icis, *f.*, tile, gutter tile

imbuō, -ere, -buī, -būtus, to wet, soak; to stain; to imbue; to instruct

immensus, -a, -um, *adj.*, immense, immeasurable, huge

immineō, -ēre, to project; to threaten; to have designs on

immodicus, -a, -um, *adj.*, huge, enormous; immoderate

immolō, (1), to sprinkle the feet of a victim for sacrifice; to sacrifice

immūtō (1), to change, alter; to substitute

impatiens, -entis, *adj.*, impatient (of); unable to endure

impediō, -īre, -īuī *or* -iī, -ītus, to entangle; to hamper; to block

imperātor, -ōris, *m.*, commander; general; commander in chief; emperor

imperium, -ī, *n.*, supreme administrative power; government; empire; command

imperō (1), to order, demand; to be in command; to govern, rule

impetrō *or* inpetrō, (1), to obtain; to achieve, accomplish, bring to pass

impōnō, -ere, -posuī, -positus, to impose, place on, lay on, set on

īmus, -a, -um, *adj.*, deepest, lowest, last; the bottom of

in, *prep.* + *abl.*, in, on, upon; during, within; (+ *acc.*) into; up to; for; respecting, with a view to; until

inaudītus, -a, -um, *adj.*, unheard-of, unprecedented; unusual

incendium, -ī, *n.*, fire; heat

incidō, -ere, -cidī, -cāsum, to happen, occur

incitō (1), to incite, spur on; to stimulate; to inspire

incohātus, -a, -um, *adj.*, only begun, unfinished, imperfect

increpō, -āre, uī, -itus, to rattle; to scold, rebuke; to protest against

incūriōsus, -a, -um, *adj.*, careless, unconcerned, indifferent; neglected

inde, *adv.*, from there, from that source, thereafter; from that cause

index, -icis, *m.*, one who reveals or points out, informer; indication, sign

indicium, -ī, *n.*, information, disclosure; evidence; proof

indīcō, -ere, -dixī, -dictus, to proclaim, announce; to summon; to impose

indigens, -entis, *adj.*, indigent; in need of

indignē, *adv.*, undeservedly; shamefully, outrageously

indūcō, -ere, -duxī, -ductus, to lead in, bring in; to seduce, mislead; to introduce

indulgens, -entis, *adj.*, indulgent, lenient

industriē, *adv.*, industriously, diligently

inēleganter, *adv.*, clumsy, infelicitious; disagreeable

ineptē, *adv.*, foolishly, absurdly, pointlessly

infāmia, -ae, *f.*, bad reputation; disrepute; disgrace

infāmis, -is, -e, *adj.*, infamous, notorious, disgraceful

infans, -antis, *m./f.*, child

infensus, -a, -um, *adj.*, bitterly hostile; furious

inferior, -ior, -ius, *adj.*, lower, farther down; subsequent, more recent

inferō, inferre, intulī, illātus, to bring in, carry in; to enter; **sē inferō,** to go to, enter

infirmus, -a, -um, *adj.*, weak, faint, feeble; trivial

infrā, *prep.* + *acc.*, below; inferior to; smaller than; (*adv.*) below, underneath;

ingens, -entis, *adj.*, huge, vast; great; a great amount of; very important; proud

ingerō, -ere, -gessī, -gestus, to carry in, throw in, heap; to force, thrust

inguen, -inis, *n.*, groin; sexual organs; swelling

initium, -ī, *n.*, beginning; entrance

iniungō, -ere, iniunxī, iniunctus, to join, attach, fasten

inlinō, -ere, -lēuī, -litus, to cover; smear (on)

inlūcescō, -ere, -xī, to grow light, begin to shine, dawn

inopīnanter, *adv.*, unexpectedly

inpensa, -ae, *f.*, expense, cost, outlay; waste; contribution

inprofessus, -a, -um, *adj.* that has not professed or declared himself

inquam, to say

inquiētō (1), to disquiet, disturb

inquīrō, -ere, -quīsīuī *or* **-quīsiī, -quīsītus,** to search for, inquire into; to examine

insānia, -ae, *f.*, insanity, madness, frenzy; mania; excess

insānus, -a, -um, *adj.*, insane; crazy; absurd; foolish; inspired

insequor, -ī, -cūtus sum, to follow immediately behind; to attack; to reproach

inserō, -ere, -uī, -tus, to insert, introduce, include

insidiae, -ārum, *f. pl.,* to ambush, plot, trap

insidiātor, -ōris, *m.,* soldier in ambush; plotter, subversive

insignis, -is, -e, *adj.,* conspicuous, distinguished; prominent; singular

insinuō (1), to bring in secretly, sneak in

inspiciō, -ere, -spexī, -spectus, to inspect, look into, examine; to watch; to consider

instans, -antis, *adj.,* pressing, urgent

instituō, -ere, -uī, -ūtus, to fix, set; to establish; to build; to appoint; to govern

institūtum, -ī, *n.,* plan, program; custom; principle; decree; stipulation; purpose

instruō, -ere, -xī, -ctus, to build up, construct; to furnish, prepare, fit out

insula, -ae, *f.,* island; apartment building

insum, -esse, -fuī, to be there, exist

insuō, -ere, -suī, -sūtus, to sew up; to sew up in

intemperans, -antis, *adj.,* intemperate, without restraint; lewd

intempestīuus, -a, -um, *adj.,* untimely; unseasonable; poorly timed

inter, *prep + acc.,* between, among; during

interdum, *adv.,* sometimes, now and then, occasionally; meanwhile

interim, *adv.,* meanwhile; for the moment; sometimes; however; anyhow

interpellō (1), to interrupt, break in on; to disturb

interrogō (1), to ask, question; to sue; to seek information from

interrumpō, -ere, -rūpī, -ruptus, to break apart, break up; to divide; to interrupt

intersum, -esse, -fuī, to be present, assist, take part; to differ

interuallum, -ī, *n.,* interval, space, distance; gap; interval of time

intimus, -a, -um, *adj.,* innermost; deepest; closest

intrōdūcō, -ere, -duxī, -ductus, to bring in, lead in; to introduce

introeō, -īre, -īuī *or* **-iī, -itum,** to enter

inualidus, -a, -um, *adj.,* weak; feeble; dim; ineffectual

inueniō, -īre, -uēnī, -uentus, to find, light upon, discover

inuītō (1), to invite, entertain; to summon; to ask; to encourage

inuoluō, -ere, -uī, -ūtus, to
wrap up; to involve; envelop;
to overwhelm

iocur *or* **iecur, -inoris,** *n.,* liver;
anger; lust

iocus, -ī, *m.,* joke

ipse, -a, -um, *pron.,* himself,
herself, itself; self; the very,
just; even; in person

īrascor, -ārī, to get angry
(with), fly into a rage

irrīdeō, -ēre, -sī, -sus, to laugh
at, ridicule; to laugh

irruō, -ere, -ī, to rush in, attack

is, ea, id, *pron. adj.,* he, she, it;
this one, that one; this, that

iste, -a, -ud, *pron.,* that of
yours, that

istōc, *adv.,* there, to where you
are

ita, *adv.,* thus, so, in this
manner, in that way

Italus, -a, -um, *adj.,* Italian

itaque, *adv.,* and so; and thus;
accordingly, therefore,
consequently

item, *adv.,* besides, likewise;
moreover

iter, -ineris, *n.,* journey, trip;
walk, march; route

iubeō, -ēre, iussī, iussus, to
order; to bid, ask, tell; to
decree

Iūdaicus, -a, -um, *adj.,* Jewish;
of Judaea

iūdicium, -ī, *n.,* trial, court;
sentence; opinion, decision;
judgment; taste

iugulum, -ī, *n.,* throat

Iūlius, -a, -um, *adj.,* Julius, a
nomen; Julian; **lex Iūlia,**
law passed by Caesar or
Augustus

iungō, -ere, iunxī, iunctus, to
join, unite, connect, clasp

Iuppiter, Iouis, *m.,* Juppiter

iurgium, -(i)ī, *n.,* quarrel, abuse

iūs, iūris, *n.,* law, the laws;
justice, right; law court; **iūs
dīcere,** to sit as judge, hold
court

iuuenta, -ae, *f.,* youth

iuuentūs, -ūtis, *f.,* youth, prime
of life, manhood; young
people, the young

iuxtā, *prep.* + *acc.,* close to; next
to; near; (*adv.*) nearby, in
close proximity

Kalendae, -ārum, *f. pl.,* Kalends
(1st day of the month)

lac, lactis, *n.,* milk; milky sap

lacerō (1), to lacerate, tear,
mangle; to batter, damage;
to abuse

lactēs, -ium, *f. pl.,* small
intestines

laetus, -a, -um, *adj.,* glad,
cheerful, rejoicing; happy;
fortunate; fertile; fat

laeuus, -a, -um, *adj.,* left, on the
left side; awkward, stupid;
ill-omened; lucky

lāna, -ae, *f.,* wool; working in
wool

largus, -a, -um, *adj.,* abundant,
plentiful; large, much

lascīuus, -a, -um, *adj.*, playful, frisky; licentious, horny

laudātiō, -ōnis, *f.*, commendation; eulogy, funeral oration

laureus, -a, -um, *adj.*, of laurel

lautus, -a, -um, *adj.*, expensive, elegant, fine; refined, fashionable

lectīca, -ae, *f.*, litter

lectīcula, -ae, *f.*, small litter, small couch

lector, -ōris, *m.* reader

lectus, -a, -um, *adj.*, select, choice

lectus, -ī, *m.*, bed, couch, dining couch

lēgātiō, -ōnis, *f.*, embassy; staff appointment; command of a legion; governorship

lēgātus, -ī, *m.*, ambassador; deputy; governor of an imperial province

lēgō (1), to commission; to dispatch; to delegate

legō, -ere, lēgī, lectus, to read, recite; to gather, collect

lēniō, -īre, -īuī *or* -iī, -ītus, to soothe, alleviate, calm; to calm down

lēnitās, -ātis, *f.*, mildness, gentleness; clemency

lepidus, -a, -um, *adj.*, charming, delightful, nice, neat; witty, amusing

lētālis, -is, -e, *adj.*, fatal, mortal, lethal

leuiter, *adv.*, lightly; slightly; gently

lex, lēgis, *f.*, law, bill, motion; condition

libellus, -ī, *m.*, booklet, pamphlet; letter, petition; placard

libens, -entis, *adj.*, willing; ready; glad, merry

liber, -brī, *m.*, book, work, treatise; catalogue, register

līberālitās, -ātis, *f.*, generosity, munificence; grant, gift

līberē, *adv.*, freely; frankly; ungrudgingly

līberī, -ōrum, *m. pl*, children; sons

lībertīnus, -a, -um, *adj.*, of the status of a freeman; (*m.*), freedman; ex-slave

libīdinōsus, -a, -um, *adj.*, willful; arbitrary; lustful, lecherous

libīdō, -inis, *f.*, desire, inclination, pleasure; will; caprice, fancy; lust

licentia, -ae, *f.*, license, freedom; unruly behavior, lawlessness

licet, -ēre, -uit, it is permitted, it is lawful

lingua, -ae, *f.*, tongue; speech, language, dialect; eloquence

lītigō (1), to squabble; to go to court

litō (1), to propitiate, atone for; obtain favorable omens from a sacrifice

littera, -ae, *f.*, letter

litterārius, -a, -um, *adj.*, of writing; (*m.*) ludus litterārius, elementary school

lītus, -oris, *n.,* seashore, beach, coast

Līuius, -a, -um, *adj.,* Livius, a *nomen*; especially of the historian Livy

locuplēs, -plētis, *adj.,* rich (in)

locuplētō (1), to make rich, enrich; to embellish

locus, -ī, *m.,* place, spot, site

longus, -a, -um, *adj.,* long; tall; protracted

loquor, loquī, locūtus sum, to say; to talk of; to tell; to mention; to speak

lōrīcātus, -a, -um, *adj.,* wearing a breastplate; mail-clad

Lūcius, -ī, *m.,* Lucius, a *praenomen* (abbreviated **L.**)

lūcubrātōrius, -a, -um, *adj.,* suitable for nocturnal studies

lūculus, -ī, *m.,* small grove

lucusta *or* **locusta, -ae,** *f.,* locust; lobster

lūdō, -ere, -sī, -sus, to play, to amuse oneself with; to imitate; to deceive

lūmen, -inis, *n.,* light, lamp; torch; daylight; eye

lūna, -ae, *f.*; moon; month; night; crescent

Lūsītānī, -ōrum, *m. pl.,* the Lusitanians, a people of western Iberia

Lūsītānia, -ae, *f.,* Lusitania, a province in western Iberia

lux, lūcis, *f.,* light; life; daylight; **prīma lux,** daybreak, dawn

luxuria, -ae, *f.,* luxuriance; luxury; extravagance, excess, sumptuousness

māchina, -ae, *f.,* large mechanism, machine; crane; siege engine

Maecēnās, -ātis, *m.,* Maecenas, a *nomen*; especially of Maecenas, friend of Augustus

magis, *adv.,* more, to a greater extent, in a higher degree; rather

magnitūdō, -inis, *f.,* magnitude; size; extent; greatness; importance; high rank

magnō opere, *adv.,* greatly, very much; particularly; strongly

magnus, -a, -um, *adj.,* large, great, big

māiestās, -ātis, *f.,* majesty, dignity, grandeur; sovereignty; authority

māior, -or, -us, *adj.,* bigger, larger; greater; more important

Māius, -a, -um, *adj.,* May, of May

male, *adv.,* badly, wrongly; unfortunately; extremely; unsuccessfully; cruelly

malus, -a, -um, *adj.,* bad, evil; adverse; ugly; abusive

mandō (1), to hand over; to commit, entrust; to command, commission

mandō, -ere, -dī, -sum, to chew, bite

maneō, -ēre, -sī, -sus, to remain, stay; to last, endure, persist; to await

manifestus, -a, -um, *adj.*, manifest, clear, distinct

manus, -ūs, *f.*, hand, band, collection

Marcus, -ī, *m.*, Marcus, a *praenomen* (abbreviated **M.**)

mare, -is, *n.*, sea; saltwater

marītus, -ī, *m.*, husband

marmoreus, -a, -um, *adj.*, marble, made of marble; marble-like

Martius, -a, -um, *adj.*, March, of March; of Mars

māter, -tris, *f.*, mother; matron; motherland; native city

māteria, -ae, *f.*, matter, stuff, material; lumber; subject matter; opportunity

māternus, -a, -um, *adj.*, maternal, mother's

mathēmaticus, -ī, *m.*, mathematician; astrologer

mātricīda, -ae, *m.*, murderer of one's mother

mātrimōnium, -ī, *n.*, matrimony, marriage

mātūrus, -a, -um, *adj.*, ripe, mature; opportune, at the right time; early

mātūtīnus, -a, -um, *adj.*, morning, early

Maurētānia, -ae, *f.*, Mauretania, a country of northwest Africa

maximē, *adv.*, very, most, especially, particularly; just, precisely, exactly

maximus, -a, -um, *adj.*, biggest, largest, most important, greatest

medeor, -ērī, to heal, cure

medicus, -ī, *m.*, doctor, surgeon

mediocris, -is, -e, *adj.*, medium, average, ordinary; undistinguished

meditor, -ārī, -ātus sum, to think over, reflect on; to practice; to have in mind

medius, -a, -um, *adj.*, middle, central, the middle of; moderate; ordinary; undecided

Meleager, -grī, *m.*, Meleager

melior, -or, -us, *adj.*, better, kinder, more gracious

meminī, -isse, to remember

memor, -oris, *adj.*, mindful, remembering; having a good memory

memoria, -ae, *f.*, memory; remembrance; period of recollection, time; past event

mensa, -ae, *f.*, table; meal, course; dinner; guests at table; bank; altar

mentiō, -ōnis, *f.*, mention

mentior, -īrī, -ītus sum, to invent, fabricate; to feign; to act deceitfully

mereō, -ēre, -uī, -itus, *or* **mereor, -ērī, -itus sum,** to deserve, merit, be entitled to; to win, gain; to earn; to serve (as a soldier)

merīdiānus, -a, -um, *adj.*, midday, noon; southern

merum, -ī, *n.,* undiluted wine

meus, -a, -um, *adj.,* my

mīles, -itis, *m.,* soldier; army

mīlia, -ium, *n. pl.,* thousands

mīmus, -ī, *m.,* mime; farce

minae, -ārum, *f. pl.,* threats

Minerua, -ae, *f.,* Minerva

minimē, *adv.,* least of all, very little; by no means, certainly not

minister, -trī, *m.,* servant, attendant (at table); agent; subordinate

ministrō (1), to serve, wait on

minor, -or, -us, *adj.,* smaller, less; shorter; inferior

Mīnōs, -ōis, *m.,* Minos, the king of Crete

minuō, -ere, -uī, -ūtus, to diminish, lessen; to weaken; to modify; to offend against

misceō, -ēre, miscuī, mixtus, to mix, blend; to associate; to unite sexually

mittō, -ere, mīsī, missus, to send, let fly; to utter; to release; to discharge; to send for

Mnestēr, -ēris, *m.,* Mnester, a famous pantomimic actor

moderātiō, -ōnis, *f.,* restraint; moderation

modestus, -a, -um, *adj.,* moderate, restrained, modest

modicus, -a, -um, *adj.,* moderate; small; unassuming; puny; ordinary

modo, *adv.,* only, merely; just now, just recently; if only, provided that

modulor, -ārī, -ātus sum, to regulate the time of; to measure rhythmically; to sing

modus, -ī, *m.,* measured amount, quantity; way; kind; **in modum,** in the manner of; **eius modī,** of that kind

moechus, -ī, *m.,* adulterer

Moesia, -ae, *f.,* Moesia, a province south of the Danube

mōlēs, -is, *f.,* mass, bulk, pile; massive structure; pier; burden, effort

mōmentum, -ī, *n.,* movement; critical time; moment

moneō, -ēre, -uī, -itus, to call to mind, remind; to advise; to warn

monīle, -is, *n.,* necklace; collar

monimentum *or* **monumentum, -ī,** *n.,* memorial, monument, statue, tomb

mons, -tis, *m.,* mountain; hill; mountain range; heap

monstruōsus, -a, -um, *or* **monstrōsus, -a, -um,** *adj.,* unnatural; monstrous, strange

mora, -ae, *f.* delay, pause

morbus, -ī, *m.,* disease, sickness, ailment; fault, vice

mōrigerō, -āre *or* **mōrigeror, -ārī, -ātus sum,** to be compliant, gratify

moror, -ārī, -ātus sum, to delay, detain, hold the attention of, occupy; to prevent

mors, mortis, *f.,* death; destruction; corpse; bloodshed

morsus, -ūs, *m.,* bite; grip; gnawing pain

mortuus, -a, -um, *adj.,* dead, deceased; decayed; half-hearted

mōs, mōris, *m.,* custom, usage; nature; manner; rule, regulation

mōtus, -ūs, *m.,* motion, movement; change; revolt

mox, *adv.,* soon, subsequently

mullus, -ī, *m.,* red mullet

multiplex, -icis, *adj.,* winding; serpentine; varied; versatile

multum, *adv.,* much, a lot, greatly; often, frequently

multus, -a, -um, *adj.,* many a, much, great; abundant; numerous

mūnus, -eris, *n.,* service; duty; function; favor; public entertainment; gladiatorial show

mūrēna, -ae, *f.,* moray, kind of eel

murmillō, -ōnis, *m.,* kind of gladiator

mūsica, -ae, *f.,* music; the art of music

Mūsīum *or* **Mūsēum, -ī,** *n.,* Museum, an institute for research in Alexandria

mūtō (1), to change, shift, alter; to exchange; to modify; to vary

mūtuō, *adv.,* mutually; jointly

mūtuus, -a, -um, *adj.,* mutual, reciprocal, interchangeable; borrowed, lent

nam, *conj.,* for; for in that case; yes, to be sure; now, on the other hand

namque, *conj.,* for in fact; for no doubt

nanciscor, -ī, nanctus sum, to get, obtain; to come across; to experience

narrō (1), to tell, relate, narrate; to describe, tell about

nascor, -ī, nātus sum, to be born; to begin; to be produced; to be found

nātūra, -ae, *f.,* nature; character, temperament; distinctive feature; sex organs

nauarchus, -ī, *m.,* commander of a warship

nāuis, -is, *f.,* ship

nāuō (1), to do or perform energetically; **operam nāuāre,** to act energetically

nē, *adv.,* not, **nē ... quidem,** not even; (*conj.*), that not, lest

Neāpolis, -is, *f.,* Neapolis, Naples

nec *or* **neque,** *adv.,* not; *conj.,* nor, and not; **nec ... nec** neither ... nor

necdum, *conj.,* and not yet, nor yet

necessārius, -a, -um, *adj.,* necessary; urgent; closely related

necō (1), to kill, slay

nēdum, *conj.,* much less, still less; not to say

neglegō, -ere, -lēxī, -lēctus, to be unconcerned about; to neglect; to fail to; to overlook

negōtium, -ī, *n.,* business, occupation, employment; matter, affair; commerce

nēmō, -inis, *m./f.,* no one, nobody; a person of no consequence; a nobody

nemus, -oris, *n.,* cluster of trees, grove

nepōs, -ōtis, *m.,* grandson; nephew; descendant

neptis, -is, *f.,* granddaughter; female descendant

neque. *See* **nec**

nequeō, -īre, -īuī *or* **-iī,** to be unable to

Nerō, -ōnis, *m.,* Nero, a *cognomen* in the Claudian *gens;* especially of the emperor Nero

nex, necis, *f.,* death; murder, slaughter

nī, *adv.,* not; (*conj.*) that not; if not, unless

nihil, *n.,* nothing

nimius, -a, -um, *adj.,* very much, very great; too great; intemperate; extravagant

Nioba, -ae, *f.,* Niobe

nisi, *conj.,* unless, if not; except

nō, -āre, -āuī, to swim, float; to sail; to fly

nōbilis, -is, -e, *adj.,* familiar; noted; famous; fine; noble, well-born

nōbilitās, -ātis, *f.,* fame, renown; noble birth; nobility; the nobles; excellence

Nōla, -ae, *f.,* Nola, a town in Campania

nōmen, -inis, *n.,* name; title; reputation; title

nomos, -ī, *m.,* tune, melody

nōn, *adv.,* not, no, by no means

nōnāgēnārius, -a, -um, *adj.,* having or consisting of ninety; ninety years old

nōnnūllus, -a, -um, *adj.,* some, a certain amount of; not a few

nōnnumquam, *adv.,* sometimes

nōnus, -a, -um, *adj.,* ninth

nōs, *pron.,* we

noster, -tra, -trum, *adj.,* our, our own

notō (1), to mark; to write down; to brand; to reproach

nōtus, -a, -um, *adj.,* known, well-known; notorious; familiar

nouus, -a, -um, *adj.,* new; young; unexpected; strange; unheard-of

nox, noctis, *f.,* night; sleep; death; ignorance

noxa, -ae, *f.,* harm, injury, offense; guilt, responsibility

nūbēs, -is, *f.* cloud, gloom, veil

nūbilis, -is, -e, *adj.,*
marriageable
nūdus, -a, -um, *adj.,* naked,
lightly clothed; poor; simple
nullus, -a, -um, *adj.,* no; not,
not at all; non-existent
numerus, -ī, *m.,* number; class;
group
nummus, -ī, *m.,* coin; cash,
money
nunc, *adv.,* now; nowadays,
today; now, in view of
this; **nunc . . . nunc,** at one
moment . . . at another
nuncupō (1), to declare, specify;
to nominate, appoint (as heir)
nūntiō (1), to bring word of;
to announce; to declare; to
report
nuptiae, -ārum, *f. pl.,* marriage,
wedding
nympha, -ae, *f.,* nymph

ob, *prep.* + *acc.,* before, in front
of, on account of, for the
sake of, in return for
obeō, -īre, -īuī *or* -**iī, -itus,**
to go to meet; to travel; to
review; to die
obēsitās, -ātis, *f.,* fatness,
stoutness
obēsus, -a, -um, *adj.,* obese;
swollen; crude
obferō, -ferre, -tulī, -lātus,
to offer, bring forward; to
present, show
obiciō, -ere, -iēcī, -iectus, to
throw before; to expose; to
cite, throw in one's teeth

obiectō (1), to impute to; to
bring a charge of against
obiurgō (1), to scold, rebuke,
reprimand; to correct; to
order
obnoxius, -a, -um, *adj.,*
submissive, servile;
obedient; at the mercy of;
exposed to
obscūrus, -a, -um, *adj.,*
obscure, dark; not openly
expressed; unintelligible
obses, -idis, *m./f.,* hostage;
guarantee; pledge
obsignō (1), to seal, to sign and
seal; to stamp
obsōnium, -ī, *n.,* purchasing of
food; provisions
obstrepō, -ere, -uī, -itus, to
shout at, interrupt with
shouts; to protest
obtestātiō, -ōnis, *f.,* invocation;
solemn appeal
obueniō, -īre, -uēnī, -uentus,
to come up, happen; to come
one's way
obuius, -a, -um, *adj.,* in the way;
exposed; ready; accessible
obuoluō, -ere, -uī, -ūtus, to
wrap up, cover up
occāsiō, -ōnis, *f.,* opportunity;
good time, right moment;
chance; pretext
occīdō, -ere, -cīdī, -cīsus, to
kill, murder; to ruin
occulō, -ere, -uī, -tus, to hide,
cover up, cover
occultus, -a, -um, *adj.,* hidden,
secret

occupātus, -a, -um, *adj.,* occupied, busy, engaged

occupō (1), to occupy, seize; to grasp; to gain

Ōceanus, -ī, *m.,* ocean

octo, *adj.,* eighteen

oculus, -ī, *m.,* eye; sight, vision

Oedipūs, -odis, *m.,* Oedipus, the king of Thebes

offendō, -ere, -dī, -sus, to hit; to offend, shock; to annoy, disgust

offerō, offerre, obtulī, oblātus, to offer, bring forward; to cause; to inflict; to deliver

officiō, -ere, -fēcī, -fectum, to get in the way of; to obstruct

officium, -ī, *n.,* service, duty, function; ceremony; courtesy; post; body of officials

ōlim, *adv.,* once, once upon a time; at the time; for a good while; now and then

omittō, -ere, omīsī, omissus, to let go; to let fall; to abandon; to overlook; to discard

omnis, -is, -e, *adj.,* all, every, the whole

onerārius, -a, -um, *adj.,* carrying freight

onerō (1), to load, load down; to burden

onus, -eris, *n.,* burden; load; expenditure

opera, -ae, *f.,* activity, task, effort; **operam dāre,** to devote one's attention to

opīnor (1), to suppose, imagine, conjecture

opitulor, -ārī, -ātus sum, to bring help to, assist

opperior, -īrī, -tus sum, to wait for; to wait

oppidum, -ī, *n.,* town

oppōnō, -ere, -posuī, -positus, to put, place, station; to oppose; to cover

opprimō, -ere, -pressī, -pressus, to press down; to overwhelm, destroy

oppugnō (1), to assault, attack, storm

ops, opis, *f.,* power, might; aid; weight

optineō, -ēre, -tinuī, -tentus, to hold on to; to maintain; to win; to secure

optō (1), to choose, select; to pray for; to wish for

opus, -eris, *n.,* work; building; work of art; worksmanship; achievement

ōrātiō, -ōnis, *f.,* speaking; speech; language

orchestra, -ae, *f.,* area in front of the theather stage; senatorial seating in theater

ordō, -inis, *m.,* line, row; series; arrangement; rank; class; system, routine; turn

Orestēs, -is, *m.,* Orestes, the son of Agamemnon and Clytemnestra

orīgō, -inis, *f.,* origin, source; birth; lineage, descent

ornāmentum, -ī, *n.,* equipment;
trappings; ornament,
decoration

ornō (1), to equip, fit out,
furnish; to outfit; to adorn;
to attire

ōs, ōris, *n.,* mouth; voice, speech;
expression; face, look; front

os, ossis, *n.,* bone

osculor, -ārī, -ātus sum, to kiss;
to embrace; to value, prize

osculum, -ī, *n.,* kiss; mouth, lips

ostendō, -ere, -dī, -tus *or* **-sus,**
to hold out; to show, display;
to expose; to make known

Ostia, -ae, *f.,* Ostia, the port
town of Rome at the mouth
of Tiber river

ostrea, -ae, *f.,* oyster

pābulum, -ī, *n.,* feed, fodder;
nourishment

paciscor, -iscī, -tus sum, to
bargain for, agree upon; to
stipulate; to strike a bargain

paene, *adv.,* almost, nearly

paenitentia, -ae, *f.,* repentance,
regret

palam, *prep.+ abl.,* before,
in the presence of; (*adv.*)
openly, publicly, plainly;

Palātium, -ī, *n.* Palatine Hill;
imperial residence on the
Palatine, palace

pallaca, -ae, *f.,* concubine

Pāniscus, -ī, *m.,* little Pan, a
minor rustic deity

pantomīmus, -ī, *m.,* performer
in pantomime

papilla, -ae, *f.,* nipple; teat;
breast

parasīticus, -a, -um, *adj.,*
parasitical

parātus, -a, -um, *adj.,* prepared,
ready; available; well-versed
(in)

parens, -entis, *m.,* parent,
father; ancestor; grandfather

parō (1), to prepare; to get,
procure; to purchase

parricīdium, -ī, *n.,* parricide;
murder; assassination; high
treason

pars, -tis, *f.,* part, portion,
share; function, duty; (*pl.*)
part, role, task

Parthī, -ōrum, *m. pl.,*
Parthians

Parthia, -ae, *f.,* Parthia, a
country of west Asia

particeps, -ipis, *adj.,* sharing in,
taking part in

parturiō, -īre, -īuī, to teem
with; to bring forth; to be in
labor

parum, *n. and adv.,* a little, too
little, insufficiently

paruus, -a, -um, *adj.,* small,
tiny; unimportant

Pāsiphaa, -ae, *f.,* Pasiphae, the
daughter of the Sun

passim, *adv.,* here and there; all
over the place; at random,
without order

passus, -ūs, *m.,* step, pace;
footstep; track

pateō, -ēre, -uī, to stand open,
open

pater, -tris, *m.*, father

paternus, -a, -um, *adj.*, father's; paternal; ancestral; native

patina, -ae, *f.*, dish, pan

patricius, -a, -um, *adj.*, patrician

paucus, -a, -um, *adj.*, few, little

paulātim, *adv.*, little by little, by degrees; a few at a time

paulisper, *adv.*, for a little while

paulum, *adv.*, a little, somewhat

paulus, -a, -um, *adj.*, a small, little

pāuō, -ōnis, *m.*, peacock

pax, pācis, *f.*, peace; peace treaty; harmony, tranquility; pardon

peccō (1), to make a mistake; to make a slip in speaking; to be wrong; to sin

pectus, -oris, *n.*, heart, breast, chest; mind; soul; understanding

Pedius, -a, -um, *adj.*, Pedius, a Roman *nomen*; lex Pedia: Pedian law

pendō, -ere, pependī, pensus, to weigh; to pay; to ponder; to value, esteem; nihil pensī habēre, to have no scruples

pēnis, -is, *m.*, tail; penis

per, *prep.* + *acc.*, through, throughout, during; by; under pretense of

peragō, -agere, -ēgī, -actus, to complete; to accomplish; to pierce

peragrō, (1) travel through, traverse; to spread

perdūcō, -ere, -duxī, -ductus, to lead, guide; to bring; to bring to bed, seduce

pereō, -īre, -iī, -itus, to pass away, die; to perish; to be lost

perferō, -ferre, -tulī, -lātus, to carry through; to deliver; to bring news of

perfidia, -ae, *f.*, treachery, perfidy

perfricō, -āre, -uī, -ātus, to rub all over

perīculum, -ī, *n.*, danger

perlegō, -ere, -lēgī, -lectus, to scan; to read through; to recount

permaneō, -ēre, -sī, -sus, to remain; to last, continue

perpetrō (1), to accomplish, carry out, perform

perpetuus, -a, -um, *adj.*, perpetual, continuous; general; whole

persequor, -ī, -secūtus sum, to follow, follow up; to chase after

perseuērō (1), to persist in

persōna, -ae, *f.*, mask; part, character; pretense; personality; person

persōnātus, -a, -um, *adj.*, wearing a mask, masked

pertinax, -ācis, *adj.*, stubborn, steadfast, very tenacious

pēs, pedis, *m.*, foot

pestilentia, -ae, *f.*, pestilence, plague; unhealthful atmosphere

petō, -ere, -īuī *or* **-iī, -ītus,** to make for, head for; to attack; to demand, lay claim to

phalerātus, -a, -um, *adj.,* wearing medals; decorated

Pharus, -ī, *m.,* Pharos, an island off Alexandria with a great lighthouse; lighthouse

phāsiāna, -ae, *f.,* pheasant

Philippensis, -is, -e, *adj.,* of or associated with Philippi, a town in Macedonia

phoenīcopterus, -ī, *m.,* flamingo

pictūra, -ae, *f.,* painting; embroidery

pinguis, -is, -e, *adj.,* fat; fatty; rich, fertile, luxuriant; dense; stupid

piscātor, -ōris, *m.,* fisherman; fishmonger

pisciculus, -ī, *m.,* little fish

piscis, -is, *m.,* fish

Pīsō, -ōnis, *m.,* Piso, a *cognomen*

plāga, -ae, *f.,* blow, wound; gash

plānē, *adv.,* clearly, distinctly; legibly; quite; certainly

plaustrum *or* **plostrum, -ī,** *n.,* wagon; cart

plausus, -ūs, *m.,* clapping, flapping; applause

plebs, plēbis, *f.,* the plebeians, common people; the masses, proletariat

plēnus, -a, -um, *adj.,* full; filled

plērusque, -aque, -umque, *adj.,* a very great part of; the greater part of; most

plostrum. *See* **plaustrum**

plumbeus, -a, -um, *adj.,* of lead; leaden; oppresive

plūrēs, -ēs, -a, *adj.,* more; several; too many

plūrifāriam, *adv.,* extensively, in many places

plūrimum, *adv.,* very much, especially; commonly, generally; **cum plūrimum,** at most

plūrimus, -a, -um, *adj.,* many a; most; very much; very great

plūs, plūris, *adj.,* more

poena, -ae, *f.,* punishment; penalty; compensation; hardship, loss

polliceor, -ērī, -itus sum, to promise

Pompēiānus, -a, -um, Pompeian, of or belonging to a Pompeius

pōmum, -ī, *n.,* fruit; fruit tree

pōnō, -ere, posuī, positus, to put, set; to post; to build; to lay down; to smooth

pons, -tis, *m.,* bridge; gangway; drawbridge

popīna, -ae, *f.,* low-class restaurant; cookshop

populus, -ī, *m.* the people; nation; public; crowd

porrigō, -ere, -rexī, -rectus, to reach out; to stretch out; to offer, present

poscō, -ere, poposcī, to ask, request; beg; to ask for in marriage; to demand; to need

possum, posse, potuī, to be able

post, *prep* + *acc.*, after, since; behind; (*adv.*) behind; backwards; later; next;

posteā, *adv.*, afterwards, after this, after that

posterior, -or, -us, *adj.*, later, next; following; latter, posterior; inferior

posterus, -a, -um, *adj.*, following, ensuing, next, subsequent

postquam, *conj.*, after; when

postrēmō, *adv.*, at last, finally

postrīdiē, *adv.*, on the day after, on the following day

postulō (1), to demand, claim; to expect; to require

potentia, -ae, *f.*, force, power; influence

potestās, -tātis, *f.*, power, capacity, dominion; possibility, opportunity

pōtiō, -ōnis, *f.*, drinking; drink; drose

potissimum, *adv.*, chiefly, especially

potius, *adv.*, rather, more, by preference

pōtō (1), to drink; to absorb

pōtulentus, -a, -um, *adj.*, drinkable; tipsy

prae, *prep.* + *abl.*, before, in front of; compared with; by reason of; in consequence of; (*adv.*) before, in front of; **prae sē ferre** to display, manifest

praebeō, -ēre, -uī, -itus, to hold out, offer; to supply, give; to show

praecipitō (1), to throw down headfirst; to hasten; to rush headfirst

praecipuē, *adv.*, especially, chiefly

praeclārus, -a, -um, *adj.*, very clear; very nice; splendid; excellent; famous

praedor, -ārī, -ātus sum, to raid, plunder, loot

praefectūra, -ae, *f.*, supervision, superintendence; prefecture

praefectus, -ī, *m.*, prefect, commander; **praefectus praetōriī,** commander of the praetorian guard

praeferō, -ferre, -tulī, -lātus, to hold out, carry in front; to offer; to display; to prefer

praegrandis, -is, -e, *adj.*, huge, very great

praemittō, -ere, -mīsī, -missus, to send out ahead, send in advance; to send word

praemium, -ī, *n.*, prize, reward, recompense; exploit; gift

praepinguis, -is, -e, *adj.*, very fertile; very fat

praepōnō, -ere, -posuī, -positus, to place in front of; to put in command of

praeruptus, -a, -um, *adj.*, precipitous, abrupt

praesaepe, -is, *n.*, stall, stable, crib; manger

praeses, -idis, *m.,* guard, guardian; governor

praestantia, -ae, *f.,* excellence; preeminence, superiority

praestituō, -ere, -tuī, -tūtus, to fix or set up beforehand; to put in charge

praestō, -āre, -stitī, -stitus, to be superior to; to show, give evidence of; to display

praetendō, -ere, -dī, -tus, to stretch in front of oneself; to give as pretext, allege

praeter, *prep.+ acc.,* past, by, along; surpassing; despite; in addition to; except; exclusive of; *(conj.)* besides, other than;

praetereā, *adv.,* besides, moreover

praetereō, -īre, -iuī *or* **-iī, -itus,** to go past, pass by, to go by

praetextātus, -a, -um, *adj.,* wearing the toga praetexta;; juvenile, puerile; unseemly

praetor, -ōris, *m.,* praetor, a magistrate at Rome

praetōriānus, -a, -um, *adj.,* of or belonging to the praetorian cohorts

praetōrium, -ī, *n.,* general's quarters; imperial bodyguard, praetorian guard; palace

praetōrius, -a, -um, *adj.,* of the commander-in-chief or emperor; praetor's; belonging to the praetorian cohorts

praetūra, -ae, *f.,* praetorship; propraetorship

prandium, -ī, *n.,* breakfast; lunch

prasinus, -a, -um, *adj.,* green

prex, precis, *f.,* prayer; request; intercession; curse

prīdiānus, -a, -um, *adj.,* of the day before

prīdiē, *adv.,* the day before

prīmum, *adv.,* first; in the first place; at first; for the first time

prīmus, -a, -um, *adj.,* first; foremost; distinguished; leading; earliest; nascent

princeps, -ipis, *m.,* leader, chief; emperor

principātus, -ūs, *m.,* first place; post of commander in chief; principate; rule

principium, -ī, *n.,* beginning, start; origin; preamble

prior, -or, -us, *adj.,* previous, preceding; basic; better

prīuātus, -a, -um, *adj.,* private, person; individual

prīuātus, -ī, *m.,* private citizen; one who is not a ruler, a subject

prīuignus, -ī, *m.,* stepson

prius quam *or* **priusquam,** *conj.,* before

prō, *prep. + abl.,* before, in front of; instead of; just as; according to; in comparison with; for; in lieu of

probō (1), to approve, commend, esteem

procax, -ācis, *adj.*, pushing,
impudent; undisciplined

prōcērus, -a, -um, *adj.*, tall, long

prōclāmō (1), to yell out; to
exclaim

prōconsulātus, -ūs, *m.*,
proconsulship, proconsulate

prōcreō (1), to procreate, beget;
to produce

prōcūrātor, -ōris, *m.*,
manager, administrator;
agent; governor of a minor
province

prōdeō, -īre, -iī, -itum, to go
out, come out, go forth; to
appear in public; to appear

prōdigium, -ī, *n.*, unnatural
event, prodigy; monstrous
event, marvel

prōdigus, -a, -um, *adj.*,
wasteful, lavish

prōdō, -ere, -didī, -ditus,
to bring out, bring forth,
produce; to reveal

prōdūcō, -ere, -duxī, -ductus,
to bring out, produce; to
prolong, extend

proelior, -ārī, -ātus sum, to
battle

prōfectiō, -ōnis, *f.*, setting out,
departure

prōfectus, -ūs, *m.*, progress,
success

prōferō, -ferre, -tulī, -lātus, to
bring forward, put off, defer;
extend

profiteor, -ērī, -fessus sum, to
declare publicly, acknowledge;
to confess; to register

profugus, -a, -um, *adj.*,
fugitive; banished; exiled;
nomadic

profundō, -ere, -fūdī, -fūsus,
to pour, pour out; to give
vent to

profundum, -ī, *n.*, depth; deep,
deep sea

profundus, -a, -um, *adj.*,
deep, boundless, vast;
dense; high

prōgnātus, -a, -um, *adj.*, born,
descended

prōgredior, -ī, -gressus sum, to
go forth, go out, set out

prohibeō, -ēre, -uī, -itus, to
hold back, check, prevent; to
prohibit; to keep away

prōmiscuus, -a, -um,
adj., promiscuous,
indiscriminate; in common,
open to all

prōmittō, -ere, -mīsī, -missus,
to send forth; to promise,
guarantee; to give hope of

pronepōs, -ōtis, *m.*, great-
grandson

prōnuntiō (1), to proclaim,
announce; to promise; to
deliver, recite

prōnus, -a, -um, *adj.*, leaning,
inclined; inclined towards;
disposed toward

propīnō (1), to make a toast and
hand over the cup

propinquitās, -ātis, *f.*,
proximity, nearness,
vicinity; relationship;
affinity

propior, -or, -us, *adj.*, nearer, closer; later, more recent; more nearly resembling

prōpōnō, -ere, posuī, -positus, to exhibit; to put or place forward, propose; to plan

propter, *prep.+ acc.*, near, close, next to; on account of, for the sake of

prōripiō, -ere, -ripuī, -reptus, to drag forth, drag out; to rush

prōsāpia, -ae, *f.*, stock, race, line

prōsequor, -ī, -secūtus sum, to escort, attend, to pursue; to chase; to go on with

prōsiliō, -īre, -uī *or* **-iī** *or* **-īuī,** to jump forward; to jump up

prōstō, -āre, -stitī, -stitum, to offer for sale; to prostitute oneself

prōsus *or* **prorsus, -a, -um,** *adj.*, straight; **prōsa ōrātiō,** prose

prōuerbium, -ī, *n.*, proverb

prōuincia, -ae, *f.*, province; sphere of administration; office, duty; command

prōuinciālis, -is, -e, *adj.*, provincial, of a province

prout, *conj.*, as, just as; in so far as; in as much as

proximus, -a, -um, *adj.*, nearest, next, following; preceding

Ptolemaeus, -ī, *m.*, Ptolemy, a name of kings of Egypt and a king of Mauretania

pūbēs, -is, *f.*, private parts; puberty; adult population

pūblicē, *adv.*, publicly; officially; on behalf of the state, for the state; at public expense

pūblicō (1), to confiscate; to throw open to the general public; to prostitute

pūblicus, -a, -um, *adj.*, public, of the people; common; of the state, national; vulgar

puella, -ae, *f.*, girl, girlfriend; sweetheart

puer, -erī, *m.*, boy, lad; slave

pueritia, -ae, *f.*, childhood; boyhood

pūgiō, -ōnis, *f.* dagger

pulcher, -cra, -crum, *adj.*, beautiful, handsome

pūniō, -īre, -īuī *or* **-iī, -ītus,** to punish, avenge

purgō (1), to cleanse; clean; to clear, remove; to excuse; to refute

purpureus, -a, -um, *adj.*, purple, crimson, royal purple

pūrus, -a, -um, *adj.*, pure, clean, clear; plain, naked, natural; absolute

Puteolānus, -a, -um, *adj.*, of Puteoli, a town near Naples

putō (1), to trim, prune; to think, ponder, consider

quadrāgintā, *adj.*, forty

quadrifāriam, *adv.*, in four ways; in four places; in fours

quadrīgārius, -a, -um, *adj.*, connected with chariot racing

quadringēnī, -ae, -a, *adj.*, four hundred each

quaerō, -ere, -sīuī *or* **-siī, -sītus,** to look for, search for; to get; to demand; to examine

quaestōrius, -a, -um, *adj.*, quaestor's, of a quaestor; employed in a quaestor's office; having quaestorian rank

quaestūra, -ae, *f.*, quaestorship, a magistracy in Rome

quālis, -is, -e, *adj.*, what sort of, what kind of; of such a kind, such as, as; as for example

quāliscumque, -iscumque, -ecumque, *adj.*, of whatever kind; of any kind whatsoever; any at all

quam, *adv.*, how, how much; as, than

quamquam *or* **quanquam,** *conj.*, although

quamuīs, *adv.*, however, no matter how; ever so

quandōque, *adv.*, whenever

quantopere, *adv.*, by how much, how much; with how great effort; how carefully

quantuluscumque, quantulacumque, quantulumcumque, *adj.*, however small, however unimportant

quantus, -a, -um, *adj.*, how great, how much, of what size, of what importance

quārē, *adv.*, by what means, how; in what way; why; whereby

quartus, -a, -um, *adj.*, fourth

quasi, *adv.*, as it were, so to speak; about, nearly; (*conj.*), on the grounds that; as would be the case if

quātenus, *adv.*, how far, to what point; as far as; to what extent

quater, *adv.*, four times

-que, *conj.*, and

querceus, -a, -um, *adj.*, of oak

queror, -ī, questus sum, to complain about, complain of; to lament; to sing sadly

quī, qua, quod, *adj.*, some, any

quī, quae, quod, *pron.*, who, which, that; (*adj.*) which, what?

quīcumque, quaecumque, quodcumque, *pron.*, whoever, whosoever

quīdam, quaedam, quiddam, *pron.*, a certain, certain

quīdam, quaedam, quoddam, *adj.*, a certain; a kind of, what one might call

quidem, *particle*, certainly, indeed; in fact

quiēs, -ētis, *f.*, rest, calm, quiet, sleep, death

quīlibet, quaelibet, quodlibet, *adj.*, whatever or whichever you please; any

quīn, *adv.*, why not; in fact; (*conj.*) so that not; that

quinquāgēsimus, -a, -um, *adj.*, fiftieth

quinque, *adj.*, five

quintus, -a, -um, *adj.*, fifth
Quintus, -ī, *m.*, Quintus, a
    praenomen (abbreviated **Q.**)
quis, quid, *pron.*, who, which
    one; anyone
quisnam, quaenam, quidnam,
    pron., who, tell me?; what,
    tell me?; who; what
quisquam, quidquam *or*
    quicquam, *pron.*, anyone,
    anything
quisque, quaeque, quidque *or*
    quodque, *pron.*, each, each
    one, everybody
quō, *adv.* (*interr.*) where, to
    what place; (*conj.*) where, to
    which place; in order that
quōcumque, *adv.*, to whatever
    place, wherever
quod, *conj.*, because, since; as
    for the fact that; the fact
    that; insofar as
quōlibet, *adv.*, anywhere you
    please; anywhere at all
quondam, *adv.*, once, at one
    time, formerly; at times;
    someday
quoniam, *conj.*, because, seeing
    that, now that
quoque, *adv.*, also, too; even
quotannīs, *adv.*, every year
quotiens, *adv.*, how many
    times; as often as,
    whenever

rāmulus, -ī, *m.*, twig
rapiō, -ere, -uī, -tus, to seize
    and carry off; to snatch, to
    hurry; to ravish; to ravage

rārus, -a, -um, *adj.*, thin;
    scattered; few; uncommon;
    scarce
ratiō, -ōnis, *f.*, calculation,
    account; matter; affair,
    scheme; fashion
recīdō, -ere, -dī, -sus, to cut
    back, cut off, cut away, cut
    down; to abridge
reciperō *or* **recuperō** (1), to
    regain, recover, get back
recipiō, -ere, -cēpī, -ceptus,
    to acquire; to accept; to
    recover; **sē recipere,** to
    retreat to
recitātiō, -ōnis, *f.*, reading
    aloud, recitation
recitō (1), to read out; to read
    aloud, recite
rectē, *adv.*, in a straight line;
    rightly, correctly; suitably;
    good, very good
recūsō (1), to raise objections
    to, reject, refuse; to make a
    rebuttal
redūcō, -ere, -duxī, -ductus, to
    lead back; to draw back; to
    escort; to withdraw
referō, referre, rettulī, relātus,
    to bring back, carry back,
    return; to reply, report
reficiō, -ere, -fēcī, -fectus, to
    rebuild, repair, restore; to
    revive, refresh; to get back
refrīgerō (1), to cool, chill;
    to refresh; to cause to lose
    zeal; (*pass.*) to be stopped or
    interrupted repeatedly
rēgāliolus, -ī, *m.*, wren

rēgius, -a, -um, *adj.*, royal; worthy of a king, princely

regō, -ere, rexī, rectus, to keep in a straight line; to guide, conduct; to manage

regredior, -ī, -gressus sum, to step or go back; to come back, return

releuō (1), to lighten; to lift up or raise again; to relieve, ease the pain of

religiō, -ōnis, *f.*, religion, religious scruple; sense of right; awe; holiness

relinquō, -ere, -līquī, -lictus, to leave behind; to bequeath; to forsake, abandon

reliquus, -a, -um, *adj.*, remaining, left over, left; subsequent

remacrescō, -ere, -uī, to shrink and become thin

remedium, -ī, *n.*, cure, remedy

reminiscor, -ī, to call to mind, remember; to be mindful of

remoueō, -ēre, -mōuī, -mōtus, to move back, withdraw; to remove, set aside

rēmus, -ī, *m.*, oar

renūntiō (1), to report; to announce; to retract; to reject; to take back a message

renuō, -ere, -ī, to nod refusal to; to turn down, say no to

repente, *adv.*, suddenly; unexpectedly, without warning

reperiō, -īre, repperī, repertus, to find, meet with, discover

repertor, -ōris, *m.*, discoverer, inventor; author

repetō, -ere, -īuī *or* **-iī, -ītus,** to head back to; to return to; to repeat, undertake again

repetundae, -ārum, *f. pl.*, money extorted; extortion

repleō, -ēre, -ēuī, -ētus, to refill, replenish; to fill to the brim

reposcō, -ere, to demand back; to ask for, claim; to require

repraesentō (1), to present again; to show, display; to rush; to depict

reprehendō, -ere, -ī, -sus, to hold back; to restrain; to blame; to convict

repulsa, -ae, *f.*, defeat (at the polls); rebuff; cold shoulder

rēs, reī, *f.*, thing, object, matter, affair, circumstance, situation, fact

residuus, -a, -um, *adj.*, remaining, left

respectus, -ūs, *m.*, backward glance; refuge; respect; regard

respiciō, -ere, -spexī, -spectus, to look back at; see behind oneself; to look at

respondeō, -ēre, -dī, -sus, to answer; to say in reply; to say in refutation

restituō, -ere, -tuī, -tūtus, to set up again; to restore, rebuild; to revive; to repair

restitūtiō, -ōnis, *f.*, restoration; reinstatement, pardon; recall

restrictus, -a, -um, *adj.*, tied back, tight; stingy; drawn back

resūmō, -ere, -psī, -ptus, to resume, recover

retegō, -ere, -texī, -tectus, to uncover, expose

reuertor, -ī, -uersus sum, to turn back, turn around; to come back, return

reuocō (1), to call back, recall; to cancel; to withdraw

reus, -ī, *m.*, defendant; plaintiff; criminal

rex, rēgis, *m.*, king; patron

Rhēnus, -ī, *m.*, the Rhine River

rīsus, -ūs, *m.*, laugh, laughter, smile; laughingstock

rīuālis, -is, *m.*, one who uses the same stream; a rival (especially in love)

rōbustus, -a, -um, *adj.*, hardwood; oak; robust; strong; tough; firm

rogō (1), to ask, beg, request; to introduce, propose

Rōma, -ae, *f.*, Rome

Rubicō(n), -ōnis, *m.*, Rubicon, the river marking boundary of Italy and Gaul

rubor, -ōris, *m.*, redness; blush; sense of shame

ruīna, -ae, *f.*, tumbling down, collapse, fall; destruction

rūpēs, -is, *f.*, cliff

rursus, *adv.*, back, backwards; on the contrary; on the other hand; in turn; again

rūs, rūris, *n.*, the country, countryside, lands, fields; farm, estate

Sabīnus, -a, -um, *adj.*, of the Sabines or their country

sacrificium, -ī, *n.*, sacrifice

sacrificō (1), to sacrifice

sacrum, -ī, *n.*, holy object, sacred vessel; temple; act of worship, religious service; festival

saeculāris, -is, -e, *adj.*, centennial

saepe, *adv.*, often

saepiō, -īre, -sī, -tus, to fence in, hedge in; to surround, encircle; to fortify

saepius, *adv.*, more frequently; more (times) than is normal

saeuitia, -ae, *f.*, rage, fierceness; brutality; savageness

sagum, -ī, *n.*, coarse mantle; military uniform

salsāmentārius, -ī, *n.*, seller of salted fish

saltō (1), to dance

salūtō (1), to greet, wish well; to send greetings to; to pay respects to; to welcome

sānē, *adv.*, sanely, reasonably; certainly, truly

Sarmatae, -ārum, *m. pl.*, the Sarmatians

satira, -ae, *f.*, literary medley of prose and poetry; satire

satis, *adv.*, enough, sufficiently; adequately

saucius, -a, -um, *adj.,* wounded; offended; drunk; madly in love

scaena, -ae, *f.,* stage; backdrop, scenery; canopy

scaenicus, -a, -um, *adj.,* of or connected with the stage; theatrical; (*m.*) actor

scarus, -ī, *m.,* scar-fish

schēma, -ae, *f.,* figure, form, style; posture, attitude

sciō, -īre, scīuī *or* **sciī, scītus,** to know; to realize; to understand

scortum, -ī, *n.,* prostitute, whore

scrībō, -ere, scripsī, scriptus, to write, draw; to write down; to register; to name

scriptum, -ī, *n.,* composition, treatise, work, book

scriptūra, -ae, *f.,* writing; composing; composition

scriptus, -ūs, *m.,* office of clerk

scrūtor, -ārī, -ātus, to search carefully, explore, examine

scurrīlis, -is, -e, *adj.,* scurrilous, offensive

sē, *pron.,* himself, herself, itself, themselves, one another

sēcessus, -ūs, *m.,* withdrawal (into seclusion); secluded place, retreat

sēcrētō, *adv.,* in private

sēcrētum, -ī, *n.,* seclusion, retirement; secluded place, secluded nature of a place; privacy; secret

secundus, -a, -um, *adj.,* following, next, second; favorable, supporting

sed, *conj.,* but

sēdātus, -a, -um, *adj.,* calm, composed

sēdēs, -is, *f.,* seat, chair, throne; residence, home

sēdūcō, -ere, -duxī, -ductus, to take aside, draw aside; to lead astray

segniter, *adv.,* without spirit or energy

sellārium, -ī, *n.,* room with seats; privy, latrine

sēmēsus, -a, -um, *adj.,* half-eaten

semper, *adv.,* always, ever

senātus, -ūs, *m.,* Senate

senescō, -ere, -uī, to get old; to decline, become feeble, lose strength

senex, -is, *adj.,* old, aged; (*m.*) old man

sensim, *adv.,* gropingly, tentatively; carefully; gradually; gently

sententia, -ae, *f.,* opinion, judgment, thought, idea, notion; saying

sentiō, -īre, sensī, sensus, to perceive, feel, hear, see; to realize; to observe

sepeliō, -īre, -pelīuī, -pultus, to bury, inter

sēpōnō, -ere, -posuī, -positus, to set aside, drop; to banish; to separate; to select

septem, *indecl. adj.,* seven

septimus, -a, -um, *adj.,* seventh

sepulcrum, -ī, *n.,* burial place, grave, tomb

sequor, sequī, secūtus sum, to follow; to escort, accompany; to pursue; to come after

seriēs, -ēī, *f.,* series, row, succession

sermō, -ōnis, *m.,* conversation, talk; discussion; gossip; language

Seruius, -ī, *m.,* Servius, a *praenomen* (abbreviated **Ser.**)

seruō (1), to watch over, preserve; to serve, protect

seruolus, -ī, *m.,* young slave

seruus, -ī, *m./f.,* slave

sescentī, -ae, -a, *adj.,* six hundred

sestertium, -ī, *n., (with numeral adjs.)* 100, 000 sesterces

sestertius, -a, -um, *adj., (with multiples of* milia) (so many) thousand sesterces

sētius, *adv.,* later, more slowly; to a lesser degree, less readily; otherwise

seuērus, -a, -um, *adj.,* severe, strict; austere; ruthless, grim; plain

sextāriolus, -ī, *m.,* small measuring vessel

sexus, -ūs, *m.,* sex

sī, *conj.,* if

sīc, *adv.,* thus, so, in this way

sīcut, *conj.,* as, just as; as it were; as for instance

sīdus, -eris, *n.,* constellation; star; heavenly body; sky

sigillum, -ī, *n.,* statuette, figurine; a relief

signātor, -ōris, *m.,* sealer, signer, witness

significō (1), to show, indicate, express, sense; to intimate; to mean

signō (1), to mark, stamp; to impress; to seal; to signify; to express

signum, -ī, *n.,* sign; indication; military standard; omen; figure; statue

silentium, -ī, *n.,* silence, inactivity

silua, -ae, *f.,* woods, forest; bush, foliage, crop; material, supply

similitūdō, -inis, *f.,* likeness, resemblance; imitation

simul, *adv.,* together; at the same time; likewise; as well

simulō (1), to imitate, copy; to represent; to put on the appearance of, to simulate

sine, *prep.+ abl.,* without

singillātim, *adv.,* singly, individually

singulāris, -is, -e, *adj.,* peculiar, special; remarkable, unusual

singulī, -ae, -a, *adj.,* single, one at a time; one by one

sinister, -tra, -trum, *adj.,* left, on the left; auspicious; inauspicious, wrong

sinus, -ūs, *m.,* indentation, curve, fold; breast, bosom, lap

sīquidem, *conj.,* if in fact; seeing that, since

sodālis, -is, *m.,* member of a fraternal organization; companion, nate, crony

sōl, sōlis, *m.,* sun; sunlight, sunshine; day

soleō, -ēre, solitus sum, to be in the habit of; to be used to

sollicitūdō, -inis, *f.,* anxiety; uneasiness; worry

sōlus, -a, -um, *adj.,* only, single, sole, alone; lonely

somnus, -ī, *m.,* sleep; night; indolence

sordidus, -a, -um, *adj.,* dirty, filthy; shabby; low; vulgar

sors, sortis, *f.,* lot; casting of lots, decision by lot; fate, destiny

sorticula, -ae, *f.,* a little lot; a small tablet or ticket

sortior, -īrī, -ītus sum, to cast lots for; to allot; to obtain by lot; to choose, select

spatium, -ī, *n.,* space, room, extent; interval, period

species, -ēī, *f.,* sight, view, outward appearance, deceptive appearance; shape, semblance

spectāculum, -ī, *n.,* sight, spectacle; public performance, show; stage play; theater

speculātus, -a, -um, *adj.,* mirrored

spernō, -ere, sprēuī, sprētus, to spurn, scorn, reject; to separate

spintria, -ae, *m.,* "squeezer," sexual acrobat

spīritus, -ūs, *m.,* breathing, breath; wind; air; life; spirit, soul; enthusiasm

splendidus, -a, -um, *adj.,* clear and bright, gleaming; noble; splendid; sumptuous

spolium, -ī, *n.,* hide, skin; spoils, booty; (*pl.*) spoils of war, booty

sponte, *adv.,* spontaneously, of its own accord

stabulum, -ī, *n.,* stable, stall; lair; hut; brothel

stadium, -ī, *n.,* running track; unit of measurement

statim, *adv.,* at once, on the spot; the moment that

statiō, -ōnis, *f.,* standing still; station, post; residence; anchorage

statua, -ae, *f.,* statue

statuō, -ere, -uī, -ūtus, to cause to stand; to stop; to erect; to establish; to decide

statūra, -ae, *f.,* stature, height

stemma, -atis, *f.,* genealogical tree, family tree, lineage

sternō, -ere, strāuī, strātus, to spread, to cover; to strike down

stīpendium, -ī, *n.,* tax, tribute, tariff; pay; military service

strigōsus, -a, -um, *adj.,* lean, shriveled; bald

stringō, -ere, strinxī, strictus, to strip, clip; to draw, draw tight; to graze, scratch

studiōsus, -a, -um, *adj.,* eager,
zealous, assiduous

stuprum, -ī, *n.,* immortality;
illicit sex; fornication

subbibō, -ere, -ī, to drink a
little

subiciō, -ere, -iēcī, -iectus, to
throw up, fling up; to add,
append

subinde, *adv.,* immediately
afterwards; promptly; from
time to time

subitō, *adv.,* suddenly,
unexpectedly; at once

sublīmis, -is, -e, *adj.,* high,
raised up; lofty; (*n.*) an
elevated position; the air

**submoueō, -ēre, -mōuī,
-mōtus,** to move up,
advance; to remove; to keep
off

subripiō, -ere, -ripuī, -reptus,
to snatch secretly, pilfer

subsellium, -ī, *n.,* seat, bench;
stool

succēdō, -ere, -cessī, -cessus, to
come to the foot of; to climb;
to succeed, follow

succendō, -ere, -dī, -sus, to set
on fire; to light

successor, -ōris, *m.,* successor

sufferus, -a, -um, *adj.,* wild

sufficiō, -ere, -fēcī, -fectus, to
supply; to be sufficient; to be
capable of

sum, esse, fuī, to be, to exist

summa, -ae, *f.,* main thing;
chief point; gist; sum,
amount; sum of money

summus, -a, -um, *adj.,* highest,
uppermost; greatest, finest;
of the highest importance

sūmō, -ere, sumpsī, sumptus,
to take up; to put on; to
begin; to consume

sumptus, -ūs, *m.,* cost, expense

supellex, -ectilis, *f.,* furniture,
household utensils;
tableware; outfit, equipment

super, *prep.* + *acc.,* over, above;
besides; beyond, more than;
(*adv.*) over, above; besides

superbus, -a, -um, *adj.,*
arrogant, haughty, snobbish;
disdainful; superb

supergredior, -ī, -gressus sum,
to walk or step over; to
surpass

superiaciō, -ere, -iēcī, -iectus, to
throw on top; to overshoot

superior, -or, -us, *adj.,* higher,
upper, past, preceding; older;
more advanced; stronger

supīnus, -a, -um, *adj.,* face-up;
lying on one's back; turned
upwards; sloping

suppetō, -ere, -īuī *or* **-iī, -ītum,**
to be at hand, be in stock, be
available

suppleō, -ēre, -ēuī, -ētus, to fill
up; to make good; to bring
to full strength

suprā, *prep.* + *acc.,* above,
beyond, on top of; more
than; (*adv.*) above, on top

suscipiō, -ere, -cēpī , -ceptus,
to catch; to support; to
accept; to undertake, take up

suspiciō, -ōnis, *f.*, suspicion, mistrust; inkling; faint indication

sustineō, -ēre, -uī, to hold up; support; to sustain; to bear, endure

suus, -a, -um, *adj.*, his own, her own, its own, their own, one's own

Syria, -ae, *f.*, Syria, a Roman province

tabella, -ae, *f.*, small board, panel; tablet to record a vote; picture, painting

tabula, -ae, *f.*, board, plank; tablet, writing tablet; painting

tālis, -is, -e, *adj.*, such, of that kind; so great; so excellent

tam, *adv.*, to such an extent; so, so much

tamen, *adv.*, yet, nevertheless, still

tamquam, *conj.*, as, just as (if); as though

tandem, *adv.*, at last, in the end, finally; tell me, please, now

tantum, *adv.*, so much, so greatly; to such a degree; only; hardly, scarcely

tantus, -a, -um, *adj.*, of such size, so big; so much; so little; so important

tardō (1), to slow down, delay; to go slow

tardus, -a, -um, *adj.*, tardy, slow; lingering; mentally slow; long drawn out

tegumentum, -ī, *n.*, cover, covering

temere, *adv.*, by chance; without cause; at random; easily

temperō (1), to exercise restraint; to restrain oneself, hold back (from)

tempestīuus, -a, -um, *adj.*, ready, ripe; timely; **conuīuium tempestīuum,** elaborate party

templum, -ī, *n.*, temple, shrine, sanctuary

temptō (1), to test, feel, probe; to attempt; to attack

tempus, -oris, *n.*, time, period, season; opportunity; right time; condition, need

tenebrae, -ārum, *f. pl.*, darkness, night; death

teneō, -ēre, -uī, -tus, to hold, keep, possess; to catch, catch out

teneritūdō, -inis, *f.*, tender age

ter, *adv.*, three times

tergum, -ī, *n.*, back; rear; hide, leather

terra, -ae, *f.*, earth; land; ground; country

terrēnus, -a, -um, *adj.*, earthly, terrestrial; earthen; (*n.*) land, ground

terreō, -ēre, -uī, -itus, to frighten, scare; to deter

territō (1), to keep frightening; to try to scare, intimidate

tertius, -a, -um, *adj.*, third

testāmentum, -ī, *n.*, testament, will

testor, -ārī, -ātus sum, to give as evidence; to show, prove; to call to witness; to testify

theātrum, -ī, *n.,* theater

Thraex, -cis, *m.,* Thracian gladiator

Thrasyllus, -ī, *m.,* Thrasyllus, an Alexadrian astrologer

Tiberius, -ī, *m.,* Tiberius, a *praenomen* (abbreviated **T.**); especially of the emperor Tiberius

tībīcen, -inis, *m.,* piper; prop, pillar

Tīburnus, -a, -um, *adj.,* of Tibur, a town east of Rome; (*m.*) legendary founder of Tibur

Tīburtīnus, -a, -um, *adj.,* of or belonging to Tibur

timiditās, -ātis, *f.,* timidity, fearfulness, cowardice

tinniō, -īre, -īuī or **-iī, -ītus,** to ring

tīrō, -ōnis, *m.,* novice; recruit (to the army)

tīrunculus, -ī, *m.,* beginner; recruit

titulus, -ī, *m.,* inscription; label; title; heading; chapter; title of honor

toga, -ae, *f.,* toga

tormentum, -ī, *n.,* windlass; catapult, artillery piece; torture rack; torture

tot, *adj.,* so many, as many

totidem, *adj.,* just so many; just as many

tōtus, -a, -um, *adj.,* the whole, all, entire

trādō, -ere, -didī, -ditus, to hand over, surrender; to deliver; to relate, recount

tragoedus, -ī, *m.,* tragic actor

trahō, -ere, -xī, -ctus, to drag, haul; to get, draw, derive; to assign, attribute to

trāiciō, -ere, iēcī, -iectus, to throw across, pass through; to move, lead across, cross over

transeō, -īre, -iī or **-iuī, -itus,** to go across

transgredior, -ī, -gressus sum, to cross, pass over

transigō, -ere, -ēgī, -actus, to pierce, run through; to finish; to transact; to accomplish

trēs, trēs, tria, *adj.,* three; a couple of

tribūnal, -ālis, *n.,* platform; tribunal; judgment seat

tribūnus, -ī, *m.* tribune

tribus, -ūs, *f.,* tribe

tribūtum, -ī, *n.,* tribute, tax; contribution

trīclīnium, -ī, *n.,* dining couch; dining room

trīduum, -ī, *n.,* three-day period, three days

trifāriam, *adv.,* in three places, on three sides; under three headings

trīgintā, *adj.,* thirty

triplex, -icis, *adj.,* threefold, triple

trirēmis, -is, -e, *adj.,* having three banks of oars; (*f.*) trireme

tristis, -is, -e, *adj.,* depressed, gloomy; bitter; stern, austere; grim, dreadful; repulsive

tropaeum, -ī, *n.,* trophy; war memorial

trucīdō, -āre, to slaughter, massacre, cut down

truncō (1), to lop off, maim; amputate

tū, *pron.,* you (*sing.*)

tum, *adv.,* then, at that time; at that moment; in those days

tumultuō (1), to make a disturbance; to be in an uproar

tumultuōsus, -a, -um, *adj.,* boisterous; turbulent; panicky

tumultus, -ūs, *m.,* commotion, uproar; insurrection

tumulus, -ī, *m.,* mound; rising; ground swell; burial mound

tunc, *adv.,* then, at that time; thereupon; consequently

turdus, -ī, *m.,* thrush

turpis, -is, -e, *adj.,* ugly, deformed; disgraceful, shameless; obscene

turris, -is, *f.,* turret; tower; castle

tūtor, -ārī, -ātus sum, to guard, protect, defend; to watch, preserve

tuus, -a, -um, *adj.,* your; yours

Tyrrhēnicos, -ē, -on, *adj.,* Etrurian, Etruscan

uacō (1), to be empty; be vacant; to be at leisure; to be unoccupied; to have time for

uagor, -ārī, -ātus sum, to wander

uagus, -a, -um, *adj.,* wandering, roaming

ualeō, -ēre, -uī, ualitūrus, to be strong; to be powerful; to be able; to be worth; to mean

ualitūdō, -inis, *f.,* state of health; good health; ill health; illness

uarius, -a, -um, *adj.,* variegated, of different colors, of different elements

uasculum, -ī, *n.,* small vessel

uastō (1), to leave desolate; to lay waste; to cut to pieces

ūbertim, *adv.,* copiously

uehō, -ere, uexī, uectus, to carry, convey, transport; to travel, ride

uel, *adv.,* even, actually; *conj.,* either, or

uēlō (1), to cover, wrap, veil

uelut *or* **ueluti,** *adv.,* as, just as, even as; as for example; like

uenēnum, -ī, *n.,* poison

uenia, -ae, *f.,* kindness, favor, goodwill; permission; pardon

ueniō, -īre, uēnī, uentum, to come

uenter, -ris, *m.,* stomach, belly

uentriculus, -ī, *m.,* belly

uepris, -is, *m.,* briar; bramble bush

uerberō (1), to flog, scourge, whip, to beat

uerbum, -ī, *n.,* word

uērē, *adv.,* truly, really

uerēcundia, -ae, *f.,* bashfulness, shyness, modesty

uereor, -ērī, -itus sum, to revere, have respect for; to fear; to feel uneasy

uerētrum, -ī, *n.,* male sexual organ

uērō, *adv.,* in fact, in truth; even; however

uersō (1), to keep turning, spin, whirl; to manipulate; (*pass.*) to come and go

uersus, -ūs, *m.,* turning; furrow; line; line, verse

uērum, *adv.,* truly; but in fact; yet

uērus, -a, -um, *adj.,* true; actual; genuine; real; fair, reasonable

uestiō, -īre, -īuī *or* **-iī, -ītus,** to dress, clothe

uestis, -is, *f.,* garment, dress; clothing; coverlet; blanket; slough

uetus, -eris, *adj.,* old, aged

uia, -ae, *f.,* way, road, street, highway

uīciēs, *adv.,* twenty times

uīcīnia, -ae, *f.,* neighborhood; nearness; proximity

uicis (*gen.*), *f.,* turn; function; plight, lot; exchange; succession

uictor, -ōris, *m.,* victor

uictōria, -ae, *f.,* victory

uīcus, -ī, *m.,* village, hamlet; ward, quarter; street, block

uideō, -ēre, uīdī, uīsus, to see, look at; to consider, realize; (*pass.*) to seem, appear

uigeō, -ēre, -uī, to thrive, flourish; to be pre-eminently successful

uigilia, -ae, *f.,* wakefulness, sleeplessness, vigil; keeping watch

uigilō (1), to spend the night awake; to make or do while awake at night; to stay awake

uīgintī, *adj.,* twenty

uilla, -ae, *f.,* country house, farm

uinciō, -īre, uinxī, uinctus, to bind, tie; to wrap; to surround; to bandage

uincō, -ere, uīcī, uictus, to conquer; to outdo; to convince; to prove; to outlive

uindicō (1), to claim formally; to avenge, punish, take vengeance upon

uīnum, -ī, *n.* wine

uir, uirī, *m.,* man; hero; husband; lover; manhood

uirid(i)ārium, -ī, *n.,* garden

uirītim, *adv.,* man by man; individually; per man

uīs, uis, *f.,* strength, power, force; attack, violence

uiscus, -eris, *n.,* (*usually pl.*) flesh; organs, innermost parts of the body

uīsus, -ūs, *m.,* faculty of sight; thing seen, sight; appearance, form

uīta, -ae, *f.,* life; way of life, means of living; manner of life; career

uitium, -ī, *n.,* fault, flaw; defect; sin; disorder

uīuō, -ere, uixī, uictum, to be alive, live; to be still alive, survive; to reside

uīuus, -a, -um, *adj.,* alive; lively; fresh

uix, *adv.,* scarcely, barely, hardly, with difficulty

uixdum, *adv.,* hardly then, scarcely yet

ulcīscor, -ī, ultus sum, to avenge oneself on, take revenge on, punish; to avenge

ullus, -a, -um, *adj.,* any

ultrā, *prep.* + *acc.,* beyond, past, more than, over and above; (*adv.*) beyond, farther

ultrō, *adv.,* to the farther side; without being asked, on one's own initiative; **ultrō (et) citrō,** to and fro

umerus, -ī, *m.,* shoulder

umquam, *adv.* ever, at any time

unde, *adv.,* from where, whence; from whom

undique, *adv.,* on all sides, from all directions; in every respect

ūnicus, -a, -um, *adj.,* one and only, sole; singular; unique; uncommon

ūniuersus, -a, -um, *adj.,* all, all together; whole, entire

ūnus, -a, -um, *adj.,* one

uocō (1), to call, name

uolitō (1), to flit around, hover; soar; move quickly

uolō, uelle, uoluī, to wish, want; to propose, determine; to hold, maintain; to be willing

uolucris, -is, *f.,* bird, fly, insect

uolūmen, -inis, *n.,* roll, book; coil, twist

uoluntārius, -a, -um, *adj.,* voluntary

uoluptās, -ātis, *f.,* pleasure, enjoyment, delight; (*pl.*) entertainments

uomitō, -āre, to vomit frequently

uomitus, -ūs, *m.,* vomiting; vomit

uōs, *pron.,* you (*pl.*)

uox, uōcis, *f.,* voice, sound, cry, call, word; expression, saying

urbānus, -a, -um, *adj.,* of the city (of Rome); courteous; sophisticated; witty; brash

urbs, urbis, *f,* city; the city of Rome

urgeō, -ēre, ūrsī, to prod on, urge forward; to press; to be hard on

ūrīna, -ae, *f.,* urine

urna, -ae, *f.,* pot, jar; water pot; voting urn; urn of fate; money jar

usque, *adv.,* all the way, right on; all the time; to the fullest extent; **usque adeō ut** to such an extent that

usquequāque, *adv.,* everywhere; in every possible situation

ūsus, -ūs, *m.,* use; enjoyment; practice; experience; custom; advantage; need

ut, *adv.,* how; such as (*conj.*) as; although; when; while; in order that; that

uterque, -traque, -trumque, *adj.*, each (of two), both

ūtor, ūtī, ūsus sum, to use; to enjoy; to practice; to treat; to handle

uulgāris, -is, -e, *adj.*, common, general; low-class; ordinary

uulgō, *adv.*, generally, publicly, everywhere

uulnerō (1), to wound, damage

uulnus, -eris, *n.*, wound, blow, strike

uultus, -ūs, *m.*, face; looks, expression, features; look, appearance

uxor, -ōris, *f.*, wife

Venereus, -a, -um, *adj.*, of Venus; of sexual love, erotic; **rēs Venereae,** sexual intercourse

Venusīnus, -a, -um, *adj.*, of Venusia, a town in south Italy

Vergilius, -ī, *m.*, Vergil, name of a *gens*; especially of the poet Vergil

Vespāsiānus, -ī, *m.*, Vespasian, a *cognomen*; especially of the emperor Vespasian

Vesuuius, -a, -um, *adj.*, of Vesuvius; **mōns Vesuuius,** Mount Vesuvius

Vindelicus, -a, -um, *adj*, of the Vindelici, a people living between the Alps and Danube

Viriāthīnus, -a, -um, *adj.*, of Viriathus, a Lusitanian who fought Rome

Xerxēs, -is, *m.*, Xerxes, a Persian king (485–65 BCE)

ℬℭ **LATIN** Readers

Series Editor: RONNIE ANCONA, HUNTER COLLEGE

Other Readers Also Now Available

A Lucan Reader
Selections from CIVIL WAR
SUSANNA BRAUND
(2009) ISBN 978-0-86516-661-5

A Terence Reader
Selections from Six Plays
WILLIAM S. ANDERSON
(2009) ISBN 978-0-86515-678-3

A Plautus Reader
Selections from Eleven Plays
JOHN HENDERSON
(2009) ISBN 978-0-86516-694-3

A Livy Reader
Selections from AB URBE CONDITA
MARY JAEGER
(2010) ISBN 978-0-86515-680-6

A Sallust Reader
Selections from BELLUM CATILINAE,
BELLUM IUGURTHINUM, and HISTORIAE
VICTORIA E. PAGÁN
(2009) ISBN 978-0-86515-687-5

A Roman Verse Satire Reader
Selections from Lucilius, Horace,
Persius, and Juvenal
CATHERINE C. KEANE
(2010) ISBN 978-0-86515-685-1

Forthcoming in 2011 and Beyond

An Apuleius Reader
ELLEN D. FINKELPEARL
ISBN 978-0-86515-714-8

A Caesar Reader
W. JEFFREY TATUM
ISBN 978-0-86515-696-7

A Cicero Reader
JAMES M. MAY
ISBN 978-0-86515-713-1

A Latin Epic Reader
ALISON KEITH
ISBN 978-0-86515-686-8

A Martial Reader
CRAIG WILLIAMS
ISBN 978-0-86515-704-9

An Ovid Reader
CAROLE E. NEWLANDS
ISBN 978-0-86515-722-3

A Propertius Reader
P. LOWELL BOWDITCH
ISBN 978-0-86515-723-0

A Roman Army Reader
DEXTER HOYOS
ISBN 978-0-86515-715-5

A Roman Women Reader
SHEILA K. DICKISON
and JUDITH P. HALLETT
ISBN 978-0-86515-662-2

A Seneca Reader
JAMES KER
ISBN 978-0-86515-758-2

A Tacitus Reader
STEVEN H. RUTLEDGE
ISBN 978-0-86515-697-4

A Tibullus Reader
PAUL ALLEN MILLER
ISBN 978-0-86515-724-7

**VISIT THE SERIES WEBSITE FOR UPDATES
ON AVAILABLE VOLUMES:**
www.bolchazy.com/readers